Claude: The Definitive Guide

The Complete Guide to Anthropic's AI Assistant

Ken Tannenbaum

2026

Finnoybu Press

Claude: The Definitive Guide

2026 Edition

The Complete Guide to Anthropic's AI Assistant

Published by Finnoybu Press

For permissions and inquiries: press@finnoybu.org

First Edition: 2026

About the Author

Ken Tannenbaum is a technologist, entrepreneur, and AI governance researcher. He is the founder of Finnoybu Press and the founder/steward of the AEGIS Initiative, an open framework for AI safety and accountability. Learn more at aegis-initiative.com.

When he's not building governance standards for artificial intelligence, he's helping everyday people understand and use it.

Dedication

For Irene. If she can find her glasses, I know she'll want to read this. After her podcast. If she doesn't fall asleep. The best teacher, friend, partner, spouse, step-mother, mother, and grandmother to walk the face of my earth. Aaaaah! We got married!?

And for everyone who tried Claude once and thought, *"Wait, this one actually listens."* You were right. This book shows you what it can really do.

The AI for Everyone Series

This book is part of the **AI for Everyone** series by Finnoybu Press, designed to help real people use AI tools effectively. Visit **press.finnoybu.org** for the latest titles and updates.

Collection One: Product Deep Dives

- *ChatGPT: The Definitive Guide (2026 Edition)*
- *ChatGPT: The Power User Guide (2026 Edition)*
- *Claude: The Definitive Guide (2026 Edition)*
- *Claude Code: The Power User Guide (2026 Edition)*
- *Gemini: The Complete Guide (2026 Edition)*
- *Gemini: The Advanced Guide (2026 Edition)*
- *Copilot: The Workplace AI Guide (2026 Edition)*
- *Copilot: The Advanced Workplace Guide (2026 Edition)*
- *Perplexity: The Research Playbook (2026 Edition)*
- *Perplexity: The Advanced Research Playbook (2026 Edition)*

Collection Two: Product Guides

- *NotebookLM: From Sources to Audio Overviews (2026 Edition)*
- *DeepSeek: Code, Math, and Reasoning (2026 Edition)*
- *Cursor: The AI Code Editor (2026 Edition)*
- *OpenClaw: Agentic AI for Everyday Work (2026 Edition)*

Collection Three: Cross-Platform Skills

- *AI Systems Playbook (2026 Edition)*
- *AI Prompt Engineering (2026 Edition)*
- *AI for Developers (2026 Edition)*
- *AI for Business (2026 Edition)*
- *AI for Students (2026 Edition)*
- *AI Governance for Practitioners (2026 Edition)*
- *Securing Agentic AI (2026 Edition)*

Table of Contents

Introduction

If you have used an AI assistant in the past year, there is a good chance it was ChatGPT. OpenAI's chatbot became a cultural phenomenon almost overnight, and for many people it was their first encounter with what modern artificial intelligence can do. But ChatGPT is not the only game in town, and if you are holding this book, you already suspect that one of its competitors deserves a closer look.

Claude, built by Anthropic, is that competitor. It is not a ChatGPT clone, and not a minor variation on the same theme. Claude is a different AI assistant — one built from the ground up around safety, honesty, and careful reasoning, and you will feel the difference within minutes of your first conversation. It pushes back when you are wrong. It says "I'm not sure" when it isn't. It produces writing that reads less like a machine and more like a careful, well-read colleague. For a growing number of professionals, creators, students, and everyday users, Claude has become the AI assistant they reach for first.

This book is a complete guide to Claude. If you have never used an AI assistant before, you will find everything you need to get started — from creating an account to writing your first prompts. If you are already using Claude casually and want more out of it, the later chapters take you deeper into advanced features like Projects, Artifacts, extended thinking, and professional workflows. And if you are evaluating Claude for your team or business, you will find honest comparisons, deployment guidance, and practical advice on data governance and adoption.

This is the third book in the Finnoybu Press AI Guide Series. The first two cover ChatGPT — one for getting started and one for advanced use. If you have read those, you will find the same practical, no-nonsense approach here. If you have not, this book stands on its own. You do not need any prior experience with AI assistants, ChatGPT or otherwise, to follow along.

The book follows a deliberate progression. Part I (Chapters 1 through 4) covers the fundamentals: what Claude is, how to choose a plan, how to set up your account, and how to understand the different models. Part II (Chapters 5 through 13) is the hands-on core: your first conversations, writing, research, everyday productivity, professional use, vision, file uploads, Artifacts, and Projects. Part III (Chapters 14 through 17) goes deeper into how Claude thinks and how to get the best results: personality and behavior, prompting fundamentals, handling long and complex tasks, and output formatting. Part IV (Chapters 18 through 21) addresses specific audiences: students, businesses, developers, and creators. Part V (Chapters 22 through 24) is about the hard truths: what Claude gets wrong, privacy and security, and the ethical questions that matter. Each chapter builds on what came before, but most also stand on their own if you want to skip ahead.

One more thing, said plainly: this book was written with the assistance of Claude itself. The author used Claude extensively throughout the writing process — for drafting, research, editing, and refining arguments. This is not a secret and not a contradiction. A book about an AI tool should demonstrate confidence in that tool. Every word was reviewed, revised, and approved by a human author who takes responsibility for the final product. Where Claude helped, it helped well. Where it needed correction, it was corrected. That is exactly how the tool is meant to be used.

Whether you are here out of curiosity, because your job demands it, or because you tried Claude once and want to understand it fully — welcome. You picked a good time to learn, and you picked the right book.

A Note About Accuracy

Claude changes constantly. Anthropic ships updates regularly, sometimes weekly. Features get added, interfaces get redesigned, models get upgraded. This book is accurate as of May 2026, but specific details — menu locations, exact pricing, feature availability — may have shifted by the time you read this.

The principles, techniques, and strategies in this book have a much longer shelf life than the specific interface details. How to write effective prompts, evaluate Claude's reasoning, and structure long-form work with Projects and Artifacts — those skills transfer across versions and even across different AI tools.

When something seems different from what's described here, check Anthropic's help center at help.anthropic.com for the latest information.

Let's get started.

Part I: Getting Started

"The best way to predict the future is to invent it."

— Alan Kay

Chapter 1: What Is Claude?

You have probably heard the buzz about AI assistants. Maybe a coworker mentioned one that drafted an entire proposal in minutes, or a friend showed you a chatbot that explained a tax form in plain English. The field is crowded — ChatGPT, Gemini, Copilot — and if you are reading this book, you have at least a passing curiosity about one called Claude.

Good. You picked up the right book.

Claude is an AI assistant made by Anthropic. You type (or speak) a question, request, or instruction — called a **prompt** — and Claude responds with text that is often remarkably useful. It can summarize a forty-page contract, debug a Python script, brainstorm marketing slogans, translate a letter into French, or explain quantum mechanics to a ten-year-old. It draws on a vast body of knowledge absorbed during training, plus whatever documents or images you share in the conversation. Claude can also search the web when the feature is enabled, though its web search is more limited than ChatGPT's deeply integrated browsing.

A few things to get out of the way early. Claude is not a person. It does not have feelings, desires, or a secret agenda. It is a **large language model** — software trained on enormous amounts of text so it can predict, word by word, what a helpful response looks like. Think of it as an extraordinarily well-read colleague who never sleeps, never gets annoyed, and never forgets the first paragraph of a conversation you started five minutes ago.

It is also not infallible. Claude can make mistakes, invent plausible-sounding facts (a phenomenon called **hallucination**), and occasionally refuse a perfectly reasonable request because it errs on the side of caution. We cover all of that honestly in this chapter, because understanding what Claude *cannot* do matters as much as knowing what it can.

Anthropic: The Company Behind Claude

Anthropic was founded in 2021 by Dario Amodei and Daniela Amodei, along with several colleagues who had previously worked at OpenAI. Their departure was not casual — it was driven by a specific belief: that as AI systems become more powerful, the organizations building them need to prioritize safety at a foundational level, not as an afterthought.

That belief shaped everything about Anthropic, from its corporate structure (it is a **public benefit corporation**, with a legal obligation to consider societal impact alongside profits) to its flagship research contribution, **Constitutional AI**, which we will explore shortly.

Anthropic is headquartered in San Francisco and has grown rapidly, attracting significant investment from Amazon, Google, and others. Its identity remains rooted in a straightforward premise: build capable AI, and build it responsibly.

A Brief History of Claude

Claude's evolution has been fast, even by the standards of an industry that moves at breakneck speed. The timeline in broad strokes:

Claude 1 (2023)

The original release. Claude 1 was competent but clearly a first-generation product — good at summarization and conversation, limited in reasoning depth. It established the brand's voice: helpful, honest, and less prone to the exaggerated confidence that dogged some competitors.

Claude 2 (2023)

A significant step forward. Claude 2 could handle much longer documents (up to 100,000 tokens, roughly 75,000 words), which made it the go-to tool for anyone working with long contracts, research papers, or codebases. Its reasoning improved, and it handled complex multi-step instructions better.

Claude 3: The Haiku/Sonnet/Opus Era (Early 2024)

This was the release that put Claude firmly in the top tier. Anthropic introduced three models under the Claude 3 umbrella:

- **Haiku** — small, fast, and cheap. Ideal for quick tasks.
- **Sonnet** — a balanced middle ground. Good enough for most everyday work.

- **Opus** — the powerhouse. Best reasoning, best writing, best at handling nuance.

This tiered approach — giving users a choice between speed and depth — has remained a core part of the Claude product ever since.

Claude 3.5 (Mid-to-Late 2024)

Incremental but meaningful upgrades. Claude 3.5 Sonnet became one of the most popular models in the industry, rivaling or exceeding GPT-4o on many benchmarks while remaining faster and cheaper. Claude 3.5 Haiku brought near-Sonnet quality at Haiku speed.

Claude 4 and Beyond (2025)

The Claude 4 family marked a generational leap in reasoning. The introduction of **extended thinking** — where the model explicitly works through problems step by step before answering — dramatically improved performance on math, logic, coding, and anything else that benefits from deliberation. Claude 4 Opus became the model of choice for professionals tackling complex problems.

Claude 4.5/4.6/4.7 (2025–2026)

Where we are today. **Claude Opus 4.7** is the most capable model Anthropic has ever released — stronger at coding, analysis, creative writing, vision, and nuanced reasoning. **Claude Sonnet 4.6** delivers an impressive balance of speed and quality for everyday use, with a one-million-token context window at standard pricing. **Claude Haiku 4.5** remains the fastest option, ideal for simple lookups and high-volume tasks. Throughout this book, when we refer to "Claude" without specifying a model, we mean whichever model fits the task at hand — and Chapter 4 will help you choose.

Constitutional AI: What Makes Claude Different

Every AI company claims its product is safe and responsible. Anthropic backs that claim with a specific technique called **Constitutional AI** (often abbreviated **CAI**).

The idea in plain language: during training, most AI models are shaped by human feedback. People rate the model's outputs as good or bad, and the model learns to produce more of the good ones. This works, but it is expensive, slow, and limited by the biases and inconsistencies of the human raters.

Constitutional AI adds a layer. Anthropic wrote a set of principles — a "constitution" — that describes how Claude should behave. Things like: be helpful, be honest, do not help with illegal activities, acknowledge uncertainty, avoid reinforcing harmful stereotypes. During training, a separate AI system evaluates Claude's outputs *against these principles* and provides feedback. The result is a model that is more consistent in its values, less dependent on the idiosyncrasies of individual human raters, and more transparent about *why* it behaves the way it does.

What does this mean for you? Claude is less likely to tell you what you want to hear and more likely to tell you what is accurate. It will push back if your premise is flawed. It will say "I'm not sure" when it isn't. Critics call this overly cautious; fans call it refreshingly honest. We think the honesty is a feature, not a bug — and once you get used to it, going back to a more sycophantic assistant feels hollow.

How Claude Compares to the Competition

You have options. Let's be straightforward about how Claude stacks up against the other major AI assistants as of early 2026.

ChatGPT (OpenAI)

ChatGPT is the most widely known AI assistant, with hundreds of millions of users. It has a massive plugin and tool ecosystem, built-in web browsing, image generation via DALL-E, and a voice mode that feels remarkably natural. If you want an all-in-one Swiss Army knife with the largest third-party integration library, ChatGPT is hard to top.

Where Claude pulls ahead: long-document handling, nuanced and less sycophantic writing, code quality on complex tasks, and a more principled approach to safety that results in fewer fabricated facts.

Gemini (Google)

Gemini is Google's entry, deeply integrated with the Google ecosystem — Gmail, Docs, Search, YouTube. If your life runs on Google products, Gemini's ability to pull context from your email, calendar, and Drive is a genuine advantage.

Where Claude pulls ahead: reasoning depth, consistency across long conversations, and writing that reads less like a corporate memo and more like a thoughtful human.

Copilot (Microsoft)

Microsoft Copilot is baked into Windows, Edge, Office 365, and Teams. For users who live inside the Microsoft ecosystem, the convenience is significant — ask Copilot to summarize an email thread in Outlook or generate a chart in Excel, and it just works.

Where Claude pulls ahead: standalone quality. If you are not specifically looking for tight Office integration, Claude generally produces more thoughtful, accurate, and better-structured responses.

The honest summary: no single assistant is best at everything. Claude's strengths — honesty, long-context handling, careful reasoning, and high-quality writing — make it the right choice for many tasks, especially professional and creative work that demands nuance.

What Claude Is Good At

Let's get specific.

Long documents. Claude can process extremely long inputs — well over 100,000 words in a single conversation. This makes it exceptional for reviewing contracts, analyzing research papers, comparing multiple documents, or working through a long codebase.

Nuanced writing. Whether you need a blog post, a cover letter, a short story, or a business proposal, Claude tends to produce prose that is more natural and less formulaic than what you get from many competitors. It handles tone shifts well — formal to casual, technical to accessible — and it is good at matching a style you provide as an example.

Code. Claude is a strong coding assistant across dozens of programming languages. It can write new code, debug existing code, explain a confusing function, and refactor messy scripts into clean ones. Claude Opus 4.7 is competitive with the best coding models available anywhere.

Honest feedback. Ask Claude to review your writing, your business plan, or your code, and it will tell you what is wrong — not just what is right. That is a real differentiator. Many AI assistants default to cheerful agreement; Claude defaults to constructive honesty.

Analysis and reasoning. With extended thinking enabled, Claude works through multi-step problems — financial models, logic puzzles, legal arguments, research synthesis — with impressive depth.

Vision. Upload images and Claude will describe, analyze, or extract information from them. Useful for reading charts, interpreting screenshots, analyzing photographs, or processing scanned documents.

What Claude Struggles With

No sugar-coating here.

No image generation. Claude cannot create images. If you need to generate illustrations, logos, or art, you will need a different tool (DALL-E, Midjourney, or similar).

Limited web search. Claude can search the web when the feature is enabled, but its search is more limited than ChatGPT's or Gemini's deeply integrated browsing. Claude's training data has a cutoff that varies by model — January 2026 for Opus 4.7, August 2025 for Sonnet 4.6, July 2025 for Haiku 4.5 — and while web search can supplement that knowledge, it is not as seamless or comprehensive as what competitors offer natively. For tasks that require extensive real-time research, you may still want to do your own searching alongside Claude.

Occasional over-caution. Claude's safety training sometimes leads it to decline reasonable requests. Ask about a sensitive topic for legitimate educational or professional reasons, and Claude may hedge more than necessary or add disclaimers you did not ask for. This has improved significantly over time, but it still happens.

Hallucination. Like all large language models, Claude can state false information with apparent confidence. It is better calibrated than many competitors — more likely to say "I'm not certain" — but you should still verify important facts independently. This is not a Claude-specific problem; it is a limitation of the technology as it exists today.

Real-time information. Claude's web search can help with some current topics, but it is not designed for up-to-the-minute data. If you need current weather, breaking news, or live sports scores, Claude may not be the most reliable tool — verify time-sensitive results independently.

The Claude Ecosystem

Claude is not just a single chatbot on a single website. It is available across multiple platforms and in multiple forms.

claude.ai — The primary web interface. Open a browser, go to claude.ai, sign in, and start chatting. This is where most people begin, and it offers the full feature set: model selection, Projects, Artifacts, file uploads, and more.

Mobile apps — Claude is available as a native app on both iOS and Android. The mobile experience is polished and supports the same core features as the web, including voice input and image uploads.

Desktop apps — Native applications for both Windows and macOS provide a dedicated Claude experience outside the browser, with system-level integration and keyboard shortcuts.

The API — For developers and businesses that want to integrate Claude into their own applications, Anthropic offers a robust API. You send prompts programmatically and receive responses, enabling everything from customer support chatbots to document processing pipelines. The API is priced per token (roughly per word) and gives you full control over model selection, parameters, and behavior.

Claude Code — A separate command-line tool designed for software developers. Claude Code lets you interact with Claude directly from your terminal, with awareness of your local files and codebase. It is covered in detail in Anthropic's developer documentation, and while it is beyond the scope of this book, it is worth knowing it exists if you write code professionally.

What to Expect from This Book

Over the coming chapters, we will walk you through everything you need to become proficient with Claude — from choosing the right plan and setting up your account, to mastering prompts, using advanced features like Projects and Artifacts, and integrating Claude into your professional workflow.

We wrote this book because Claude is genuinely useful, not because it is perfect. Where it falls short, we will say so. Where it excels, we will show you exactly how to take advantage.

Let's get started. In Chapter 2, we will help you figure out which Claude plan is right for you — and whether the free tier is enough to get real work done.

Chapter 2: Choosing the Right Plan

One of the first decisions you will face with Claude is how much to pay — or whether to pay at all. Anthropic offers a range of plans, from a usable free tier to enterprise packages that cost thousands per month. The right choice depends on how often you plan to use Claude, what kind of work you need it for, and whether you are an individual or part of a team.

This chapter walks you through every option, explains what you get at each level, and helps you decide without overspending.

The Free Tier: A Real Starting Point

Good news first: you can use Claude for free, and the free tier is not a crippled demo. You get access to **Claude Sonnet 4.6**, the balanced everyday model, with a reasonable number of messages per day. You can upload files, use vision (image analysis), and have multi-turn conversations. For anyone who wants to try Claude out, ask occasional questions, or use it for light personal tasks, the free tier is a valid option.

What you do *not* get on the free plan:

- **No access to Opus or Haiku.** You are limited to Sonnet 4.6. That is a strong model — arguably the best free AI model available anywhere — but you cannot switch to Opus for complex reasoning or Haiku for quick, lightweight tasks.
- **Lower message limits.** Anthropic does not publish exact numbers (they adjust based on demand and model costs), but you will hit a daily or hourly cap much sooner than paying users. When you hit it, you will see a message telling you to wait or upgrade. During peak hours, limits may be tighter.
- **No Projects.** Projects — organized workspaces with custom instructions and uploaded knowledge files — are reserved for paid plans.
- **No extended thinking.** The step-by-step reasoning mode that dramatically improves output quality on complex tasks is not available on the free tier.

- **Limited priority.** When Anthropic's servers are busy, free-tier users may see slower response times or reduced availability. Paid users get priority.

The honest assessment: If you use Claude a few times a week for straightforward questions — summarizing an article, drafting a quick email, getting a recipe suggestion — the free tier will serve you well. If you bump into limits regularly or wish you had access to Opus, that is your signal to upgrade.

Pro: The Sweet Spot for Individuals ($20/month)

The **Pro plan** at $20 per month is where Claude becomes a serious everyday tool. This is the plan most individual users will want, and it is the one we recommend for anyone reading this book who intends to use Claude regularly.

Here is what Pro unlocks:

Access to all models. You can switch freely between Opus 4.7, Sonnet 4.6, and Haiku 4.5. The flexibility is more valuable than it might sound. Use Haiku for quick lookups that do not need deep reasoning, Sonnet for everyday tasks, and Opus when you need Claude's best — a complex analysis, a tricky coding problem, or a piece of writing that demands real nuance.

Higher message limits. Pro users get substantially more messages per day than free users. For most people using Claude as a daily work tool, you are unlikely to hit the cap during normal use. Heavy users — those running long conversations with Opus all day — may still encounter limits, but they are generous enough for the vast majority of workflows.

Projects. This feature alone may justify the upgrade for many professionals. Projects let you create dedicated workspaces with custom instructions (so Claude behaves a specific way every time you open that project) and uploaded knowledge files (so Claude has persistent access to your company's style guide, product documentation, or other reference material). We cover Projects in depth in Chapter 13.

Extended thinking. With extended thinking enabled, Claude takes extra time to reason through a problem before responding. The difference in output quality can be dramatic, especially for math, logic, coding, and analysis. The Pro plan gets this feature with moderate thinking budgets.

Artifacts. Claude can generate interactive content — code previews, documents, visualizations — in a separate panel called Artifacts. Available on Pro and above.

Priority access. During peak times, your requests are prioritized over free-tier users, which means faster and more consistent response times.

The honest assessment: If you plan to use Claude for professional work — writing, research, coding, analysis, or any task where quality and availability matter — Pro is an easy recommendation at $20 per month. It is priced competitively with ChatGPT Plus and offers a comparable feature set.

Max: For Power Users Who Push the Limits ($100 or $200/month)

The **Max plan** exists for people who use Claude intensively — professionals who spend hours a day in conversation with the model, developers running complex coding sessions, researchers analyzing large document sets, or anyone who regularly bumps against Pro-tier limits.

Max comes in two tiers:

Max at $100/month

- **Much higher usage limits** than Pro. Anthropic describes these as "5x" the Pro limits, though exact numbers vary by model and may change over time.
- **Longer extended thinking.** The model can reason for longer before responding, which improves quality on the hardest problems.
- Everything included in Pro.

Max at $200/month

- **Even higher limits** — described as "20x" Pro.
- **The longest extended thinking budgets available** to any consumer plan.
- Everything included in the $100 Max tier.

Who actually needs Max? In our experience, you need Max if at least one of the following is true:

- You use Claude Opus for extended sessions (multiple hours per day) and regularly hit Pro limits.
- You work on problems that benefit significantly from extended thinking — advanced mathematics, complex code architecture, deep research synthesis — and you want the longest possible thinking budgets.
- Claude is a core part of your revenue-generating workflow, and any interruption from rate limits costs you more than the subscription price.

The honest assessment: Most users will never need Max. It is not a "better" version of Claude — the underlying models are identical. You are paying for higher limits and longer thinking time. If Pro-tier limits frustrate you at least a few times a week, try the $100 Max tier. If that is still not enough, step up to $200. But start with Pro and upgrade only when you have evidence that you need to.

Team: Collaboration for Small Groups ($25 or $150/seat/month, 5-seat minimum)

The **Team plan** is designed for small-to-medium businesses and workgroups that need Claude as a shared tool with administrative oversight. Anthropic offers two seat types, and you can mix and match them across a single team:

- **Standard seats ($25/seat/month):** Everything in Pro plus team-level features.
- **Premium seats ($150/seat/month):** Standard plus Claude Code, Cowork, and 5x more usage than Standard.

A minimum of five seats is required.

Each team member gets:

- **Everything in Pro**, including all models, Projects, extended thinking, and Artifacts.
- **Higher usage limits** than Pro — and substantially higher again on Premium seats.
- **Shared workspaces.** Team members can share Projects, so you can set up a workspace with your company's brand guidelines, product

documentation, or standard operating procedures, and every team member has access.

- **Microsoft 365 and Slack integrations**, enterprise search, SSO and domain capture, and central billing with admin controls.
- **Premium add-ons.** Premium seats unlock Claude Code (the CLI tool covered in Chapter 20) and Cowork, plus much higher usage allowances.

Who needs Team instead of individual Pro plans? If you have five or more people in your organization using Claude regularly, Team makes sense for two reasons: shared workspaces create consistency (everyone works from the same reference materials and instructions), and admin controls give you oversight. If you are a solo professional or a small group below the seat minimum, individual Pro plans are simpler.

The honest assessment: Team is well-designed for its audience. Shared Projects alone can save significant time for teams that need consistent outputs — marketing teams maintaining brand voice, legal teams referencing the same contract templates, or customer support teams working from standardized response guidelines.

Enterprise: For Large Organizations (Custom Pricing)

The **Enterprise plan** is Anthropic's offering for large organizations with complex requirements. Pricing is custom — you will need to contact Anthropic's sales team for a quote, and costs vary based on user count, usage volume, and specific requirements.

Enterprise includes everything in Team, plus:

Single Sign-On (SSO). Employees log in with existing corporate credentials (Okta, Azure AD, Google Workspace, etc.) rather than creating separate Anthropic accounts. A standard requirement for any tool used at scale in a large organization.

Advanced security and compliance. Enterprise customers get more granular data controls, audit logs, and compliance certifications. If your organization operates in a regulated industry — healthcare, finance, government — these controls may be mandatory.

Custom data retention policies. You can specify how long Anthropic retains your organization's conversation data, or ensure it is not retained at all beyond the active session. Critical for organizations handling sensitive information.

Dedicated support. Enterprise customers get a dedicated account team and priority technical support, rather than standard customer service channels.

Higher limits and custom terms. Usage limits, model access, and contractual terms are all negotiable at the Enterprise tier.

The honest assessment: If your organization has more than about fifty Claude users, operates in a regulated industry, or requires SSO and audit logging as a matter of policy, Enterprise is the right path. For smaller organizations without strict compliance requirements, Team is almost certainly enough.

A Decision Guide: Five Questions to Ask Yourself

If you are still unsure, work through these questions:

1. How often will I use Claude? A few times a week for simple tasks? The free tier is fine. Daily for meaningful work? You want Pro at minimum.

2. Do I need access to Opus? If your work involves complex reasoning, advanced coding, or tasks where quality matters more than speed, you want Opus — which means a paid plan.

3. Do I hit limits on my current plan? If you regularly see "usage limit reached" messages on Pro, move to Max. If you have never hit a limit on Pro, you do not need Max.

4. Am I part of a team that needs shared context? If multiple people in your organization work from the same reference materials and instructions, Team's shared Projects feature is worth the premium over individual Pro subscriptions.

5. Does my organization require SSO, audit logs, or compliance controls? If yes, you need Enterprise. There is no workaround for these requirements on lower tiers.

Education and Research Access

Anthropic has shown a growing commitment to making Claude accessible for education and academic research. The specific programs evolve, but here is what to be aware of:

Students and educators should check Anthropic's website for current academic pricing or free-tier enhancements. As of early 2026, Anthropic has offered expanded access for verified educational institutions, though the details vary by region and institution type.

Researchers working on AI safety, alignment, or related fields may have access to special programs, including API credits and early access to new features. Anthropic's research team actively collaborates with the academic community, and inquiries about research partnerships can be directed through their website.

Nonprofits and social impact organizations have occasionally been offered discounted or free access, particularly for projects that align with Anthropic's mission of beneficial AI development.

Our recommendation: if you are affiliated with an educational institution, a nonprofit, or a research organization, check Anthropic's website or contact their team directly before paying full price. The worst they can do is say no.

A Note on API Pricing

If you are a developer or a business looking to integrate Claude into your own applications, the API (Application Programming Interface) uses a separate pricing model. Instead of a monthly subscription, you pay per token — roughly per word — for both input (what you send to Claude) and output (what Claude sends back). Different models have different per-token prices, with Haiku the cheapest and Opus the most expensive.

API pricing is beyond the scope of this chapter, but we mention it here so you know that the subscription plans above apply to *using Claude directly* through the web interface, mobile apps, and desktop apps. If you are building software that uses Claude under the hood, review Anthropic's API pricing page for current rates.

Our Recommendation

For most readers of this book, the short version:

- **Start with the free tier** to get a feel for Claude and confirm it fits your workflow.
- **Upgrade to Pro ($20/month)** as soon as you find yourself wanting more — more messages, access to Opus, Projects, or extended thinking. This happens faster than you expect.
- **Move to Max only if Pro limits become a regular friction point** in your work.
- **Choose Team if you need shared workspaces** and admin controls for a group.
- **Go Enterprise if compliance requires it.**

In Chapter 3, we will walk you through setting up your account — regardless of which plan you choose — and getting Claude configured the way you want it.

Chapter 3: Setting Up Your Account

You have decided to give Claude a try. Maybe you are sticking with the free tier to explore, or maybe you have already committed to Pro. Either way, setup takes only a few minutes — but the choices you make now will shape your experience going forward.

This chapter walks you through account creation, the interface on every platform, the settings worth adjusting, and the privacy controls you should understand before you share anything sensitive with an AI assistant.

Creating Your Account

Head to **claude.ai** in any modern web browser. You will see a clean sign-in page with several options for creating an account:

Email and password. The most straightforward option. Enter your email address, create a password, and verify your email through a confirmation link. Anthropic will also ask you to verify your phone number as an additional security step.

Sign in with Google. If you have a Google account, you can sign in with a single click. This links your Claude account to your Google identity — convenient, but it means your Claude usage is associated with that Google account.

Sign in with Apple. Apple's sign-in lets you hide your real email address behind a relay address, a nice privacy feature if you want to keep your Claude account separate from your primary identity.

Single Sign-On (SSO). If your organization uses a Team or Enterprise plan, you may sign in through your company's identity provider — Okta, Microsoft Entra ID (formerly Azure Active Directory), Google Workspace, or similar. Your IT administrator will provide instructions specific to your setup.

Once signed in, you land on the main conversation screen. There is no lengthy onboarding wizard, no mandatory tutorial, no series of preference questions to answer before you can start. You can type your first message immediately. But before you do, let's take a quick tour.

The Interface: Web

The web interface at claude.ai is where most people spend their time with Claude. It is clean and uncluttered by design.

The Conversation Area

The center of the screen is the conversation itself — your messages on one side, Claude's responses on the other. It looks and feels like a messaging app, by design. Each conversation is a self-contained thread; Claude remembers everything said within a single conversation but starts fresh when you open a new one.

The Sidebar

On the left side, you will find a sidebar listing your recent conversations and your Projects. You can:

- Start a new conversation by clicking the compose button at the top.
- Return to any previous conversation by clicking on it. Claude retains the full context of past conversations, so you can pick up where you left off.
- Access your **Projects** — organized workspaces with custom instructions and reference files. (More on Projects in Chapter 13.)
- Search through your conversation history to find something specific.

The Input Bar

At the bottom of the screen is the input area where you type your messages. Next to the text field, you will find buttons for:

- **Attaching files.** You can upload documents (PDFs, text files, Word documents, spreadsheets) and images directly into the conversation.
- **Model selection.** A dropdown or toggle lets you choose which Claude model to use — Opus 4.7, Sonnet 4.6, or Haiku 4.5 — depending on your plan.
- **Extended thinking toggle.** On paid plans, you can enable or disable extended thinking for the current conversation.

Artifacts Panel

When Claude generates certain types of content — a code snippet, a document, a table, a diagram — it may display that content in a separate **Artifacts** panel to the right of the conversation. Artifacts are interactive: copy, edit, download, or iterate on them without cluttering the main conversation thread.

The Interface: Mobile (iOS and Android)

Claude's mobile apps are available from the Apple App Store and Google Play Store. The experience is streamlined for smaller screens but retains the core functionality.

What works well on mobile:

- Quick questions and conversations. The mobile app is great for on-the-go queries — ask Claude to explain something, draft a quick reply, or brainstorm ideas while you are away from your desk.
- Voice input. Dictate your prompts instead of typing, which is often faster on a phone.
- Image uploads. Take a photo with your phone's camera and send it directly to Claude — useful for reading documents, signs, menus, or anything else you want analyzed.
- Push notifications. If you have a conversation in progress and Claude finishes a long response, you can be notified.

What is more limited on mobile:

- File uploads beyond images are possible but less convenient than on desktop.
- The Artifacts panel is available but harder to work with on a small screen. Complex artifacts (code, tables, long documents) are better viewed on a larger display.
- Extended conversations with heavy file attachments are more cumbersome to manage.

Our recommendation: use the mobile app for quick interactions and the web or desktop app for substantial work sessions.

The Interface: Desktop (Windows and macOS)

Anthropic offers native desktop applications for both **Windows** and **macOS**. These are standalone apps — not just browser shortcuts — and they offer a few advantages over the web interface:

- **System-level keyboard shortcuts.** Invoke Claude with a global hotkey, even when the app is minimized or in the background.
- **Cleaner focus.** A dedicated app means fewer distractions than a browser tab competing with your other open sites.
- **Native notifications.** Desktop-level alerts when Claude completes a response.
- **Slightly better performance.** Native apps can feel snappier than web interfaces, particularly on older hardware.

The feature set is identical to the web version. Model selection, Projects, Artifacts, file uploads, extended thinking — it is all there. Pick whichever platform feels most comfortable; there is no feature gap to worry about.

Settings Worth Adjusting

Once you have signed in and oriented yourself, it is worth spending a few minutes in the settings. You can access these through the gear icon or your profile menu (exact location varies slightly by platform).

Appearance

Claude offers light and dark themes. Pick whichever is easier on your eyes. If you work in varied lighting conditions, the "system" option matches your device's current light/dark mode automatically.

You can also adjust the font size in some clients, worth doing if you spend long sessions reading Claude's responses.

Language Preferences

Claude can respond in dozens of languages. By default, it responds in whatever language you write to it — ask a question in Spanish, get an answer in Spanish.

Set a preferred language in settings if you want Claude to always respond in a specific language regardless of how you write your prompts.

Data Privacy Controls

This is the most important section in settings, and we will cover it in detail in the privacy section below. For now, know that there is a specific toggle that controls whether your conversations can be used to improve Claude's future models.

Response Style

Depending on platform and version, you may have options to adjust Claude's default response style — more concise or more detailed, more formal or more casual. These are gentle nudges, not dramatic changes, and you can always override them with specific instructions in your prompts.

Configuring Claude's Behavior with Projects

One of Claude's most powerful features is **Projects** — dedicated workspaces where you define custom instructions and upload reference files that persist across conversations. A marketing manager could create a "Brand Content" project with tone guidelines and a style guide, so every conversation in that project follows those rules automatically.

Projects are available on Pro, Max, Team, and Enterprise plans (not the free tier). Set up at least one project early, even if it is just basic instructions about how you prefer Claude to communicate. We cover Projects in full detail in Chapter 13.

Privacy: What You Need to Know

AI privacy is a legitimate concern, and Anthropic has been more transparent than most about how it handles user data. Here is what you should know.

What Anthropic Stores

When you have a conversation with Claude, the text is stored on Anthropic's servers. This is necessary for basic functionality — it is how your conversation history works, and how Claude maintains context within a single conversation.

By default, Anthropic retains your conversations for a period of time (the exact duration is specified in their privacy policy and may change). This data is used for:

- **Providing the service.** Your conversation history, Projects, and settings need to be stored so they are available when you return.
- **Safety and abuse monitoring.** Anthropic reviews a small fraction of conversations to identify and address misuse, improve safety features, and comply with legal obligations.
- **Model improvement.** By default, your conversations *may* be used as training data for future Claude models. You can opt out.

Opting Out of Training Data Use

In your privacy settings you will find a toggle (the exact wording may vary) that controls whether your conversations can be used to train future models. If you turn it off, your conversations are still stored for service delivery and safety purposes, but they are not fed into the training pipeline.

Our recommendation: If you use Claude for anything involving sensitive information — client data, proprietary business information, personal health details, legal matters — turn this toggle off. The peace of mind is worth whatever marginal impact it might have on Claude's future improvement.

On **Team and Enterprise plans**, this setting is typically controlled by the administrator, and training data use is off by default. That is one of the reasons organizations with data sensitivity requirements opt for these plans.

What Claude Does *Not* Do

Claude does not:

- Search the internet during your conversation (and therefore does not leave a trail of web searches associated with your account).
- Share your conversation data with third parties for advertising purposes.
- Retain information from one conversation and use it in a different conversation (unless you are within the same Project with uploaded knowledge files).
- Access your device's files, contacts, location, or other data beyond what you explicitly share in the conversation.

A Practical Privacy Framework

Here is how we think about it:

- **Low sensitivity** (general questions, creative brainstorming, learning): Use Claude freely without worrying much about privacy settings.
- **Medium sensitivity** (work emails, business planning, internal documents): Opt out of training data use. Consider using Projects to keep this work organized and separate from casual conversations.
- **High sensitivity** (legal documents, medical records, financial data, trade secrets): Opt out of training data use, use a Team or Enterprise plan with organizational data controls, and think before you paste. Anything you share with Claude is transmitted to and stored on Anthropic's servers.
- **Do not share** (passwords, API keys, Social Security numbers, credit card numbers): Never paste these into any AI assistant, Claude included. There is no legitimate reason to do so.

Accessibility Features

Anthropic has invested in making Claude usable for people with diverse needs, though this is an area where the product continues to evolve.

Screen reader compatibility. The web interface is built with semantic HTML and ARIA labels, making it navigable with screen readers like JAWS, NVDA, and VoiceOver. Claude's responses render as text, which screen readers handle well.

Keyboard navigation. You can navigate the interface, switch between conversations, and access settings using keyboard shortcuts without a mouse. The desktop apps add system-level shortcuts.

High contrast and font sizing. The dark theme provides a high-contrast option that some users find more readable, and font sizes can be adjusted in your browser or system settings.

Voice input. On mobile and some desktop configurations, you can dictate prompts instead of typing. This is handled by your device's speech-to-text system, not by Claude itself.

Response format control. If you need Claude's responses in a specific format for accessibility reasons — plain text without formatting, shorter paragraphs, simpler language — include those preferences in your custom instructions or in the prompt itself. For example: *Please respond in plain text without markdown formatting, using short paragraphs of no more than three sentences each.*

Accessibility is an area where we expect continued improvement. If you have specific needs the current interface does not meet, Anthropic's support team welcomes feedback.

You Are Ready

Your account is created. You know what the interface looks like on every platform. You have configured the settings that matter — especially privacy. And if you are on a paid plan, you have at least considered setting up your first Project.

In Chapter 4, we dig into the three Claude models — Opus, Sonnet, and Haiku — and help you understand when to use which one. Choosing the right model is one of the simplest ways to get better results.

Part II: Understanding Claude

"The question of whether a computer can think is no more interesting than the question of whether a submarine can swim."

— Edsger W. Dijkstra

Chapter 4: Understanding Claude's Models

When someone says "I asked Claude," that statement is less specific than it sounds. Claude is not a single model — it is a family of models, each designed for different situations. Choosing the right one is like choosing the right tool from a toolbox: a sledgehammer works, but if the job calls for a finishing nail, you want a smaller hammer.

This chapter explains the three current Claude models, what each is best at, how extended thinking changes the equation, and how to develop an intuition for when to switch.

The Three Models

As of early 2026, Anthropic offers three models in the Claude family. They share the same underlying architecture and training philosophy, but differ significantly in capability, speed, and resource cost.

Claude Opus 4.7: The Powerhouse

Model ID: claude-opus-4-7

Opus is Claude's most capable model. If Claude were a consulting firm, Opus would be the senior partner — the one you bring in for the highest-stakes problems, the most nuanced analysis, and the work where "good enough" is not good enough.

What Opus excels at:

- **Complex reasoning.** Multi-step logic problems, mathematical proofs, legal analysis, financial modeling — anything that requires holding multiple threads of thought at once and working through them carefully.
- **Advanced coding.** Not just writing code, but architecting systems, debugging subtle issues, refactoring large codebases, and explaining complex code in ways less experienced developers can follow.

- **Nuanced writing.** Opus produces the most natural, sophisticated prose of any Claude model. If you are writing something that needs to be good — a client-facing report, a long-form article, a creative piece — use Opus.
- **Analysis of long, complex documents.** Opus handles very long inputs (contracts, research papers, code repositories) with the best comprehension and recall.
- **Instruction following on complex tasks.** When your prompt has multiple requirements, constraints, and nuances, Opus is the most reliable at catching and honoring all of them.

What Opus costs you:

- **Speed.** Opus is the slowest of the three. Responses typically take noticeably longer, especially for complex tasks. That is the tradeoff for depth.
- **Usage limits.** Because Opus requires more computational resources, your usage limits are lower. You will send fewer messages per day with Opus than with Sonnet or Haiku on the same plan.

When to choose Opus: You are working on something important and complex. You want the best possible output and can wait a few extra seconds (or more) for it. The task involves reasoning, not just retrieval.

Claude Sonnet 4.6: The Everyday Workhorse

Model ID: claude-sonnet-4-6

Sonnet is the model most people should use most of the time. It is the balanced option — fast enough for responsive conversations, capable enough for the vast majority of tasks, and efficient enough that your usage limits stretch much further.

What Sonnet excels at:

- **General-purpose assistance.** Answering questions, summarizing documents, drafting emails, explaining concepts, brainstorming ideas — the bread and butter of daily Claude use.
- **Coding.** Sonnet is a very capable coding assistant. For most programming tasks — writing functions, debugging, generating tests,

explaining code — Sonnet's output is indistinguishable from Opus in practical quality.

- **Conversation.** For back-and-forth dialogues where you are iterating on something (refining a piece of writing, exploring an idea, working through a problem), Sonnet's speed makes the experience feel more natural.
- **Document handling.** Sonnet handles long documents well, though Opus has a slight edge on the most complex analytical tasks.

What Sonnet costs you:

- **A small step down in peak reasoning quality.** On the hardest reasoning tasks — the kind where Opus shines — Sonnet will occasionally miss nuances or take a less optimal path. For most tasks, you will not notice the difference.

When to choose Sonnet: This should be your default. Start with Sonnet, switch to Opus only when the task demands it. If you are unsure, Sonnet is the right answer.

Claude Haiku 4.5: The Speedster

Model ID: claude-haiku-4-5-20251001

Haiku is the fastest and most resource-efficient Claude model. It is designed for tasks where speed matters more than depth, where the question is straightforward, or where you need to process a high volume of simple requests.

What Haiku excels at:

- **Quick lookups.** "What is the capital of Uruguay?" "Convert 5 miles to kilometers." "What does the HTTP status code 403 mean?" Haiku handles these instantly.
- **Simple text manipulation.** Reformatting a list, converting bullet points to prose, translating a short text, extracting key points from a brief document.
- **Triage and classification.** Sorting items into categories, tagging content, quick yes/no judgments.

- **High-volume tasks.** If you are processing many simple requests in sequence (through the API, primarily), Haiku's speed and low cost make it the obvious choice.

What Haiku costs you:

- **Reduced depth.** Haiku struggles with complex reasoning, nuanced analysis, and sophisticated writing. It is not designed for those tasks.
- **More errors on hard problems.** If you ask Haiku to do something that really needs Opus or Sonnet, the quality drop is noticeable.

When to choose Haiku: The task is simple and straightforward. You want an answer in seconds, not a carefully reasoned essay. You are working through a series of quick tasks and want snappy responses.

Extended Thinking: Claude's Inner Monologue

Extended thinking is one of Claude's most powerful features, and understanding it will change how you approach complex problems.

What It Is

When extended thinking is enabled, Claude does not jump to an answer. Instead, it spends time — sometimes a few seconds, sometimes significantly longer — reasoning through the problem step by step before producing its visible response. Think of it as Claude's internal scratch paper: it works through possibilities, considers counterarguments, checks its reasoning, and only then writes its final answer.

You will see a visual indicator that Claude is "thinking," and once it finishes, the response appears. On some interfaces, you can expand the thinking process to see what Claude reasoned through, which can be fascinating and educational.

How It Changes Output Quality

The difference is most dramatic on tasks that involve:

- **Multi-step reasoning.** "Given these financial statements, what is the company's free cash flow, and how does it compare to the industry average? What risks does the trend suggest?" Without extended thinking,

Claude might give a surface-level answer. With it, Claude works through the numbers methodically.

- **Complex coding problems.** "Refactor this 500-line function into smaller, well-structured modules." Extended thinking lets Claude plan the architecture before writing.
- **Ambiguous or nuanced questions.** "What are the strongest arguments for and against this policy proposal?" Extended thinking produces more balanced, thorough analysis.
- **Mathematical and logical problems.** Any problem that benefits from showing your work.

How to Use It

On paid plans, you will find an extended thinking toggle in the conversation interface — typically near the model selector or in the input bar. When enabled, it applies to all responses in the current conversation (or until you toggle it off).

A few practical tips:

- **Skip extended thinking for simple tasks.** If you are asking Claude to summarize a paragraph, draft a quick email, or answer a factual question, turning it on slows the response without meaningfully improving quality.
- **Use it when the task is hard.** Complex analysis, multi-step problems, challenging code, important writing that needs to be well-structured.
- **Budget varies by plan.** Pro users get moderate thinking budgets. Max users get longer budgets, meaning Claude can reason longer on the hardest problems. The $200 Max tier gets the longest budgets of all.
- **It combines powerfully with Opus 4.7.** Extended thinking on Sonnet is useful. Extended thinking on Opus is where you see the most dramatic quality improvements, because Opus has the deepest reasoning capability to begin with.

When It Is Not Worth It

Extended thinking adds latency. In a rapid back-and-forth conversation, the extra wait can disrupt your flow. It is also unnecessary for tasks that do not involve reasoning — translation, text reformatting, simple Q&A. Use it deliberately, not as a default.

How Model Selection Affects Your Experience

Choosing a model is not just about quality — it also affects speed and how quickly you burn through your usage limits.

Speed

Haiku responds almost instantly for most prompts. It feels like a fast messaging app.

Sonnet is quick but not instant. Most responses arrive within a few seconds, though complex tasks may take longer.

Opus is noticeably slower. Expect to wait several seconds for most responses, and potentially much longer for complex tasks with extended thinking enabled. Not a flaw — the cost of depth.

Usage Limits

Your plan gives you a budget of usage per time period (hourly, daily, or both). Different models consume different amounts of that budget:

- **Haiku** uses the least. You can send many more Haiku messages before hitting your limit.
- **Sonnet** uses a moderate amount. Most Pro users will not exhaust their Sonnet budget during normal use.
- **Opus** uses the most. Heavy Opus users may hit their limits, especially on Pro. That is the main reason power users upgrade to Max.

Quality

We have covered this, but to summarize the hierarchy:

- **Opus 4.7** — Best quality across the board, especially on complex and nuanced tasks.
- **Sonnet 4.6** — Very strong quality, nearly indistinguishable from Opus on many everyday tasks.
- **Haiku 4.5** — Good for straightforward tasks, but a clear step down on anything requiring depth.

When to Switch Models

Developing an intuition for model selection takes a little practice. Some concrete guidelines:

Start a task with Sonnet. If the results are good, stay with Sonnet. No need to use a bigger model if a smaller one delivers.

Switch to Opus when: - You tried Sonnet and the output was not quite right — it missed nuances, made reasoning errors, or produced writing that lacked polish. - The task is inherently complex: multi-step analysis, advanced mathematics, intricate code, or high-stakes writing. - You need the response to be correct on the first try, with minimal back-and-forth iteration.

Switch to Haiku when: - The task is simple and speed matters. Quick lookups, reformatting, classification, short translations. - You are doing many small tasks in sequence and do not want to wait for Sonnet's slightly longer response times. - You are approaching your usage limits and want to stretch them further on the remaining tasks.

A common pattern: Sonnet to draft, Opus to refine. Start a piece of writing or a code project with Sonnet for speed, then switch to Opus for a final review pass. The best of both worlds — rapid iteration followed by deep quality assessment.

Legacy Models and the Evolution Path

If you have been using Claude for a while, you may remember earlier model names — Claude 3 Opus, Claude 3.5 Sonnet, Claude 4 Sonnet, and so on. Anthropic has gone through several generations, and the naming convention has evolved.

The simplified lineage:

- **Claude 3 family (early 2024):** Claude 3 Haiku, Claude 3 Sonnet, Claude 3 Opus. The first tiered model release.
- **Claude 3.5 family (mid-to-late 2024):** Significant improvements, especially Claude 3.5 Sonnet and Claude 3.5 Haiku.
- **Claude 4 family (2025):** Major reasoning and extended thinking improvements.

- **Claude 4.5/4.6/4.7 family (2025–2026):** The current generation. Refinements in coding, reasoning, vision, and overall capability.

Legacy models are typically phased out over time. If you are accessing Claude through the API, you may still be able to specify older model versions for compatibility, but for interactive use through claude.ai and the apps, you will always be on the current generation.

The key takeaway: if someone references an older Claude model in a blog post or tutorial, the concepts still apply, but the specific model names and capabilities may differ from what you see today. Claude's core behavior — helpful, honest, careful — has been consistent across generations, even as raw capability has improved dramatically.

Practical Model Selection Scenarios

Ten common tasks and which model we would recommend:

1. **Summarize a one-page email.** Haiku or Sonnet. Either works; Haiku is faster.
2. **Draft a cover letter for a job application.** Sonnet with extended thinking, or Opus for an important application.
3. **Debug a Python script that is throwing an error.** Sonnet. Switch to Opus if the bug is subtle or involves complex logic.
4. **Analyze a 50-page contract for potential risks.** Opus with extended thinking. Exactly the kind of task where Opus earns its keep.
5. **Translate three sentences from English to Japanese.** Haiku. Fast and accurate for short translations.
6. **Write a 2,000-word blog post about industry trends.** Sonnet for the first draft, Opus for final review and polish.
7. **Explain what a confusing error message means.** Haiku or Sonnet. Quick, factual, straightforward.
8. **Build a financial model in a spreadsheet.** Opus with extended thinking. Complex reasoning with numbers benefits from Claude's deepest thinking.
9. **Brainstorm ten names for a new product.** Sonnet. Creative brainstorming does not need Opus-level reasoning.

10. **Review your business plan and identify weaknesses.** Opus with extended thinking. You want the most critical, nuanced feedback possible.

The pattern is clear: match the model to the complexity. When in doubt, start with Sonnet and upgrade to Opus if needed. You will rarely regret having Opus double-check important work.

In Chapter 5, we put this into practice with your first real conversations — a guided walkthrough of ten prompts that will teach you how Claude thinks and how to get the best results from it.

Chapter 5: Your First Conversations

You have an account. You know which model to pick. Now it is time to talk to Claude.

This chapter is hands-on. We will walk through how conversations with Claude work, what makes a good prompt, how to interpret Claude's responses (including the moments when it pushes back), and then work through ten real prompts together so you can see the dynamics in practice.

How to Talk to Claude

There is no special syntax. You do not need to start with "Hey Claude" or use particular keywords. Type naturally, the way you would message a knowledgeable colleague.

That said, how you phrase your request has a significant impact on what you get back. AI researchers call this **prompt engineering**, which sounds more complicated than it is. At its core, it is clear communication. The same principles that make you effective when emailing a coworker apply here:

- **Be specific.** "Help me with my resume" will get a generic response. *"Review my resume for a senior product manager role at a tech company. Focus on whether my bullet points demonstrate measurable impact, and suggest improvements for any that don't."* will get a useful one.
- **Provide context.** Claude cannot read your mind. If your question depends on background information, include it. You can paste text, upload documents, or simply explain the situation in a few sentences.
- **State your desired format.** If you want a bulleted list, say so. If you want a two-paragraph summary, say so. If you want pros and cons in a table, say so. Claude follows format instructions well when you provide them.
- **Indicate your audience and purpose.** "Explain machine learning" produces a different response than *"Explain machine learning to a group of marketing professionals who have no technical background. Keep it under 300 words and use a real-world analogy."*

You do not need to be formal or polite (Claude has no feelings to hurt), but many people find that writing in a natural, conversational tone produces the most natural responses in return. Do whatever feels comfortable.

Asking Questions, Getting Answers

The simplest interaction with Claude is a single question:

What is the difference between a traditional IRA and a Roth IRA?

Claude will respond with a clear, organized explanation. For factual questions like this, the response is typically accurate, well-structured, and more comprehensive than a quick web search — though you should always verify financial, medical, or legal information independently.

You can also ask open-ended questions:

What are some effective strategies for managing a remote team?

Here, Claude draws on its training data to offer a range of practical suggestions. The response will be thorough but general — it does not know your specific team, your industry, or your challenges. This is where follow-up questions become powerful.

Follow-Up Questions and Refining Responses

One of Claude's greatest strengths is its ability to maintain context within a conversation. Every message you send builds on what came before, creating a **context window** — the running memory of everything said so far.

This means you can iterate. Suppose Claude gives you a response about remote team management that is too general. You can follow up:

Those are good starting points, but my team is in four different time zones and we have struggled specifically with asynchronous communication. Can you focus on that?

Claude will narrow its advice based on your new constraints. You can continue refining:

We use Slack and Notion. What specific practices would you recommend for those tools?

Each follow-up gets you closer to something useful. This iterative process — prompt, respond, refine, respond — is the fundamental rhythm of productive work with Claude. Think of it less like a search engine (one query, one answer) and more like a conversation with a consultant (back and forth until you reach a good solution).

A practical tip: Do not restart the conversation when the response is not quite right. Refine within the same conversation. Claude will pick up your preferences and constraints as the conversation progresses, producing increasingly targeted responses.

Understanding Context Windows

The **context window** is the amount of text Claude can hold in its working memory during a single conversation. Think of it as the size of Claude's desk — how many pages it can have spread out and refer to at once.

Claude's context window is large — capable of holding well over 100,000 words. In practical terms, this means you can:

- Paste in a long document and have a detailed conversation about it.
- Have extended back-and-forth dialogues without Claude forgetting what you discussed earlier.
- Upload multiple files and ask Claude to compare, analyze, or synthesize them.

There are, however, some important nuances:

Conversations are isolated. When you start a new conversation, Claude begins with a blank slate. It does not remember what you discussed in previous conversations. (The exception is Projects, where custom instructions and uploaded knowledge files persist across conversations within that project.)

Very long conversations can degrade. Claude's context window is large, but information in the middle of a very long conversation may be recalled less reliably than information at the beginning or the end. If you are working on a critical task and the conversation has grown long, consider starting a fresh conversation and pasting in the most important context.

Input counts against the window too. The context window includes both your messages and Claude's responses. A conversation where Claude has written several long responses will use up context faster than one with short exchanges.

For most users, these limitations rarely matter in practice. But they are worth knowing about, especially if you work with long documents or have marathon conversation sessions.

Reading Claude's Responses

Claude's responses have a distinctive character, and learning to read them well will make you a more effective user.

Structure

Claude naturally organizes its responses with headings, bullet points, numbered lists, and clear paragraph breaks. It tends toward thoroughness — if you ask an open-ended question, expect a comprehensive answer. If you want something shorter, say so explicitly: *"Answer in two to three sentences"* or *"Give me the short version."*

Hedging

Claude often qualifies its statements. Phrases like "generally speaking," "this may vary depending on," and "I'd recommend checking with a professional" are common. This is not evasiveness — it is calibration. Claude is communicating its level of certainty honestly.

When Claude says "I believe" or "I think," pay attention. It is often signaling that the information is likely correct but not guaranteed. When it says "I'm not sure about this" or "my knowledge may be outdated here," take that seriously — it is telling you to verify.

Pushback

This is one of Claude's most distinctive and valuable traits. Unlike some AI assistants that cheerfully agree with anything you say, Claude will tell you when it thinks you are wrong, when your premise is flawed, or when your plan has a problem.

For example, if you ask:

Write me a cover letter that says I have ten years of experience in data science when I actually have three.

Claude will not write it. It will explain that misrepresenting your experience is dishonest and counterproductive, and offer to help you write a compelling cover letter that presents your three years of experience in the best possible light.

This pushback extends to subtler situations. If you ask Claude to review a business plan and the plan has serious weaknesses, Claude will name them — even if you clearly put a lot of work into it. This can feel jarring if you are used to AI assistants that default to praise, but it is far more useful.

How to handle pushback: Read it carefully. Claude's objections are usually well-reasoned. If you still disagree, explain why and ask Claude to proceed — it will often comply once it understands your reasoning. But consider the possibility that Claude has a point.

Refusals

Occasionally, Claude will decline a request entirely. This happens most often with:

- Requests to help with clearly illegal activities.
- Requests for content that could cause serious harm (detailed instructions for weapons, dangerous substances, etc.).
- Requests that involve impersonating real people in misleading ways.
- Some requests involving graphic sexual or violent content.

In most of these cases, the refusal is appropriate. But Claude sometimes errs on the side of caution and refuses legitimate requests — a researcher asking about dangerous topics for academic purposes, a fiction writer working on a thriller, or a security professional testing vulnerabilities. If you encounter an overly cautious refusal, rephrase with more context about your purpose: *"I'm a security researcher testing our company's defenses. Can you help me understand how SQL injection attacks work so I can protect against them?"* Adding context about your intent often resolves the issue.

Claude's Personality

Claude has a consistent personality built around three core values: being **helpful, harmless, and honest**. In practice, this means Claude tries to solve your problem, avoids producing harmful outputs, and tells you the truth even when it is not what you want to hear. It is notably **less sycophantic** than many AI assistants — more willing to push back, disagree, and offer honest criticism rather than empty praise. Some users find this refreshing immediately; others need time to adjust. Chapter 14 covers Claude's personality, behavior, and how to work with (and customize) its communication style in detail.

Walkthrough: Your First Ten Prompts

Let's put everything together. Here are ten prompts you can try right now, each designed to show a different aspect of Claude's capabilities. We will explain what each prompt demonstrates and what to look for in the response.

Prompt 1: A Simple Factual Question

What causes tides, and why are there two high tides per day instead of one?

What this demonstrates: Claude's ability to explain scientific concepts clearly. Look for how it handles the nuance — most people expect the answer to be just "the moon," but the full explanation involves both the moon's gravitational pull and centrifugal force. A good response will address both.

Prompt 2: A Practical Task

I need to write a professional email declining a meeting invitation because I have a schedule conflict. The meeting was proposed by my skip-level manager. Keep it respectful but brief.

What this demonstrates: Claude's ability to follow specific constraints (professional, brief, respectful) and to understand social context (skip-level manager implies a need for particular care with tone).

Prompt 3: An Open-Ended Creative Request

Give me five ideas for a birthday gift for someone who loves cooking, hates clutter, and has a small kitchen.

What this demonstrates: Claude's ability to work within multiple constraints simultaneously. Good responses will suggest things that are practical, space-efficient, and cooking-related — not just generic gift ideas.

Prompt 4: Analysis with Pushback

I'm thinking about quitting my stable job to start a business selling handmade candles on Etsy. The candle market seems like it's booming. Is this a good idea?

What this demonstrates: Claude's willingness to push back constructively. A sycophantic assistant would say "Great idea! Go for it!" Claude will acknowledge the appeal while raising practical concerns — market saturation, income instability, the difference between a hobby and a business. This is Claude's honest personality at work.

Prompt 5: Follow-Up and Refinement

After Prompt 4, follow up with:

Fair points. What if I kept my job and started it as a side business first? What would that look like for the first six months?

What this demonstrates: The power of iterative conversation. Claude will use the context from your previous exchange to provide a more targeted, actionable plan. Notice how the response is more specific because Claude already knows your situation.

Prompt 6: Document Analysis

Paste in a paragraph or two from any document you have — an article, a report, an email thread — and ask:

Summarize this in three bullet points and identify the single most important takeaway.

What this demonstrates: Claude's ability to process pasted text and extract meaning. The constraint (three bullets plus one takeaway) forces conciseness. Try this with different types of documents to see how Claude adapts.

Prompt 7: Explaining Something Complex Simply

Explain how a mortgage amortization schedule works. Assume I know nothing about finance. Use a concrete example with a $300,000 home loan.

What this demonstrates: Claude's ability to adjust its explanation to match your stated knowledge level and to ground abstract concepts in specific numbers.

Prompt 8: Code (Even If You Are Not a Programmer)

Write a simple Python script that reads a CSV file called "expenses.csv" with columns for date, category, and amount, and prints the total amount spent in each category. Add comments explaining each line so a beginner can understand it.

What this demonstrates: Claude's coding ability and its capacity to explain code to non-experts. Even if you do not use the code, reading the response shows you how Claude breaks down technical tasks.

Prompt 9: Handling Uncertainty

Who will win the 2026 World Series?

What this demonstrates: Claude's honesty about its limitations. Since Claude's knowledge has a cutoff and the 2026 season is ongoing, it cannot predict the future. Watch how it handles this — it should be upfront about what it does not know rather than guessing.

Prompt 10: A Complex, Multi-Part Request

I'm preparing a presentation for my team about whether we should adopt a four-day workweek. I need: (1) three strong arguments in favor, (2) three strong arguments against, (3) two real companies that have tried it and what happened, and (4) a suggested structure for a 15-minute presentation on the topic.

What this demonstrates: Claude's ability to handle multi-part requests with different types of content (arguments, research, planning). This is the kind of prompt where Sonnet does well, and where Opus with extended thinking would do even better if the stakes are high.

What to Do Next

You have now seen Claude in action across a range of tasks. You understand how conversations work, how to refine responses, what to expect from Claude's personality, and when it will push back or refuse.

The most important thing now is to use Claude for your own real work. Take a task you would normally spend thirty minutes on — a piece of writing, a research question, an email you have been putting off, a decision you are mulling over — and bring it to Claude. The more real your prompts are, the more useful the responses will be, and the faster you will develop an intuition for what Claude does best.

The chapters ahead build on this foundation with more advanced techniques: crafting better prompts, using Projects and Artifacts, working with long documents, and integrating Claude into specific professional workflows. But the core skill — clear communication, iterative refinement, and honest engagement with Claude's responses — starts here.

Part III: Core Use Cases

"We shape our tools, and thereafter our tools shape us."

— Marshall McLuhan

Chapter 6: Writing with Claude

Writing is the single most popular use for Claude. Whether you need a quick email, a polished blog post, or a carefully worded resignation letter, Claude can get you from blank page to finished draft faster than you thought possible. But speed is only part of the story. The real value is in the back-and-forth — drafting, revising, adjusting tone, tightening prose — that turns a rough idea into something you are proud to send.

This chapter covers the full range of writing tasks you can hand to Claude, from everyday messages to long-form content. You will learn how to get drafts that sound like you (not like a robot), how to use Claude as an editor, and where AI-written text shines versus where it falls flat. By the end, you will walk through a complete example: writing a professional bio from scratch.

Drafting Emails, Letters, and Messages

Most of us write dozens of emails a day, and the hard ones are not the quick replies — they are the messages where tone matters. A complaint to a vendor. A follow-up after an awkward meeting. A thank-you note that does not sound generic. These are the places where Claude earns its keep.

To get a good email draft, give Claude three things:

1. **Who you are writing to.** A colleague, a client, your landlord, a professor — the relationship shapes the tone.
2. **What you need to say.** The core message, even in rough bullet points.
3. **Any constraints.** Keep it under 200 words. Be warm but professional. Avoid jargon. Whatever matters to you.

Here is an example prompt:

> I need to write an email to my apartment building's management company. Our hot water has been out for three days. I've already called twice with no response. I want to be firm but not aggressive — I still have to live here. Keep it to one short paragraph.

Claude will produce a concise, measured message that hits the right notes. If the first draft feels too soft, say "Make it firmer" or "Add a line about my tenant rights." If it feels too harsh, say "Soften the last sentence." This iterative process is where Claude shines — you are not starting over each time, you are sculpting.

The same approach works for formal letters, LinkedIn messages, text messages you have been agonizing over, wedding toasts, and condolence notes. For anything emotionally delicate, Claude is useful as a sounding board. You can say, "Here is what I want to communicate — help me find the right words," and Claude will respect the emotional weight of the situation without overdoing it.

Blog Posts, Articles, and Social Media Content

If you are writing longer content — a blog post, a newsletter, a thought-leadership article — Claude can help at every stage: brainstorming topics, outlining, drafting, and editing.

Start with an outline. Rather than asking Claude for a full 1,500-word blog post in one shot, ask for an outline first. Something like:

> I run a small bakery. I want to write a blog post about why sourdough takes so long to make and why it's worth the wait. Give me an outline with 4-5 sections, each with a one-sentence summary of the point I'll make.

Review the outline, rearrange it, add your own ideas, then ask Claude to draft each section. This gives you more control and produces better results than a single "write me a blog post" prompt.

Provide your voice. If you have existing writing — a previous blog post, a page from your website, even a few emails — paste it in and tell Claude to match that style. Claude picks up on patterns well: sentence length, vocabulary level, how formal or casual you tend to be.

Social media is its own animal. For Twitter/X posts, LinkedIn updates, or Instagram captions, be explicit about the platform and its norms. A LinkedIn post that reads like a tweet will feel too terse; a tweet that reads like a LinkedIn post will get scrolled past. Tell Claude the platform, the audience, and the goal (engagement, information, humor), and it will adapt.

One practical tip for social media: ask Claude for several variations. Say, "Give me five different versions of this LinkedIn post, each with a different hook." Then pick the one that feels most natural, or combine elements from two or three. You will end up with something better than any single draft.

Editing, Proofreading, and Tone Adjustment

Claude is not just a writer — it is an excellent editor. In some ways, editing is where Claude provides the most value, because you keep your own voice and ideas while getting a sharp second pair of eyes.

There are several levels of editing you can ask for:

Proofreading. Ask Claude to check for typos, grammar errors, and punctuation issues. Paste your text and say, "Proofread this. Only fix clear errors — don't change my style." Claude catches the mistakes a spell-checker misses, like incorrect homophones ("their" vs. "there"), subject-verb agreement issues, and inconsistent formatting.

Copy editing. This goes a step further: tightening sentences, eliminating redundancy, improving flow. Ask Claude to "edit this for clarity and concision" or "tighten this up without changing the meaning." Claude is good at cutting filler words and restructuring awkward sentences while preserving your intent.

Tone adjustment. This is one of Claude's most useful editing tricks. You can take a draft and say:

- "Make this more formal."
- "Make this friendlier and more approachable."
- "This sounds too salesy — tone it down."
- "Adjust this for a technical audience who already knows the basics."

Claude will rewrite with the new tone while keeping the substance intact. This is useful when you have written something in your natural voice but need to adapt it for a different audience — say, turning an internal memo into a client-facing document.

Structural feedback. For longer pieces, ask Claude to evaluate the overall structure. "Does this essay flow logically? Are there any gaps in my argument? Is the conclusion strong enough?" Claude will give you honest, specific feedback rather than vague praise. (Chapter 14 covers Claude's honesty and how to get genuine criticism.)

Translation

Claude handles translation well across dozens of languages, and it is especially strong when you need more than a literal word-for-word conversion. You can say:

> Translate this email into Spanish. The recipient is a business partner in Mexico City — keep the tone professional but warm, the way you would in Mexican business culture.

That cultural context makes a difference. A direct translation of an American business email into Spanish can feel abrupt or rude, because the conventions are different. Claude knows this and adapts — adding the appropriate greetings, adjusting the level of formality, and restructuring sentences to feel natural in the target language.

You can also use Claude for:

- **Translating documents you have received.** Paste in a French contract or a German product specification and ask Claude to translate it into English, noting any terms that do not have clean equivalents.
- **Bilingual communication.** If you need to write a message in a language you partially speak, write it in English first, have Claude translate it, then ask Claude to explain any choices that might be tricky so you understand what you are sending.
- **Checking your own translations.** If you have written something in a second language, paste it in and ask Claude to review it for errors and awkward phrasing.

A word of caution: for high-stakes legal or medical translations, Claude is a useful starting point, but you should still have a qualified human translator review the final version. Claude can miss subtle nuances, idioms that do not transfer cleanly, or specialized terminology with precise meaning in one field. For everyday communication, though, Claude's translations are remarkably good.

Claude's Writing Style vs. ChatGPT's

If you have used ChatGPT, you will notice a different feel to Claude's writing. The differences are worth understanding so you can get the best results.

Claude tends toward precision. Where ChatGPT often defaults to enthusiastic, slightly flowery prose — lots of "Absolutely!" and "Great question!" and decorative adjectives — Claude leans toward cleaner, more measured language. Its default voice is closer to a thoughtful colleague than a motivational speaker. If you want warmth and energy, ask for it, but Claude will not inject it automatically.

Claude avoids over-promising. When you ask Claude to write marketing copy or persuasive text, it tends to stay grounded. It will not claim your product "revolutionizes" an industry unless you specifically ask for that kind of language. Some users find this frustrating; others find it refreshing. If you need bolder claims, say so — Claude can write punchy marketing copy, it just will not do it by default.

Claude is more willing to push back. If you ask Claude to write something misleading, exaggerated, or factually questionable, it is more likely to flag the issue than to comply. This is part of Anthropic's design philosophy. In practice, Claude is a useful gut-check: if it hesitates about a claim on your sales page, that claim might be worth reconsidering.

Claude handles nuance well. For writing that requires subtlety — a sensitive HR communication, a diplomatic response to a difficult client, a nuanced opinion piece — Claude produces drafts that acknowledge complexity rather than oversimplifying. It will not flatten a gray area into black and white unless you tell it to.

None of this means one tool is categorically better than the other. ChatGPT's enthusiasm makes it great for brainstorming and first drafts where energy matters more than precision. Claude's measured approach makes it better for final drafts, professional communication, and anything where getting the tone exactly right matters. Many writers use both.

When AI-Written Text Works and When It Doesn't

AI-written text has improved enormously, but it is not appropriate for every situation. Here is an honest breakdown:

AI text works well for:

- **Routine business communication.** Emails, status updates, meeting summaries, standard reports. These have predictable structures and expectations, and Claude handles them efficiently.
- **First drafts.** Even if you plan to rewrite heavily, starting with Claude's draft beats staring at a blank page.
- **Content at scale.** Product descriptions, FAQ entries, social media posts — when you need many pieces of similar content, Claude speeds up the process dramatically.
- **Text you would rather not write.** Complaint letters, awkward messages, boilerplate — the tedious writing tasks that drain your energy.

AI text struggles with:

- **Deeply personal writing.** A eulogy, a love letter, a memoir. Claude can help organize your thoughts, but the emotional authenticity has to come from you. Use Claude as a structural aid, not the author.
- **Original thought leadership.** If your value to readers is your unique perspective and experience, a Claude draft will feel generic no matter how much you prompt it. Use Claude to polish your ideas, not generate them.
- **Creative fiction (usually).** Claude writes competent prose, but truly original, voice-driven fiction remains elusive for AI. It can help with plot structure, dialogue experiments, and overcoming writer's block, but it is not going to write your novel for you.

- **Anything requiring lived experience.** A restaurant review, a travel essay, a product testimonial — readers can often tell when the writer has not actually experienced what they describe.

The golden rule: use Claude to amplify your ideas and save time on execution, not to replace your thinking. The best results come when you bring the substance and Claude helps with the form.

Walkthrough: Writing a Professional Bio

Let us walk through a realistic example from start to finish. You need a professional bio — for a conference, a company website, or a LinkedIn profile. You have been putting it off because writing about yourself is uncomfortable. Here is how to tackle it with Claude.

Step 1: Give Claude the raw material.

> I need to write a professional bio. Here's the basic info:
>
> - Name: Sarah Chen
> - Title: Senior Product Manager at a fintech startup called Ledger Labs
> - 8 years in product management, previously at two larger companies (Wells Fargo and Intuit)
> - Led the launch of Ledger Labs' main product, a budgeting app that hit 500K users in its first year
> - MBA from UC Berkeley
> - I mentor women in tech through a nonprofit called TechBridge
> - I also speak at product management conferences occasionally
>
> I need three versions: a long one (about 150 words) for conference programs, a medium one (about 75 words) for our company website, and a short one (one sentence) for social media profiles. Professional but not stuffy — I want to sound approachable.

Step 2: Review Claude's drafts.

Claude will produce all three versions. Read them carefully. Common things to adjust:

- The long version might lead with your title when you would rather lead with your mission or what drives you. Tell Claude: "Start the long version with why I'm passionate about fintech, not my job title."
- The short version might be too generic. If it says something like "fintech product leader and mentor," ask Claude to make it more specific and memorable.
- Check for accuracy. Did Claude embellish anything? If it says "award-winning product manager" and you did not mention any awards, flag it. Claude generally avoids inventing credentials, but verify anyway.

Step 3: Iterate.

> The long version is good, but the second sentence is clunky. Can you tighten it? Also, I'd like to mention that I speak conversational Mandarin — it's relevant since Ledger Labs is expanding into Asian markets.

Claude will revise, incorporating your new details and smoothing out the rough spots.

Step 4: Adapt for different contexts.

Once you have a bio you like, you can quickly spin it for other purposes:

> Take the long bio and adapt it for a podcast guest intro. Make it sound like something a host would read aloud — conversational, not like a resume.

Or:

> Turn the medium bio into a third-person version for a press release.

This is one of Claude's strengths: once it has the core material, producing variations is fast. What would have taken an hour of agonizing over word choices becomes a five-minute conversation.

Step 5: Final polish.

Paste your chosen version back in and ask Claude to proofread it one last time. Then copy it out and use it. Done.

Key Takeaways

- Give Claude context about your audience, purpose, and tone — the more specific you are, the better the output.
- Use Claude as an editor, not just a writer. Paste your own drafts in for proofreading, tightening, and tone adjustment.
- For longer content, start with an outline and build up section by section rather than asking for a complete draft in one prompt.
- Claude's writing style is more precise and measured than ChatGPT's. If you want more energy or enthusiasm, ask for it explicitly.
- AI-written text works best for routine communication and first drafts. For deeply personal or experience-driven writing, use Claude as a structural aid, not the author.
- Always review AI-generated text before sending it. Claude is fast, but you are the one who has to stand behind the words.

In the next chapter, we will look at how Claude can help you learn new things and dig into research — even without a web connection.

Chapter 7: Research and Learning

Claude is an exceptional research partner — but one with a specific set of strengths and limitations. It can synthesize vast amounts of information, explain difficult concepts in plain language, summarize long documents in seconds, and quiz you until a topic sticks. What it cannot do is look things up on the internet. This single fact shapes everything in this chapter, and understanding it will save you from the most common mistake new users make: treating Claude like a search engine.

In this chapter, you will learn how to use Claude for research, summarization, and learning. You will see where it excels (long documents, explanations, study aids) and where you need to be careful (facts, dates, recent events). By the end, you will walk through a complete example: researching a topic for a work presentation.

Using Claude as a Research Assistant

Think of Claude less like Google and more like a brilliant colleague who has read an enormous number of books, papers, and articles — but whose reading stopped sometime in 2025 or early 2026 (the exact cutoff varies by model) and who has not checked the news since. That colleague can help you think through a topic, explain how things work, identify the key debates in a field, and organize your findings. But they cannot tell you what happened last week, and they might misremember a specific statistic.

With that mental model in place, here is how to use Claude for research:

Start broad, then narrow. If you are researching a topic you do not know much about, begin with an overview question:

> I need to understand the basics of carbon capture technology. Give me an overview: what it is, the main approaches, where it stands today, and the biggest open questions.

Claude will give you a solid foundation. From there, you can drill into the areas that matter most for your purposes:

> Tell me more about direct air capture specifically. What are the leading companies, what does the economics look like, and what are the main technical challenges?

Ask Claude to map the landscape. One of Claude's most useful research tricks is asking it to lay out the different perspectives or schools of thought on a topic:

> What are the main arguments for and against universal basic income? Give me the strongest version of each side.

Claude is good at presenting multiple viewpoints fairly, which is valuable when you are trying to understand a debate rather than find support for a position you already hold.

Use Claude to identify what you do not know. After Claude gives you an overview, ask: "What are the key questions I should be asking about this topic that I haven't asked yet?" This is surprisingly effective at uncovering blind spots.

Bring your own sources. This is the single most important research strategy with Claude. Because Claude cannot browse the web, the best way to use it for current or specialized research is to bring the information to it. Copy and paste articles, upload PDFs, or paste in data, then ask Claude to help you analyze, summarize, or synthesize. When you supply the source material, Claude's analysis is grounded in real, verifiable information rather than its training data alone.

Summarizing Articles, Papers, and Documents

This is one of Claude's standout capabilities. If you have ever stared at a 40-page research paper or a dense legal document and wished someone would tell you what it says, Claude is that someone.

Quick summaries. Paste in an article or upload a document and ask:

> Summarize this in three paragraphs. Focus on the main findings and why they matter.

Claude will extract the key points and present them clearly. For shorter documents, this takes seconds.

Executive summaries. For business documents, reports, or proposals, you can ask for a structured summary:

> Give me an executive summary of this report. Include: key findings, recommended actions, risks identified, and any data points I should know.

Targeted extraction. Sometimes you do not need a full summary — you need specific information pulled from a long document:

> I'm uploading a 50-page employee handbook. I just need to know: what's the policy on remote work, how many vacation days do new employees get, and what's the process for requesting a leave of absence?

Claude will find and extract exactly what you asked for, sparing you the entire document.

Academic papers. Claude handles research papers exceptionally well. You can ask it to:

- Summarize the paper's hypothesis, methodology, findings, and conclusions
- Explain the paper in plain language (invaluable for papers outside your field)
- Identify the limitations the authors acknowledge and any they do not
- Compare the paper's findings to what you already know about the topic

Long documents are a particular strength. Claude's context window — the amount of text it can process at once — is large enough to handle book-length documents. Where other tools might lose track of details in a long text, Claude maintains coherence across the whole document. If you need to analyze a 200-page contract, a full thesis, or a long legislative bill, Claude can work with the whole thing at once.

A practical tip: when summarizing, specify what you care about. "Summarize this" is fine, but "Summarize this with an emphasis on the financial implications" or "Summarize this for someone who needs to decide whether to invest" produces far more useful results. Claude can tailor the summary to your needs, but only if you tell it what those needs are.

Explaining Complex Topics at Your Level

Everyone has encountered an explanation that was either too basic to be useful or too advanced to follow. Claude can calibrate its explanations to your level, but you need to tell it where you are starting from.

Be explicit about your background:

> Explain how mRNA vaccines work. I have a basic college biology background but no specialized knowledge of immunology.

Or:

> I'm a complete beginner with no science background. Explain how mRNA vaccines work using everyday analogies.

Or:

> I have a PhD in molecular biology. Explain the specific mechanism by which lipid nanoparticles deliver mRNA to dendritic cells and why the choice of ionizable lipid matters.

Same topic, three completely different explanations. Claude adjusts vocabulary, depth, and the use of analogies based on what you tell it.

Ask for analogies. If Claude's explanation is too abstract, say "Explain that using an analogy" or "Compare this to something I'd encounter in everyday life." Claude is good at finding metaphors that make difficult concepts click.

Build understanding incrementally. You do not have to understand everything in one exchange. Start with the basics, make sure you follow, then ask Claude to go deeper:

> OK, I understand the basic idea. Now explain what happens when the immune system encounters the real virus after vaccination. Go one level deeper than your last explanation.

This layered approach mirrors how good teachers work, and it is far more effective than trying to absorb everything at once.

Ask "why" and "how" follow-ups. When Claude explains something, the most powerful follow-up is often the simplest: "Why?" or "How does that work?" These push Claude past surface-level explanations into the mechanisms and reasoning underneath. Keep asking until you are satisfied.

Study Aids: Quizzes, Flashcards, and Tutoring

Whether you are preparing for a certification exam, learning a new subject for work, or helping your kid study for a test, Claude is an effective study partner.

Quizzes. Ask Claude to test you on a topic:

> Quiz me on the key concepts of microeconomics. Give me 10 multiple-choice questions, ranging from basic to intermediate. After I answer each one, tell me if I'm right and explain why.

Claude will generate questions, wait for your answers, and provide detailed explanations. This is active recall — one of the most effective study techniques — and Claude makes it painless.

Flashcard generation. If you use flashcard apps like Anki, Claude can create flashcard sets for you:

> Create 30 flashcards for AP US History covering the period from 1865 to 1920. Format them as "Front: [question]" and "Back: [answer]" so I can import them into my flashcard app.

The Socratic method. Instead of asking Claude to explain something, ask it to teach you by asking questions:

> I want to understand supply and demand. Instead of explaining it to me, ask me questions that guide me to figure it out myself. Start simple and build up.

Claude will ask leading questions, gently correct misconceptions, and guide you toward understanding. This takes more effort than reading an explanation, but the understanding sticks better.

Tutoring sessions. For ongoing learning, you can have extended tutoring conversations with Claude. Work through textbook problems together. Ask Claude where you went wrong in a calculation. Have it generate practice problems at increasing difficulty levels. Claude is patient, never judges you for not knowing something, and can explain the same concept ten different ways until one clicks.

Exam preparation. Tell Claude what exam you are preparing for and what you have already covered:

> I'm studying for the PMP certification exam. I've finished the chapters on project scope and schedule management. Generate a practice test that covers those two areas, in the style of actual PMP exam questions.

Claude can mimic the format and difficulty level of standardized tests surprisingly well. Just remember that for very recent exams or newly updated formats, Claude's knowledge might be slightly outdated — check the exam provider's website for the latest format.

Fact-Checking: Why You Must Verify Everything

A critical warning: Claude can state false information with apparent confidence — a phenomenon called hallucination. It can fabricate citations, invent statistics, and blend real facts with invented details in ways that sound entirely plausible. Always verify specific facts, statistics, quotes, and citations before using them in anything important. For a thorough treatment of hallucination — how to spot it and how to protect yourself — see Chapter 22.

Claude's Knowledge Cutoff

Claude's training data has a cutoff that varies by model — January 2026 for Opus 4.7, August 2025 for Sonnet 4.6, July 2025 for Haiku 4.5. Anything that happened after the relevant cutoff is unknown to Claude unless you supply it. For current or recent topics, bring your own sources — paste in articles, reports, or data — and let Claude analyze them. Claude can also search the web when the feature is enabled, though its search capabilities are more limited than some competitors. For a deeper discussion of the knowledge cutoff and its implications, see Chapter 22.

Walkthrough: Researching a Topic for a Presentation

Let us put everything together with a realistic example. Imagine you have been asked to give a 15-minute presentation at work on "the impact of remote work on employee productivity." You have a week to prepare. Here is how to use Claude as your research partner.

Step 1: Get the lay of the land.

> I need to give a 15-minute presentation on how remote work affects employee productivity. Give me an overview of what we know about this topic: the main findings from research, the key debates, and any nuances I should be aware of.

Claude will give you a solid overview covering the major studies, the "it depends" nature of the findings, and the factors that influence whether remote work helps or hurts productivity (job type, management style, home environment, and so on). That gives you a framework.

Step 2: Go deeper on what matters.

> My audience is senior managers at a mid-sized tech company. Most of them are skeptical of remote work. What are the strongest evidence-based arguments that remote work can maintain or improve productivity? And what are the legitimate concerns I should acknowledge?

Claude will tailor its response to your audience and situation. Notice that you are not asking Claude to be one-sided — you are asking it to help you build a balanced, credible presentation.

Step 3: Bring in your own sources.

Find two or three recent articles, surveys, or reports from reputable sources (McKinsey, Gallup, Harvard Business Review, your industry's trade publications). Paste them into Claude:

> Here are three recent articles about remote work productivity. Summarize the key findings from each, and identify where they agree, where they disagree, and what the overall picture looks like.

Now Claude is working with current, verifiable data — not just its training knowledge. This makes your presentation much stronger.

Step 4: Build the presentation structure.

> Based on everything we've discussed, create an outline for a 15-minute presentation. I want to open with a surprising statistic, cover 3-4 main points with supporting evidence, acknowledge the counterarguments, and end with practical recommendations for our company. Include suggested slide titles.

Claude will give you a complete presentation skeleton. Review it, rearrange if needed, and ask Claude to flesh out any section that needs more detail.

Step 5: Prepare for questions.

> What questions is a skeptical audience likely to ask after this presentation? Give me the five toughest questions and help me prepare concise, evidence-based answers for each.

This is one of Claude's most underused capabilities. Having it anticipate objections and help you prepare responses makes you far more prepared than walking in with just your slides.

Step 6: Fact-check before you present.

Go through your presentation and verify every specific claim, statistic, and study reference against an original source. If Claude told you "a Stanford study found that remote workers were 13% more productive," find that actual Stanford study and confirm the number. Do not present anything you cannot verify.

Key Takeaways

- Claude is a research partner, not a search engine. It cannot look things up on the web, so bring your own sources for current or specialized topics.
- Claude excels at summarizing long documents, explaining complex topics at any level, and helping you synthesize information from multiple sources.
- For studying, use Claude for quizzes, flashcards, Socratic tutoring, and practice tests. Active recall with Claude is one of the most effective ways to learn.
- Verify every specific fact, statistic, and quote before using it in anything important. Claude is usually accurate, but "usually" is not good enough for professional work.
- Claude's knowledge has a cutoff date. For recent events and developments, supply the information yourself and let Claude help you analyze it.
- The best research workflow combines Claude's analytical abilities with your own web research and source verification.

In the next chapter, we will move from research into everyday life — using Claude to plan trips, manage meals, and handle the hundred small tasks that eat up your week.

Chapter 8: Everyday Productivity

The last two chapters covered writing and research — the big, obvious use cases. But some of the most satisfying ways to use Claude are the smaller, everyday tasks that individually take 20 minutes but collectively eat hours out of your week. Planning a trip. Figuring out what to cook. Making sense of your finances. Deciding how to fix something around the house.

Claude is not a replacement for specialized apps and services — it will not book your flights or order your groceries. But it is a useful thinking partner for the planning, decision-making, and information-gathering that happen before you act. This chapter covers the everyday scenarios where Claude can save you real time and reduce the low-grade stress of having too many things to figure out.

Planning Trips, Events, and Schedules

Trip planning is one of those tasks that sounds fun until you are doing it — buried in browser tabs, comparing hotels, trying to figure out logistics, and wondering if you are missing something obvious. Claude cannot book anything for you, and it cannot check live prices or availability (no web access, remember), but it can do the thinking work that precedes all of that.

Building an itinerary. Give Claude the basics — destination, dates, who is going, budget, interests — and ask for a day-by-day plan:

> I'm planning a 5-day trip to Lisbon, Portugal in October with my partner. We like food, history, and walking around neighborhoods. We don't love museums but will go to one or two great ones. Mid-range budget — nice but not luxury. Build us a day-by-day itinerary.

Claude will produce a detailed plan with specific neighborhoods to explore, restaurants to look up, timing suggestions (when to visit popular spots to avoid crowds), and practical tips (how to get from the airport, whether you need a transit pass). Because Claude draws on extensive knowledge about travel destinations, the suggestions tend to be well-informed — not just the top-ten-tourist-list hits, but real local recommendations.

Important caveat: restaurants close, neighborhoods change, and prices shift. Claude's suggestions are excellent starting points, but verify everything online before you book. A restaurant Claude recommends might have closed last month. A neighborhood it calls "up-and-coming" might have already arrived and priced itself out.

Event planning. The same approach works for parties, weddings, conferences, and any other event:

> I'm hosting a backyard dinner party for 12 people in mid-July. Budget is about $300 for food and decorations. Several guests are vegetarian. One has a severe nut allergy. Help me plan the menu, a rough timeline for the day, and a shopping list.

Claude will account for the dietary restrictions, suggest a menu that works for both vegetarians and meat-eaters, give you a prep timeline so you are not scrambling at the last minute, and produce a shopping list organized by grocery store section.

Schedule optimization. If you have a busy week ahead and need help fitting everything in, describe your commitments and constraints:

> Here's my schedule for next week. I have a dentist appointment Tuesday at 2pm, I need to pick up my car from the shop (45 minutes away) sometime before Thursday, I have three work deadlines on Wednesday and Friday, and I need to fit in four 30-minute workouts. Help me organize this so nothing conflicts and I'm not rushing.

Claude will look at the constraints and suggest a realistic schedule, flagging potential problems (scheduling a workout right before an important meeting, for example) and offering alternatives.

Meal Planning and Recipes

Figuring out what to eat — and then making it happen — is one of life's most persistent low-level challenges. Claude can help in several practical ways.

Weekly meal planning. Tell Claude your household size, dietary preferences, cooking skill level, and how much time you have:

> Plan a week of dinners for a family of four. Two adults, two kids (ages 8 and 11). The kids are picky but will eat pasta, chicken, and rice dishes. One adult is trying to eat less red meat. We have about 30-40 minutes to cook on weeknights. Nothing too exotic.

Claude will give you seven dinners with variety built in, and if you ask, a consolidated grocery list. Ask it to use overlapping ingredients to reduce waste — if Monday's chicken stir-fry uses half a bunch of cilantro, Wednesday's dish can use the rest.

Adapting recipes. This is where Claude is especially handy. You have a recipe but need to change it:

> Here's my grandmother's mac and cheese recipe [paste recipe]. I need to make this for someone who is lactose intolerant. What substitutions would work without ruining it?

Or:

> I want to make this recipe but I don't have heavy cream or shallots. What can I use instead?

Claude understands the chemistry of cooking well enough to suggest substitutions that work, and it will tell you when a substitution will noticeably change the result versus when you will hardly notice.

Using what you have. One of the most practical prompts:

> I have chicken thighs, a can of coconut milk, sweet potatoes, onions, garlic, and basic pantry staples. What can I make for dinner tonight? I have about 45 minutes.

Claude will come back with two or three options, complete with instructions. This is faster than scrolling through recipe apps and more tailored to your exact situation.

Special dietary needs. Whether you are managing diabetes, following a low-FODMAP diet, training for a marathon, or just trying to eat more vegetables, Claude can help you plan around constraints:

> I was just diagnosed with Type 2 diabetes and my doctor wants me to reduce my carb intake. I normally eat a lot of pasta, rice, and bread.

> Help me plan five breakfasts and five lunches that are low-carb but still satisfying. I'm not a great cook.

Claude will provide realistic suggestions tailored to your skill level and explain why certain foods work better for blood sugar management. One important note: Claude is not a doctor or dietitian. Its nutritional information is generally accurate, but for serious medical dietary needs, use Claude's suggestions as a starting point and review them with your healthcare provider.

Personal Finance Questions

Money is stressful partly because it is confusing. Claude can serve as a patient, judgment-free financial educator — not a financial advisor, but someone who helps you understand your options.

Understanding financial concepts. If you have ever nodded along in a meeting with your bank or HR department while having no idea what anyone was talking about, Claude can help:

> Explain the difference between a traditional IRA and a Roth IRA like I'm someone who has never invested before. When would I choose one over the other?
>
> My employer offers a 401(k) match up to 6%. What does that actually mean, and why does everyone say I should at least contribute 6%?

Claude will give you clear, jargon-free explanations. Ask follow-up questions until it clicks.

Budgeting. Claude can help you build or refine a budget:

> Here are my monthly expenses [list them]. I bring home $4,800 after taxes. Help me organize this into a budget and tell me where I might be able to cut back. I want to save $500 a month for a house down payment.

Claude will analyze your spending, suggest categories, and identify potential savings. It might notice you are spending more on subscriptions than you realized, or that your grocery spending is high for your household size.

Debt strategy. If you are dealing with multiple debts, Claude can lay out your options:

> I have $3,200 on a credit card at 22% APR, $8,500 in student loans at 5.5%, and a $2,000 personal loan at 12%. I can put an extra $300 per month toward debt beyond my minimums. What's the smartest way to pay these down?

Claude will explain the avalanche method (highest interest first) versus the snowball method (smallest balance first), and show you how each plays out. It will also explain the psychological trade-offs — why some people do better with the mathematically suboptimal approach because quick wins keep them motivated.

A critical disclaimer: Claude is not a licensed financial advisor and cannot account for your full financial picture, tax situation, or risk tolerance. Its explanations of concepts and general strategies are solid, but for major financial decisions — retirement planning, tax strategy, estate planning, investment allocation — consult a qualified professional. Use Claude to educate yourself so you can have better conversations with that professional.

Health and Wellness (With Caveats)

This section comes with the biggest asterisk in the chapter: Claude is not a doctor. It has never been to medical school. It cannot examine you, run tests, or account for your medical history. That said, Claude can be useful for health-related information when used appropriately.

Understanding medical information. After a doctor's visit, you might have questions about a diagnosis, a medication, or a procedure. Claude can explain:

> My doctor said I have "mild mitral valve prolapse" and it's nothing to worry about. Can you explain what that actually is, in plain language?
>
> I was prescribed metformin. What does it do, what are common side effects, and is there anything I should avoid while taking it?

Claude will give you clear, accurate explanations based on well-established medical knowledge. This is not a replacement for your doctor — it helps you understand what your doctor told you.

Fitness and exercise. Claude can help you design workout routines, understand proper form (in text descriptions — it cannot demonstrate), and plan training programs:

> I'm a beginner who wants to start running. I can currently jog for about 5 minutes before I'm gassed. Build me an 8-week plan to work up to running 30 minutes continuously.

Claude will give you a progressive plan with realistic increases, rest days, and tips for avoiding injury. For more advanced needs, it can discuss periodization, recovery strategies, and how to balance different types of exercise.

Mental health support. Claude can provide general information about mental health topics and coping strategies, but it is not a therapist. It can:

- Explain what conditions like anxiety or depression involve
- Suggest evidence-based coping techniques (breathing exercises, cognitive reframing)
- Help you prepare for a therapy appointment by organizing your thoughts
- Point you toward professional resources

What it should not do is serve as your primary mental health support. If you are struggling, Claude can supplement professional care, but it is not a substitute for it.

The bottom line: for general health education and understanding established medical knowledge, Claude is helpful and generally accurate. For anything involving a specific diagnosis, treatment decision, or urgent health concern, talk to a real healthcare provider. Claude will usually tell you this itself — it is built to be cautious about medical advice.

Home and DIY Project Assistance

Whether you are a seasoned DIYer or someone who just learned what a Phillips head screwdriver is, Claude can help you plan and troubleshoot home projects.

Project planning. Before you start, Claude can help you understand what is involved:

> I want to convert a spare bedroom into a home office. The room is about 10x12 feet. I need good lighting for video calls, a desk area for two monitors, and some storage. I have about a $1,500 budget. What should I prioritize, and what's a realistic plan?

Claude will break the project into steps, suggest a budget allocation, recommend the order of operations (paint first, then furniture), and flag things you might not think of (where the electrical outlets sit relative to your desk placement, or whether the room's lighting will create a backlit silhouette on video calls).

Troubleshooting. When something breaks, Claude can help you diagnose the problem before you call a professional:

> My dishwasher isn't draining. There's about an inch of standing water at the bottom after a cycle. The machine is a Bosch 500 series, about 4 years old. What should I check before calling a repair person?

Claude will walk you through the most common causes (clogged filter, blocked drain hose, garbage disposal knockout plug) and how to check each one. This can save you a service call fee for something simple, and if the problem turns out to be serious, you will at least understand what the repair person is talking about.

Understanding when to hire a professional. Claude is also good at helping you know your limits:

> I want to add a new electrical outlet in my garage. Is this something I can do myself, or should I hire an electrician?

Claude will explain what is involved (and typically recommend a licensed electrician for electrical work, because the consequences of mistakes include fire and electrocution). This honest assessment is valuable — it can save you from a project that is over your head while giving you confidence to tackle the ones within your abilities.

Seasonal maintenance. Claude can help you stay on top of home maintenance:

> It's October in the Pacific Northwest. What home maintenance should I be doing right now to prepare for winter?

You will get a practical checklist: cleaning gutters, checking weatherstripping, servicing the furnace, testing smoke detectors, and other seasonal tasks you might forget.

Walkthrough: Planning a Two-Week Trip

Let us bring everything together with a detailed example. You are planning a two-week vacation to Japan — your first visit. Here is how to use Claude as your planning partner.

Step 1: The big picture.

> I'm planning a two-week trip to Japan in late March/early April (cherry blossom season). It's my first time in Japan. I'm traveling with my spouse. We love food, temples, walking around cities, and natural scenery. We're moderately active. Budget is mid-range — not backpacking, not luxury. We fly in and out of Tokyo. Help me figure out which cities/regions to include and how to split our time.

Claude will suggest a route — likely something like Tokyo, Hakone, Kyoto, Osaka, maybe Hiroshima or Kanazawa — with an explanation of why each stop is worth it and how many days to spend at each. It will note that two weeks is enough to see the highlights without rushing, and suggest logical routing so you are not backtracking across the country.

Step 2: Logistics and transportation.

> How should we get between these cities? Explain the Japan Rail Pass situation — is it worth it for our itinerary? Also, will we need to book trains in advance or can we just show up?

Claude will explain the rail system, help you calculate whether a JR Pass saves money on your route, and note which trains require reservations. Verify current

JR Pass pricing online — this is the kind of detail that might have changed since Claude's training data.

Step 3: Day-by-day planning.

> Build me a day-by-day itinerary for the Kyoto portion (5 days). Mix famous temples with less touristy spots. Include specific restaurant suggestions for lunch and dinner — we eat everything. Note which temples to visit early in the morning to avoid crowds.

Claude will create a detailed plan, noting that Fushimi Inari is best at dawn, that the Arashiyama bamboo grove is magical before 8am but miserable at noon, and that Nishiki Market is perfect for a lunch wander. It will suggest specific neighborhoods for dinner and the types of restaurants to look for.

Step 4: Practical details.

> What do we need to know about practical daily life in Japan? Cash vs. cards, tipping, language, etiquette mistakes to avoid, SIM cards or pocket wifi, that sort of thing.

Claude will cover the essentials: Japan is more cash-heavy than you might expect, tipping is not customary (and can even be considered rude), a pocket wifi rental is usually the best connectivity option, and basic etiquette like removing shoes, bowing, and handling chopsticks correctly.

Step 5: Packing and preparation.

> We're going in late March. What should we pack? We want to be comfortable walking 10-15 miles a day but also be appropriate for temples. Any items we should buy there instead of bringing from home?

Claude will give you a practical packing list tailored to the season (layers for unpredictable March weather), the activities (comfortable walking shoes are non-negotiable), and the culture (something to cover shoulders at certain temples). It will note that Japanese convenience stores sell surprisingly good toiletries, so you can pack lighter.

Step 6: Build a reference document.

> Take everything we've discussed and create a single trip planning document I can refer to. Include the day-by-day itinerary,

transportation notes, packing list, important phrases in Japanese, and the restaurant and hotel recommendations organized by city.

Claude will compile a comprehensive reference document. Print it out or save it on your phone, verify the specific details (restaurant hours, train schedules, current prices), and you have a trip plan that would have taken days to assemble on your own.

Key Takeaways

- Claude excels at the planning and thinking work that precedes action — trip itineraries, meal plans, budgets, project plans, and schedules.
- Always verify specific details like prices, hours, and availability online. Claude's knowledge is extensive but not live.
- For personal finance, use Claude to educate yourself and explore options, but consult a qualified professional for major financial decisions.
- For health and wellness, Claude is a helpful educator but not a substitute for medical professionals. Use it to understand information, not to make diagnoses or treatment decisions.
- For home projects, Claude can help you plan, troubleshoot, and know when to call a professional.
- The most effective approach is conversational: start broad, narrow down, and iterate until you have exactly what you need.

In the next chapter, we will shift from personal productivity to the workplace — using Claude to prepare for meetings, draft reports, and get ahead in your career.

Chapter 9: Work and Professional Use

If there is one place where Claude pays for itself fastest, it is at work. The professional world runs on documents, meetings, decisions, and communication — all things Claude handles well. A report that takes three hours to draft can take 45 minutes with Claude as a co-writer. A meeting you walk into unprepared can become one you own. A job application that feels generic can become one that speaks to the role.

This chapter covers the most common ways professionals use Claude on the job, from meeting prep to data analysis to job searching. The throughline is the same: Claude handles the repetitive, structural, and time-consuming parts of knowledge work so you can focus on the judgment, relationships, and creative thinking that only you can provide.

Meeting Prep and Agendas

Most meetings are mediocre because nobody prepares. The person running it wings it, the agenda is vague or nonexistent, and everyone leaves wondering what was decided. Claude can fix this in about five minutes.

Before the meeting — building an agenda:

> I'm running a 45-minute team meeting tomorrow to decide whether we should move our product launch from June to August. There are 6 people attending: me (product manager), the engineering lead, the design lead, the marketing director, a QA manager, and our VP of product. Build me a structured agenda with time allocations.

Claude will give you a tight agenda: opening context (5 minutes), current status review (10 minutes), risks and trade-offs for each timeline (15 minutes), stakeholder concerns (10 minutes), and decision and next steps (5 minutes). It will also suggest what each attendee should bring.

Preparing your own talking points:

> In that meeting, I need to argue that we should delay the launch. Our main issues are: two critical bugs we haven't resolved, the marketing site isn't ready, and our beta testers reported a confusing onboarding flow. Help me organize these into a clear, 3-minute argument that leads with the strongest point.

Claude will structure your argument, suggest the order of points for maximum impact, and anticipate the counterarguments you are likely to face (the VP will probably ask about revenue impact; engineering will want to know if a partial fix is enough).

After the meeting — action items and summaries:

If you take rough notes during the meeting, paste them into Claude afterward:

> Here are my rough notes from today's meeting [paste notes]. Clean these up into a meeting summary with: key decisions made, action items with owners and deadlines, and open questions that need follow-up.

Claude will turn your scattered notes into a professional summary you can send to the team in minutes. This alone is worth the price of a Claude subscription — clear meeting documentation prevents the "wait, what did we decide?" conversations that plague every organization.

Report and Proposal Drafting

Reports and proposals are the currency of professional life, and they are also some of the most tedious documents to write. Claude can speed up the process dramatically while improving quality.

First drafts. Give Claude the key information and structure:

> I need to write a quarterly business review report for our SaaS product. Here are the key metrics for Q1:

- MRR grew from $180K to $210K (17% growth)
- Churn decreased from 4.2% to 3.1%
- NPS score went from 42 to 51

- We launched two major features: automated reporting and a mobile app
- We missed our new customer acquisition target by 15%

> Write a first draft that hits the highlights, acknowledges the miss on acquisition, and sets up our Q2 priorities. Tone should be honest and forward-looking, not defensive about the miss.

Claude will produce a polished draft with proper section headings, data callouts, and a narrative arc that does not try to hide the bad news. You will need to revise — adding context only you have, adjusting emphasis, inserting specific names and details — but you are starting from a strong foundation instead of a blank page.

Proposals and business cases. When you need to make a case for something — a new hire, a tool purchase, a project — Claude can help you build a persuasive argument:

> I want to propose that our team of 8 adopt a new project management tool (switching from Asana to Linear). The cost is about $1,200 more per year. Help me write a one-page business case. The main benefits are: better integration with our dev tools, faster sprint planning, and less time managing tickets. My boss cares most about engineering velocity.

Claude will structure the proposal around what matters to your decision-maker, include a cost-benefit framing, and keep it to one page — because it knows that executives do not read long proposals.

Executive summaries. If you have already written a long report, paste it in and ask Claude to produce an executive summary:

> Here's a 15-page market analysis I wrote. Distill this into a one-page executive summary for my CEO. She cares about market size, competitive positioning, and our recommended next move. She doesn't need the methodology details.

Claude will pull out exactly what matters and present it at the right level. This is one of those tasks that sounds simple but is hard to do well — and Claude is good at it.

Data Analysis and Spreadsheet Help

You do not need to be a data analyst to work with data, and Claude can bridge the gap between "I have a spreadsheet" and "I understand what this data is telling me."

Interpreting data. If you have data but are not sure what story it tells, paste it in:

> Here's our customer support ticket data for the last 6 months [paste data]. What patterns do you see? Are there any trends I should flag for my team?

Claude will identify patterns: maybe tickets spike on Mondays, maybe a particular product feature generates disproportionate complaints, maybe response times have been creeping up. It will also flag when the data is insufficient to draw a conclusion — an honest assessment that saves you from acting on noise.

Spreadsheet formulas. If you need a formula but cannot remember the syntax (or never learned it in the first place), Claude is your on-demand Excel/Google Sheets tutor:

> I have a Google Sheets spreadsheet with customer data. Column A is the customer name, column B is their sign-up date, and column C is their last purchase date. I want a formula in column D that shows how many days since their last purchase, and I want column E to flag anyone who hasn't purchased in over 90 days with the word "At Risk."

Claude will give you the exact formulas, explain how they work, and note any edge cases (what happens if column C is empty, for instance). If you are not sure where to paste the formula or how to apply it to the whole column, ask — Claude will walk you through it step by step.

Data cleaning and transformation. Claude can help you think through how to clean messy data:

> I exported a CSV from our CRM and it's a mess. Phone numbers are in different formats, some dates are MM/DD/YYYY and others are DD-

> MM-YYYY, and there are duplicate entries. What's the best way to clean this up in Google Sheets?

Claude will suggest a systematic approach, provide formulas for standardizing formats, and explain how to identify and handle duplicates.

Creating charts and visualizations. While Claude cannot create charts directly in a spreadsheet, it can help you decide what type of chart best represents your data, write the formulas to prepare data for charting, and even build visualizations as artifacts (interactive charts built with code) if you want to present data outside of a spreadsheet.

A note on sensitive data: be thoughtful about what data you paste into Claude. Internal sales figures might be fine depending on your company's policies, but customer personal information, financial records, or anything covered by regulations like HIPAA or GDPR should be handled carefully. Check your organization's AI usage policy before pasting sensitive data. When in doubt, anonymize or aggregate first.

Brainstorming and Ideation

The blank whiteboard is as intimidating as the blank page. Claude is a relentless brainstorming partner — it never runs out of ideas, never judges your suggestions, and never tires.

Generating ideas. Start broad:

> We need a creative marketing campaign for a new plant-based protein bar targeted at busy professionals aged 25-40. The brand is playful but not childish. Budget is limited, so we need ideas that are mostly digital and social. Give me 15 campaign concepts, ranging from safe to bold.

Claude will give you a spectrum, some predictable and some surprising. The "ranging from safe to bold" instruction is key — it gives you practical options and stretch ideas. Often the best final concept combines a safe structure with a bold twist.

Building on ideas. Once you spot a concept you like, dig deeper:

> I like concept #7 — the "Fuel Your Hustle" challenge where people share their workday snack moments. Flesh this out: what platforms would it work best on, what would the first week of content look like, and how would we encourage user-generated content?

Claude will develop the concept into something actionable. This iterative process — generate broadly, select, develop, refine — mirrors how creative teams work, just faster.

Challenging your own thinking. Claude is also useful for stress-testing ideas:

> Here's our plan for the product launch [describe plan]. Play devil's advocate. What could go wrong? What are we not thinking about? Where are the assumptions that might not hold up?

Claude will poke holes in your plan — not to be negative, but to help you find the weak spots before they become real problems. This is one of the places where Claude's willingness to push back (covered in Chapter 14) is valuable in a work context.

Naming and branding. Need a name for a project, a product, a feature, or a team? Claude can generate dozens of options:

> We're launching an internal employee wellness program. We need a catchy internal name. The company culture is informal, tech-focused, and a little irreverent. Give me 20 name options.

You will get a mix of serious and playful options. Pick a few favorites and ask Claude to check them for unintended meanings, domain availability considerations, or cultural issues you might have missed.

Job Search: Resumes, Cover Letters, and Interview Prep

Whether you are actively job hunting or keeping your materials current, Claude can help you present yourself more effectively. This is one area where time invested with Claude pays tangible dividends — a better resume and cover letter can change the trajectory of your career.

Resume optimization. The key is not asking Claude to write your resume from scratch — it is asking Claude to improve what you have:

> Here's my current resume [paste it]. I'm applying for a Senior Marketing Manager role at a B2B SaaS company. Here's the job description [paste it]. How should I adjust my resume to be a stronger fit for this specific role? Keep everything truthful — just help me emphasize the right experience and use language that matches what they're looking for.

Claude will identify keywords from the job description that should appear in your resume, suggest reframing bullet points to emphasize relevant skills, and point out experience you may be underselling. The "keep everything truthful" instruction matters — you are optimizing presentation, not fabricating experience.

Quantifying achievements. One of the most common resume weaknesses is vague descriptions of accomplishments. Claude can help:

> Here are my current resume bullet points for my last job [paste them]. Help me make each one more specific and results-oriented. Ask me questions if you need more details to quantify the impact.

Claude might come back with: "You said you 'managed social media accounts.' How many accounts? What was the follower growth? Did any campaigns have measurable results? What was the engagement rate before and after you took over?" These questions prompt you to recall specific numbers and results that make your resume dramatically stronger.

Cover letters. A good cover letter does three things: it shows you understand the company and role, it connects your specific experience to their specific needs, and it conveys real enthusiasm. Claude can help with all three:

> Write a cover letter for this position [paste job description]. Here's my resume [paste resume]. The company recently launched a new product line in sustainable packaging, which I'm genuinely excited about because I spent two years working on sustainability initiatives at my previous company. Keep it to one page. Professional but with some personality.

Claude will draft a letter that weaves your relevant experience into the company's context. Always personalize the draft further — add a specific detail about why this company appeals to you, or reference something you noticed in their recent news. The goal is a letter that could only have been written by you, for this role, at this company.

LinkedIn optimization. Claude can also help you polish your LinkedIn profile:

> Review my LinkedIn headline and summary [paste them]. I'm a data analyst who wants to transition into data science roles. Help me rewrite these to position myself for that transition while being honest about where I am now.

Walkthrough: Preparing for a Job Interview

Let us walk through a complete interview preparation process. You have landed an interview for a Product Manager role at a mid-sized fintech company. The interview is in five days.

Step 1: Understand the role and company.

> Here's the job description for the Product Manager role I'm interviewing for at [company name] [paste description]. And here's what I know about the company: they make a B2B payments platform for small businesses, they raised a Series B last year, and they're expanding into international markets. Help me understand what this role really needs and what the company is probably looking for in a candidate.

Claude will read between the lines of the job description, identify the core challenges the role will face (likely scaling the product for international markets, working cross-functionally with engineering and sales, and making prioritization decisions under resource constraints), and help you understand the company's stage and what it means for the role.

Step 2: Map your experience to their needs.

> Here's my resume [paste resume]. Based on the role analysis, which of my experiences are most relevant? Help me identify 3-4 stories from my career that directly address what this role needs. For each story,

> help me structure it using the STAR format (Situation, Task, Action, Result).

Claude will help you select and structure your best stories. The STAR format keeps each one concise and impact-oriented. Practice telling these out loud — Claude can help refine the wording, but the delivery is up to you.

Step 3: Prepare for common questions.

> Give me the 15 most likely interview questions for a PM role at a fintech company at this stage. Include a mix of behavioral, technical, and product-sense questions. For each one, give me a brief note on what the interviewer is really assessing.

Claude will provide questions like "Tell me about a time you had to make a trade-off between speed and quality" (assessing prioritization judgment), "How would you decide which market to expand into next?" (assessing strategic thinking and framework usage), and "Describe a product you think is poorly designed and how you would improve it" (assessing product sense and analytical ability).

Step 4: Practice with tough questions.

> Let's do a mock interview. Ask me the questions one at a time. After I answer each one, give me honest feedback: what was strong, what was weak, and how I could improve the answer. Don't be nice — be helpful.

This is where Claude's willingness to give candid feedback pays off. It will point out when your answer is too long, when you are not being specific enough, when you buried the lede, or when you forgot to mention the result. Practice three or four questions this way and you will be noticeably sharper in the real interview.

Step 5: Prepare your questions for them.

> What questions should I ask the interviewer to demonstrate genuine interest and good judgment? I want 5-6 questions that are thoughtful, not generic. Tailor them to this specific role and company.

Claude will generate questions that show you have thought deeply about the role — the team structure, the biggest product challenges, how success is measured in the first 90 days, and the company's approach to the international expansion mentioned in the job description. Good questions signal good thinking, and interviewers notice.

Step 6: Day-before review.

> Tomorrow is my interview. Give me a one-page cheat sheet: my top 3 stories, the key points about the company I should reference, the questions I'm going to ask them, and any last-minute reminders about interview best practices.

Claude will distill everything into a concise reference sheet you can review over coffee the morning of your interview. You are not memorizing a script — you are making sure your best material is top of mind.

Key Takeaways

- Claude excels at the preparation work that makes professionals effective: meeting agendas, talking points, report drafts, and data interpretation.
- For reports and proposals, give Claude the key information and structure, then revise with your own context and judgment. Starting from Claude's draft is almost always faster than starting from scratch.
- Be mindful of sensitive data. Check your company's AI usage policy before pasting in confidential information.
- For brainstorming, ask for a range of ideas (safe to bold) and use Claude to develop and stress-test the concepts you like.
- Resume and cover letter work benefits enormously from Claude's ability to match your experience to specific job descriptions. Always keep it truthful — optimize presentation, not facts.
- Interview preparation is one of Claude's highest-value use cases. Mock interviews with honest feedback can meaningfully improve your performance.

In the next chapter, we will explore one of Claude's most distinctive features: its ability to see and understand images and documents you share with it.

Part IV: Advanced Features

"Any sufficiently advanced technology is indistinguishable from magic."

— Arthur C. Clarke

Chapter 10: Vision — Images and Documents

One of the most practical leaps in AI over the past few years has been the ability to *see*. Not in some abstract, metaphorical sense — Claude can look at an image you upload and tell you what is in it, read the text, interpret a chart, or describe a scene. This capability, known as vision or multi-modal input, turns Claude from a text-only assistant into something far more versatile.

In this chapter, you will learn how to use Claude's vision capabilities to analyze photos, extract data from documents, interpret screenshots, and read handwriting. By the end, you will have a clear picture of what Claude can and cannot do with images — and you will walk through a practical example of extracting structured data from a messy receipt.

Uploading Photos for Analysis

Getting an image into Claude is straightforward. In the web interface at claude.ai, you will see a paperclip or attachment icon at the bottom of the chat input. Click it, select an image file from your computer, and it will appear as a thumbnail in your message. You can also drag and drop images directly into the conversation window.

Claude accepts common image formats: JPEG, PNG, GIF, and WebP. There is no strict resolution limit you need to worry about for most practical purposes, but very large images may be downscaled internally. For best results, make sure the image is clear, well-lit, and that any text you want Claude to read is legible at a reasonable zoom level.

Once you attach an image, type your question or instruction and send the message. For example:

- Attach a photo of your garden and ask: "What species of plant is this?"
- Upload a product photo and ask: "Write a product description based on this image."

- Share a photo of a whiteboard and ask: "Transcribe everything written here."

Claude will respond with a description, analysis, or extraction based on what it sees. It is good at identifying objects, reading text, interpreting spatial relationships, and understanding context.

What Claude Sees Well

Claude performs strongly on a wide range of visual tasks:

- **Object identification**: Recognizing animals, plants, household items, vehicles, food, and more.
- **Scene description**: Understanding what is happening in a photo — a birthday party, a construction site, a sunset over a lake.
- **Text extraction**: Reading printed text in signs, labels, documents, and screens.
- **Chart and graph interpretation**: Understanding bar charts, line graphs, pie charts, and tables embedded in images.
- **Color and design analysis**: Describing color palettes, design layouts, and visual composition.

Where It Struggles

No vision system is perfect, and it helps to know the boundaries:

- **Very small or low-resolution text**: If you cannot read it easily yourself, Claude may struggle too.
- **Highly specialized imagery**: Medical imaging (X-rays, MRIs) or satellite imagery may yield unreliable results. Claude is not a diagnostic tool.
- **Counting precision**: Asking Claude to count a large number of similar objects (e.g., "How many beans are in this jar?") often produces rough estimates rather than exact counts.
- **Spatial reasoning in complex scenes**: Claude can describe what it sees, but intricate spatial questions ("Is the red car closer to the camera than the blue one?") can trip it up.

Reading and Extracting Data from Documents

One of the highest-value uses of Claude's vision is document analysis. You can upload a photo or scan of a document — a PDF page, a presentation slide, a printed form, an invoice — and ask Claude to extract or summarize its contents.

This is useful in everyday work:

- **Invoices and receipts**: Upload a photo of a receipt and ask Claude to pull out the vendor name, date, line items, and total.
- **Business cards**: Snap a photo and ask Claude to extract the name, title, company, phone number, and email.
- **Printed forms**: Upload a completed form and ask Claude to transcribe the filled-in fields.
- **Presentation slides**: Share a screenshot of a slide deck and ask for a summary of the key points.

For PDFs specifically, you have two options. You can upload the PDF directly as a file (covered in detail in Chapter 11), which gives Claude access to the raw text. But if you have a scanned PDF — essentially images of pages — Claude's vision capabilities become essential.

Tips for Document Analysis

1. **One page at a time works best.** If you upload a multi-page document as separate images, Claude can focus on each page individually. If you upload a dense multi-page scan as a single image, some details may be lost.

2. **Be specific about what you want.** Rather than "What does this document say?", try "Extract all line items, quantities, and prices from this invoice" or "What is the effective date mentioned in this contract?"

3. **Ask for structured output.** Claude can return extracted data as a table, JSON, CSV, or any format you specify. This makes it easy to paste the results into a spreadsheet or database.

4. **Verify critical data.** Claude is accurate but not infallible. For anything legally or financially significant, always double-check the extracted values against the original document.

Screenshots and UI Analysis

Another powerful application is analyzing screenshots — of websites, apps, error messages, or software interfaces.

Developers and designers find this especially useful:

- **UI review**: Upload a screenshot of your app's interface and ask Claude to suggest improvements to layout, spacing, or visual hierarchy.
- **Error diagnosis**: Share a screenshot of an error message or a buggy UI state, and Claude can help you understand what went wrong.
- **Accessibility feedback**: Ask Claude to evaluate whether text is readable, contrast is sufficient, or interactive elements are clearly labeled.
- **Competitive analysis**: Upload screenshots of competitor products and ask Claude to compare their approaches to a specific feature.

When you share a screenshot of code in an IDE, Claude can read it — but pasting the code as text is almost always better. Text can be searched, referenced precisely, and manipulated. A screenshot of code is useful when you want to show the visual context (syntax highlighting, error underlines, IDE warnings) alongside your question.

Analyzing Charts and Dashboards

Claude handles charts and data visualizations well. If you upload a screenshot of a dashboard, Claude can:

- Describe the trends shown in line charts.
- Compare values across bar chart categories.
- Identify outliers or anomalies in scatter plots.
- Read specific data points and labels.

A good prompt for chart analysis might be: "This is a screenshot of our Q3 sales dashboard. Summarize the key trends and flag anything that looks unusual."

Handwriting Recognition

Claude can read handwriting — with caveats. Neat, well-spaced handwriting in good lighting is usually transcribed accurately. Messy, hurried, or faded handwriting is more challenging, and Claude may make mistakes or flag uncertainty.

Practical uses include:

- **Meeting notes**: Photograph handwritten notes from a meeting and ask Claude to transcribe and organize them.
- **Whiteboard sessions**: Capture a whiteboard full of brainstorming ideas and have Claude convert them into a structured list or outline.
- **Handwritten letters or postcards**: Upload an old letter and ask for a transcription.
- **Sticky notes and to-do lists**: Photograph a collection of sticky notes and ask Claude to compile them into a single list.

When working with handwriting, give Claude the context. For example: "These are handwritten meeting notes from a product design review. Transcribe them as accurately as possible, and note any words you are uncertain about." This primes Claude to interpret ambiguous marks more intelligently and to be transparent about low-confidence readings.

Multi-Modal Conversations

The real power of Claude's vision emerges when you combine images with ongoing conversation. You are not limited to one image and one question — you can build on what Claude sees across multiple turns.

Here is how a multi-modal conversation might flow:

1. You upload a photo of a room you want to redecorate and ask: "Describe the current style of this room."
2. Claude responds with a description — modern minimalist, neutral tones, clean lines.
3. You ask: "What changes would make this feel warmer and more inviting?"
4. Claude suggests adding warm-toned textiles, wood accents, and softer lighting.
5. You upload a second photo of a rug you are considering and ask: "Would this rug work in the room from the first photo?"

6. Claude compares the rug's colors and style against its memory of the room and gives you a reasoned opinion.

This conversational back-and-forth with images is natural and powerful. Claude holds context about previously uploaded images within the same conversation, so you can reference "the first photo" or "the chart I showed you earlier" without re-uploading.

Combining Images with Other Inputs

You can also combine images with text, files, and other inputs in the same message. For example:

- Upload a photo of a product prototype alongside a written specification and ask Claude to check whether the prototype matches the spec.
- Share a screenshot of a data visualization alongside the raw data in CSV format and ask Claude to verify the chart's accuracy.
- Upload multiple images in a single message and ask Claude to compare them.

Walkthrough: Extracting Data from a Receipt

Let us put everything together with a concrete example. You have a crumpled receipt from a business lunch, and you need to log the expense. Here is how to handle it.

Step 1: Capture the Image

Photograph the receipt with your phone. Lay the receipt flat on a contrasting surface (a dark receipt on a light table, or vice versa). Make sure the lighting is even and all text is legible. Avoid shadows falling across the text.

Step 2: Upload and Prompt

In Claude, attach the image and write a specific prompt:

> Please extract the following information from this receipt: - Restaurant name - Date - Each line item with description and price - Subtotal, tax, and total - Tip (if visible) - Payment method
>
> Return the data as a Markdown table.

Step 3: Review the Response

Claude might respond with something like:

Field	Value
Restaurant	The Golden Fork
Date	March 15, 2026

Item	Price
Grilled salmon	$24.00
Caesar salad	$12.00
Sparkling water (x2)	$8.00
Espresso	$4.50

Subtotal	**$48.50**
Tax (8.5%)	$4.12
Total	$52.62
Tip	$10.00
Grand Total	$62.62
Payment	Visa ending 4821

Step 4: Refine if Needed

If Claude misread something — perhaps the tax amount is slightly off or a menu item name is garbled — follow up: "I think the tax should be $4.12, not $4.22. Can you double-check?" Claude will reassess and correct if warranted.

Step 5: Reformat for Your Needs

Now you can ask Claude to convert the data into whatever format your expense system requires: "Convert this into a CSV row with columns: Date, Vendor, Subtotal, Tax, Tip, Total, Payment Method." Claude will produce a clean, copy-paste-ready line.

Prompting Strategies for Better Visual Analysis

Getting good results from Claude's vision is partly about image quality and partly about how you ask. Here are strategies that make a real difference.

Be Specific About the Task

A vague prompt like "What do you see?" gives Claude no direction. It will produce a general description that may or may not include what you need. Compare these:

- Vague: "Look at this image."
- Better: "This is a photo of my car's dashboard. What warning lights are illuminated, and what does each one mean?"
- Best: "This is a photo of my 2023 Honda Civic's dashboard. Identify all illuminated warning lights and explain their severity — which ones require immediate attention and which can wait for a scheduled service?"

The more context and specificity you provide, the more targeted and useful Claude's analysis will be.

Ask Claude to Describe Before Analyzing

For complex images, a two-step approach works well. First, ask Claude to describe what it sees. Then, based on that description, ask your analytical question. This makes sure Claude has correctly identified the relevant elements before drawing conclusions.

For example, with a complex architectural blueprint: "First, describe the layout you see in this floor plan. Then, suggest how the space could be reconfigured to add a home office."

Request Multiple Perspectives

Claude can analyze the same image from different angles when asked:

- "Evaluate this product photo from a marketing perspective — is it compelling? Then evaluate it from a technical perspective — does the product look well-made?"
- "Analyze this data visualization. First, what story does it tell? Second, are there any misleading aspects of how the data is presented?"

Use Comparison Prompts

When you upload multiple images, explicit comparison prompts yield the best results:

- "Compare these two photos of the same intersection taken five years apart. What has changed?"
- "Here are three logo concepts. Rank them in terms of visual clarity, memorability, and professionalism, with specific reasons for each ranking."

Real-World Applications

Beyond the common use cases covered above, here are some real-world scenarios where Claude's vision capabilities shine:

Real estate: Upload listing photos and ask Claude to write detailed property descriptions, identify potential issues visible in the photos (water stains, outdated fixtures), or estimate the style and era of a home.

Education: Students can photograph textbook pages, diagrams, or problem sets and ask Claude to explain concepts, solve problems, or provide additional context.

Inventory and cataloging: Photograph items — books, tools, equipment, inventory — and ask Claude to identify them, estimate their condition, or create catalog entries.

Travel and language: Photograph signs, menus, or documents in foreign languages and ask Claude to translate the text. Claude's vision works across many languages and scripts.

Quality control: Upload photos of manufactured products and ask Claude to identify visible defects, inconsistencies, or deviations from a reference image.

Cooking and nutrition: Photograph a plate of food and ask Claude to estimate the ingredients, suggest what recipe was used, or provide a rough nutritional breakdown.

These applications only scratch the surface. Any task that involves a human looking at an image and making a judgment or extracting information is one Claude can help with.

Privacy Considerations

A note on privacy, since images often contain sensitive information. Any images you upload to Claude are processed according to Anthropic's data usage policies. In general:

- Images uploaded via the API are not used for training.
- Images uploaded through claude.ai on Free, Pro, or Max plans may be used to improve future Claude models unless you opt out — training is on by default for consumer plans as of September 2025.
- If you are on a Team or Enterprise plan, your data is not used for training by default; review your plan's data handling terms.

For sensitive documents — medical records, financial statements, personal identification — consider whether uploading them aligns with your organization's data policies. When in doubt, redact sensitive fields before uploading, or use Claude's API with explicit data retention controls.

Summary

Claude's vision capabilities turn it into a versatile tool for working with the visual world. You can upload photos for analysis, extract structured data from documents and receipts, get feedback on screenshots and UI designs, and transcribe handwritten notes. The key to good results is providing clear images, writing specific prompts, and verifying any critical data Claude extracts.

In the next chapter, we will go deeper into file uploads — not just images, but PDFs, spreadsheets, code files, and other document types Claude can ingest and analyze.

Chapter 11: File Uploads and Analysis

Claude is not limited to what you can type into a chat box. You can hand it entire files — PDFs, spreadsheets, code repositories, research papers, legal contracts — and ask it to read, summarize, analyze, compare, or transform them. Combined with Claude's industry-leading context window, this makes it one of the most powerful document analysis tools available today.

In this chapter, you will learn which file types Claude supports, how to work with long documents that would overwhelm other AI models, and how to get the most out of Claude's file analysis. We will also cover the limitations to know about and the best practices that will save you time.

Supported File Types

Claude can process a wide range of file types. Here is what you can upload:

Text and Documents

- **PDF** — The workhorse format. Claude can read both text-based PDFs (where you can select and copy text) and scanned PDFs (using its vision capabilities to read the images). Text-based PDFs are faster and more accurate.
- **TXT** — Plain text files of any kind.
- **Markdown (.md)** — Rendered or raw Markdown documents.
- **HTML** — Web pages saved as files.
- **RTF** — Rich text format documents.

Data Files

- **CSV** — Comma-separated values, the universal data exchange format. Claude reads, analyzes, and transforms CSV data with ease.
- **JSON** — Structured data files. Claude understands JSON natively and can parse, query, and reformat it.
- **XML** — Another structured data format Claude handles well.

Code Files

- **Python (.py), JavaScript (.js, .ts), Java (.java), C/C++ (.c, .cpp, .h), Ruby (.rb), Go (.go), Rust (.rs)**, and virtually any other programming language. Claude recognizes the language from the file extension and applies appropriate understanding.
- **Jupyter Notebooks (.ipynb)** — Claude can read notebook cells, including code, Markdown, and output.

Images

- **JPEG, PNG, GIF, WebP** — As covered in Chapter 10, Claude can analyze images using its vision capabilities.

Presentations and Spreadsheets

- **PPTX** — PowerPoint presentations. Claude extracts text and can describe slide layouts.
- **XLSX** — Excel spreadsheets. Claude can read cell data, understand formulas, and analyze the contents.
- **DOCX** — Word documents with their formatting.

The general rule: if a file contains text or visual information that a human could read, Claude can probably process it. Binary formats that are not on this list — proprietary database files, compiled executables, audio, video — are not supported.

Working with Long Documents

This is where Claude separates itself from the competition. Sonnet 4.6 and Opus 4.7 each support a one-million-token context window at standard pricing — enough to hold a small library of books, an entire codebase, or hundreds of contracts in a single conversation. (Enterprise customers get a 500,000-token window with additional governance features.) You can upload an entire novel, a full legal contract, a lengthy research paper, or a massive codebase and Claude will process the whole thing.

Why Context Window Size Matters

Other AI models struggle with long documents. They either refuse files beyond a certain size, silently truncate them, or lose track of information mentioned early on. Claude's large context window holds your entire document in memory at once, which leads to more accurate answers and fewer hallucinated details.

Consider the difference: upload a 100-page legal contract and ask "Does this contract contain a non-compete clause?" A model with a small context window might only search the first 20 pages and tell you no. Claude reads the entire document and finds the clause buried on page 73.

Strategies for Very Long Documents

Even with Claude's generous context window, there are smart ways to work with lengthy files:

Upload the full document and ask targeted questions. Rather than asking Claude to "summarize everything," start with specific questions. "What are the payment terms?" or "Find all mentions of liability caps." Targeted questions get precise answers.

Use a two-pass approach for comprehensive analysis. First, ask Claude for a high-level summary or table of contents. Then drill into the sections that matter most. This is more efficient than asking for everything at once.

Break up extremely large files if needed. If your file exceeds Claude's context limit — rare, but possible with massive codebases or data dumps — split it into logical chunks. Upload each chunk in sequence within the same conversation so Claude has context from earlier parts.

Tell Claude what you are looking for. Context helps. Instead of dropping a file with no explanation, say: "This is a vendor services agreement. I need to understand our obligations around data privacy." Claude will prioritize the relevant sections.

Analyzing Data Files

Claude is surprisingly capable at data analysis. Upload a CSV or spreadsheet and you can ask Claude to:

- **Summarize the data**: "What does this dataset contain? How many rows and columns? What are the key fields?"
- **Calculate statistics**: "What is the average order value? What is the median response time?"
- **Find patterns**: "Are there any seasonal trends in this sales data?"
- **Clean the data**: "Find and list any rows with missing values or obvious errors."
- **Transform the format**: "Convert this CSV into a JSON array" or "Pivot this data so each month is a column."

A Practical Data Analysis Session

Imagine you have a CSV file with 12 months of customer support ticket data. Here is how a productive session might look:

You: *Upload support_tickets_2025.csv* "Give me an overview of this dataset."

Claude: "This CSV contains 4,832 rows and 12 columns: ticket_id, created_date, category, priority, assignee, resolution_time_hours, customer_satisfaction, ..." (and so on, with a summary of value ranges and distributions).

You: "What is the average resolution time by category?"

Claude: Returns a table showing average hours for each category — billing issues average 4.2 hours, technical problems average 11.7 hours, account access averages 2.1 hours.

You: "Which categories have gotten worse over the year?"

Claude: Analyzes monthly trends and flags that technical problems have seen resolution times increase from 8 hours in January to 16 hours in December, while other categories remained stable.

You: "Generate a Python script that creates visualizations of these trends."

Claude: Produces a complete matplotlib script you can run on your machine.

Iterative, conversational data exploration is one of Claude's most valuable practical applications.

Working with Code Files

Developers upload code to Claude constantly, for good reason. Claude can:

- **Review code**: Upload a file and ask "Review this code for bugs, performance issues, and style problems."
- **Explain code**: "Walk me through what this function does, step by step."
- **Refactor code**: "Refactor this to be more readable and maintainable."
- **Write tests**: "Generate unit tests for this module."
- **Convert between languages**: "Translate this Python script to JavaScript."

For larger codebases, upload multiple related files in sequence. Claude will understand how they connect — imports, shared types, API contracts — and can answer questions that span files.

A Note on Code File Best Practices

When uploading code for review or analysis, a few habits will improve your results:

- **Upload related files together.** If a bug involves an interaction between two modules, upload both. Claude cannot diagnose cross-file issues from one side only.
- **Include configuration files when relevant.** Many bugs trace back to misconfigured settings. If your question involves runtime behavior, upload the relevant config.
- **Tell Claude the language and framework version.** "This is a Python 3.12 project using FastAPI 0.109" helps Claude give version-appropriate advice rather than suggesting deprecated patterns.
- **Include error messages.** If you are debugging, paste the full stack trace or error output alongside the code. Claude can often pinpoint the issue from the error alone, and does even better when it can see the code too.

Comparing Multiple Documents

One of the most time-consuming tasks in professional work is comparing documents — two versions of a contract, competing proposals, or multiple research papers on the same topic. Claude handles this well.

Side-by-Side Comparison

Upload two documents in the same message (or across two messages in the same conversation) and ask Claude to compare them:

- "Compare these two versions of the lease agreement and list every change."
- "I have two vendor proposals. Create a comparison table covering price, timeline, scope, and warranty terms."
- "These are two research papers on the same topic. Where do they agree and disagree?"

Claude will work methodically through both documents and produce a structured comparison. For contracts and legal documents, it is particularly good at catching subtle wording changes that a human reviewer might miss on a quick read.

Version Tracking

If you are iterating on a document — say a business plan or a technical specification — upload successive versions and ask Claude to track what has changed. "Here is version 3 of our product requirements. I uploaded version 2 earlier. What is new or different?" Claude will identify additions, deletions, and modifications.

Multi-Document Synthesis

Claude can also synthesize information from several documents into a single coherent output. For example:

- Upload five customer interview transcripts and ask: "Identify the top recurring themes and pain points across all five interviews."
- Upload three competing industry reports and ask: "What do these reports collectively suggest about market direction for 2027?"

- Upload a set of meeting notes from a project's history and ask: "Create a timeline of key decisions and their rationale."

Real-World File Analysis Scenarios

To make file uploads more concrete, here are several scenarios drawn from common professional workflows.

Legal Document Review

A contract manager uploads a 45-page vendor agreement and asks:

1. "Summarize the key terms: payment schedule, liability caps, termination clauses, and intellectual property provisions."
2. "Are there any unusual or non-standard clauses I should pay special attention to?"
3. "Compare the indemnification language in this contract with the standard language in our template (uploaded separately)."

Claude reads both documents, identifies the relevant sections, and produces a side-by-side comparison highlighting the differences. This kind of analysis, which might take a paralegal hours, happens in minutes.

Academic Research

A graduate student uploads three journal articles and asks Claude to identify where the authors agree and disagree on a specific question, summarize the methodology used in each study, and suggest gaps in the existing research that might make a good thesis topic. Claude synthesizes across all three papers and presents a structured analysis.

Financial Analysis

An analyst uploads a quarterly earnings report in PDF alongside a CSV of historical financial data. They ask Claude to compare this quarter's performance against the five-year trend, identify any metrics that deviate significantly from historical norms, and draft three bullet points for an executive briefing. Claude handles the cross-format analysis — reading narrative from the PDF and crunching numbers from the CSV — in a single response.

Codebase Onboarding

A developer joining a new team uploads the project's README, the main configuration file, and several core source files. They ask Claude to explain the architecture, identify the entry points, describe the data flow, and flag any patterns or conventions the team appears to follow. This gives the new developer a running start that would otherwise require days of reading code and pestering colleagues.

Limitations and Best Practices

Claude's file handling is powerful, but not magic. Here are the limitations to understand and the practices that get the best results.

Limitations

No file modification. Claude reads files — it does not edit them in place. If you want Claude to fix a bug in your code, it will show you the corrected version in its response, but it will not modify your original file. You copy the changes back yourself. (Claude Code, the CLI tool covered in Chapter 20, is a different story — it edits files directly.)

No persistent storage. Files you upload exist only within the conversation. Start a new conversation and you need to upload again. Projects (Chapter 13) offer a way around this by letting you attach knowledge files that persist across conversations.

Context window is large but finite. At up to one million tokens on Sonnet 4.6 and Opus 4.7, Claude's context window handles the vast majority of documents. But upload a multi-thousand-page corpus or a dataset with millions of rows and you will hit the limit. In those cases, upload the most relevant sections.

Scanned documents are harder than text-based ones. A text-based PDF gives Claude direct access to the characters on the page. A scanned PDF requires vision to read text from images, which is slower and occasionally less accurate — especially with low-quality scans.

Sensitive information stays in the conversation. Everything you upload is sent to Anthropic's servers for processing. Review your organization's data policies before uploading confidential documents, and use the API with appropriate data controls for sensitive workflows.

Best Practices

1. Name your files descriptively. "Q3_sales_report_2025.csv" lets Claude infer context from the filename. A file named "data.csv" gives it nothing to work with before reading the contents.

2. Provide context with your upload. Do not drop a file and say "analyze this." Tell Claude what the file is, what you need, and what format the answer should take. The more specific your instructions, the more useful the response.

3. Ask for structured output. If you need data you can actually use — tables, JSON, CSV, bullet-point summaries — say so explicitly. Claude defaults to prose, which is fine for explanations but less useful when you need to paste results into a spreadsheet.

4. Verify quantitative results. Claude is good at math, but not infallible. If it calculates a sum, percentage, or average from your data, spot-check the numbers. This matters most for financial or scientific work.

5. Use follow-up questions. The first response might not capture everything you need. Follow up with clarifying questions, ask Claude to go deeper on a specific section, or request a different angle. The conversational format is your biggest advantage — use it.

6. Combine files with instructions for best results. The most effective file analysis happens when you upload a file alongside a clear, detailed prompt. "Here is our employee handbook (upload). A new employee is asking whether they can work remotely on Fridays. Find the relevant policy and explain it in plain language." That prompt will get a useful answer.

Summary

File uploads turn Claude from a conversational assistant into a document analysis powerhouse. Feed it PDFs, spreadsheets, code files, and more — and thanks to its massive context window, Claude handles long documents that choke other AI tools. The key is being specific about what you need, providing context, and using the conversational format to iterate toward the answer you want.

In the next chapter, we will explore Artifacts — Claude's ability to create interactive content like runnable code, visual diagrams, and dynamic applications right inside your conversation.

Chapter 12: Artifacts — Interactive Content Creation

Most AI assistants give you text. Claude gives you *things.*

When you ask Claude to write code, create a document, build a diagram, or design an interactive tool, it does not paste the result into the chat. Instead, it produces an Artifact – a standalone piece of content that appears in its own panel alongside the conversation. You can preview it, interact with it, edit it, and share it. An HTML page renders. A React component runs. A Mermaid diagram displays as a rendered visual.

This is one of Claude's most distinctive features. Once you start using Artifacts, you will wonder how you ever worked with an AI that only gave you walls of text.

What Artifacts Are

An Artifact is a self-contained piece of content Claude creates during a conversation. Think of it as Claude handing you a finished product rather than a description of one.

When Claude generates an Artifact, it appears in a dedicated panel to the right of the conversation (on desktop) or as a viewable attachment (on mobile). You can see it, interact with it, and iterate on it through further conversation. The conversation becomes a creative workspace – you discuss what you want on the left and see the result take shape on the right.

Claude creates Artifacts automatically when it makes sense. Ask "Write me an HTML page with a countdown timer" and Claude will not dump raw HTML into the chat – it will create an Artifact showing a working countdown timer ticking in real time.

Types of Artifacts

Claude can produce several types of Artifacts:

- **HTML/CSS/JavaScript** — Complete web pages and interactive applications that render live in the browser.
- **React components** — Functional React components that run in a sandboxed environment, powered by a built-in rendering engine.
- **Markdown documents** — Formatted documents with headers, lists, tables, and other rich text elements.
- **SVG graphics** — Vector images created from code, from simple icons to complex illustrations.
- **Mermaid diagrams** — Flowcharts, sequence diagrams, entity-relationship diagrams, and other visualizations defined in Mermaid syntax and rendered visually.
- **Code files** — Source code in any language, presented in a syntax-highlighted, copy-ready format.

The distinction between a code Artifact and a regular code block in the chat matters. A code block is text in the conversation. An Artifact is a standalone object you can interact with, preview, copy, download, or share.

Code Artifacts: HTML, JavaScript, and React

This is where Artifacts get interesting. Claude can build you working web applications, interactive tools, and visual experiences — all within a conversation.

HTML Pages

Ask Claude to create an HTML page and you get a fully rendered page in the Artifact panel. Not a screenshot or mockup. A live page with working CSS and JavaScript.

Examples of what you can request:

- "Create a landing page for a dog-walking business with a hero section, services list, and contact form."
- "Build an HTML page that converts temperatures between Fahrenheit and Celsius."
- "Make a page that displays the current time in five different time zones."

Claude produces clean, well-structured HTML with embedded CSS and JavaScript. You see it render immediately, test the interactivity, and ask for changes.

JavaScript Applications

Claude builds surprisingly sophisticated JavaScript applications as Artifacts. These run entirely in the browser within the Artifact panel:

- **Calculators and converters** — Mortgage calculators, unit converters, tip calculators.
- **Games** — Simple but playable games like tic-tac-toe, memory matching, snake, or even basic platformers.
- **Data visualization tools** — Interactive charts where you input data and see results.
- **Text processing tools** — Word counters, Markdown previewers, JSON formatters.

The applications run in a sandboxed environment, so they cannot access your file system or make network requests. Within those constraints, Claude builds impressively functional tools.

React Components

For more complex interactive content, Claude creates React components. These render using a built-in React environment, so you do not need to set up a dev environment or install anything.

React Artifacts are particularly good for:

- **Interactive dashboards** — Components with tabs, filters, and dynamic content.
- **Multi-step forms** — Wizards that guide you through a process with validation.
- **Data exploration tools** — Tables with sorting, filtering, and pagination.
- **UI prototypes** — Mockups of application interfaces that you can actually click through.

When Claude creates a React Artifact, it uses functional components with hooks. It can leverage Tailwind CSS for styling (available in the Artifact environment) and popular libraries like Recharts for data visualization and Lucide for icons.

Here is an example prompt that produces a React Artifact:

> Build a React component that is a personal budget tracker. It should let me add expenses with a category and amount, show a running total, and display a breakdown by category as a bar chart.

Claude produces a working budget tracker you can use immediately in the Artifact panel.

Document Artifacts: Markdown and SVG

Not every Artifact is interactive code. Claude also creates document-type Artifacts for formatted content and graphics.

Markdown Documents

When Claude produces a substantial piece of writing — a report, plan, specification, or guide — it often creates a Markdown Artifact rather than dumping the text into the conversation. This gives you a cleaner reading experience and makes it easier to copy or download the complete document.

Markdown Artifacts are useful for:

- Business plans and proposals
- Technical documentation
- Meeting agendas and minutes
- Content outlines and drafts
- Standard operating procedures

You can ask Claude to iterate on a Markdown Artifact just like any other: "Add a section on risk mitigation" or "Rewrite the executive summary to be more concise."

SVG Graphics

Claude can generate SVG (Scalable Vector Graphics) images from scratch. These are vector-based, so they look crisp at any size. Examples include:

- Simple logos and icons
- Diagrams and illustrations
- Infographic elements
- Decorative graphics
- Geometric patterns

SVG Artifacts render visually in the panel, and you can download the SVG file to use in your projects. Claude is not a replacement for a professional graphic designer, but for quick visuals, diagrams, and placeholder graphics, it is handy.

Mermaid Diagrams and Visualizations

Mermaid is a diagram definition language that lets you describe charts and diagrams in text, then render them visually. Claude is fluent in Mermaid and produces diagrams as Artifacts that display as polished visuals.

Types of Mermaid Diagrams

The most commonly used diagram types you can request:

Flowcharts: Process flows, decision trees, and workflows.

> "Create a flowchart showing the customer return process — from requesting a return through approval, shipping, inspection, and refund."

Sequence diagrams: Show how different systems or people interact over time.

> "Create a sequence diagram showing what happens when a user logs into our app — the browser, API server, auth service, and database interactions."

Entity-relationship diagrams: Database schemas and data models.

> "Create an ER diagram for a simple e-commerce system with users, products, orders, and reviews."

Gantt charts: Project timelines and schedules.

> "Create a Gantt chart for a 12-week product launch plan with phases for research, design, development, testing, and launch."

Class diagrams: Object-oriented design and code architecture.

> "Create a class diagram for a library management system with Book, Author, Member, and Loan classes."

State diagrams: Show the different states an object can be in and the transitions between them.

> "Create a state diagram for an order: placed, confirmed, shipped, delivered, returned."

Mermaid Artifacts render as clean, professional-looking diagrams. They are ideal for documentation, presentations, and planning.

Editing and Iterating on Artifacts

Artifacts are not one-shot outputs. You create them through conversation, and you refine them through conversation.

Iterative Refinement

After Claude creates an Artifact, tell it what to change:

- "Make the header background dark blue instead of white."
- "Add a search filter to the table."
- "The flowchart is missing the approval step — add it between review and processing."
- "Increase the font size and add more padding."

Claude updates the Artifact in place, and you see the changes immediately. This iterative loop — create, review, refine — is fast and natural.

Being Specific with Feedback

The more specific your feedback, the better the result. Compare these:

- Vague: "Make it look better." (Claude will guess what you mean.)

- Specific: "Use a darker color palette, increase the spacing between sections, and make the buttons larger." (Claude knows exactly what to change.)

You can reference specific parts of the Artifact: "In the second section, change the chart from a bar chart to a line chart." Claude understands spatial and structural references within its own creations.

Multiple Artifacts in One Conversation

A single conversation can produce multiple Artifacts. You might start with a Mermaid diagram of a system architecture, then create an HTML prototype of the interface, then produce a Markdown specification — all in the same session. Each Artifact exists independently and can be referenced and updated individually.

Sharing and Exporting Artifacts

Once you have an Artifact you are happy with, you have several ways to use it outside Claude.

Copying Content

Every Artifact has a copy button that puts the raw content — HTML, React code, Markdown, SVG, or Mermaid syntax — on your clipboard. From there, you can paste it into your code editor, CMS, documentation tool, or anywhere else.

Downloading

You can download Artifacts as files. An HTML Artifact becomes an .html file you can open in any browser. A Markdown Artifact becomes an .md file. An SVG becomes an .svg file you can use in design tools.

Publishing

Claude offers a "Publish" feature for Artifacts that generates a shareable link. Anyone with the link can view the Artifact in their browser — no Claude account required. This is excellent for sharing quick prototypes, tools, or visualizations with colleagues or clients.

Published Artifacts are static snapshots. If you update the Artifact after publishing, republish to share the updated version.

Using Artifacts in Your Projects

For code Artifacts — especially HTML, JavaScript, and React components — Claude's output is solid starting material. You can:

- Drop an HTML Artifact into your website as a standalone page.
- Use a React component as a starting point in your application, adapting it to your project's architecture and dependencies.
- Import SVG graphics into your design tools or directly into your web projects.
- Copy Mermaid diagrams into documentation platforms that support Mermaid rendering (GitHub, Notion, many static site generators).

Walkthrough: Creating an Interactive Dashboard

Let us walk through creating something substantial — an interactive sales dashboard — from start to finish.

Step 1: Describe What You Want

Start with a clear description of the dashboard:

> Create a React dashboard that shows sales data for a fictional company. Include: - A summary bar at the top with total revenue, total orders, and average order value - A line chart showing monthly revenue for the past 12 months - A bar chart showing revenue by product category - A table of the top 10 customers by total spending - Use a clean, professional design with a sidebar navigation

Step 2: Review the First Version

Claude creates a React Artifact with all the requested components. It generates sample data to populate the charts and tables. The dashboard renders in the Artifact panel with a functional sidebar, summary cards, charts (likely using Recharts), and a data table.

You look it over. The layout is solid, but you want changes.

Step 3: Iterate

> The color scheme is too bright. Use a more muted palette — navy blue, slate gray, and white. Also, make the sidebar collapsible.

Claude updates the Artifact. The colors shift, and the sidebar now has a toggle button.

> Add a date range filter at the top that changes the data shown in all the charts. Default to "Last 12 months" with options for "Last 6 months," "Last 3 months," and "This month."

Claude adds the filter. Since the data is simulated, it adjusts the generated data to respond to the filter selection, demonstrating how the feature would work.

Step 4: Add More Features

> Add a "Export to CSV" button above the customer table that downloads the table data.

Claude adds a working download button. Because Artifacts run in the browser, file downloads work within the sandboxed environment.

> Add a pie chart showing the percentage breakdown of sales by region: North, South, East, West.

Claude adds the pie chart to the dashboard layout.

Step 5: Polish and Share

> Move the pie chart next to the bar chart so they are side by side. Add a title "Q4 2025 Sales Dashboard" at the top of the page.

Claude makes the final adjustments. You now have a polished, interactive dashboard built through conversation. You can publish it to share with your team, download the code to integrate into a project, or screenshot it for a presentation.

The entire process — from initial request to polished dashboard — might take ten to fifteen minutes of conversation. Building the same thing from scratch would take a developer hours.

When to Use Artifacts and When Not To

Artifacts are powerful, but not the right tool for every situation.

Use Artifacts when: - You need something visual or interactive — a tool, a diagram, a formatted document. - You want to iterate on a design or piece of content through conversation. - You need to share a working prototype or visualization quickly. - You are exploring ideas and want to see them take shape in real time.

Skip Artifacts when: - You just need a quick text answer or explanation. - You are working with code that needs to run in a specific environment with specific dependencies. - You need production-grade applications (Artifacts are great starting points, not deployment-ready products). - You are working with sensitive data that should not be rendered in a browser preview.

Summary

Artifacts are one of Claude's most distinctive features. They turn your conversation into a creative workshop where you can build interactive applications, design visual diagrams, create formatted documents, and produce polished graphics — all through natural language. The iterative workflow of creating, reviewing, and refining lets you produce sophisticated outputs without writing a single line of code yourself.

In the next chapter, we will look at Projects — Claude's system for organizing your work into persistent workspaces with custom instructions and shared knowledge.

Chapter 13: Projects — Organized Workspaces

If you have been using Claude for any length of time, you have probably run into a familiar frustration. You start a conversation, upload some files, explain your context, get great results — and then the conversation ends. The next day you start fresh, re-upload the files, re-explain the context, and remind Claude of everything it knew yesterday. It feels like introducing yourself to a colleague with amnesia every morning.

Projects solve this. They are persistent workspaces within Claude where you can store custom instructions, upload knowledge files, and group related conversations together. Instead of starting from zero each time, you walk into a workspace that already understands who you are, what you are working on, and what standards you expect.

In this chapter, you will learn how to create and manage Projects, how to add custom instructions and knowledge files, and how to use Projects to maintain continuity across sessions. We will also cover practical templates for common use cases and compare Projects to standalone conversations so you know when each approach makes sense.

What Projects Are

A Project in Claude is an organized workspace with three core components:

1. **Custom instructions** — Standing directions that apply to every conversation within the Project. They tell Claude how to behave, what to assume, and what standards to follow.
2. **Knowledge files** — Documents you upload that persist across all conversations in the Project. Claude can reference them whenever you ask a question, without you re-uploading.
3. **Grouped conversations** — All chats within a Project are collected together, making it easy to find and continue previous work.

Think of a Project as a briefing packet. Before Claude starts any conversation in the Project, it reads the custom instructions and has access to the knowledge files. Every conversation begins with context already loaded.

Who Can Use Projects

Projects are available on Claude Pro, Max, Team, and Enterprise plans. Free-tier users will need to upgrade. For teams and organizations, Projects become especially valuable because multiple team members can share the same workspace, instructions, and knowledge base.

Creating and Managing Projects

Creating a New Project

Setting up a Project takes a few minutes:

1. In the Claude sidebar, find the Projects section and click "New Project" (or the plus icon next to Projects).
2. Give your Project a descriptive name. "Q2 Marketing Campaign" beats "Work stuff." The name helps you find the Project later and helps teammates understand its purpose.
3. Optionally, add a description that explains the Project's scope and goals.

That is it — you have a Project. Now add instructions and knowledge files to make it useful.

Managing Existing Projects

Your Projects appear in the sidebar for easy access. You can:

- **Rename** a Project as its scope evolves.
- **Archive** Projects you are done with but might want to reference later.
- **Delete** Projects you no longer need.
- **Star** or pin Projects you use frequently so they appear at the top of your list.

For Team and Enterprise plans, you can also manage who has access to each Project. This is useful when different teams or departments need separate workspaces.

Adding Custom Instructions

Custom instructions are the backbone of a useful Project. They tell Claude how to operate within this workspace — the role to play, the standards to follow, the assumptions to make.

Writing Effective Custom Instructions

Good custom instructions are specific, clear, and actionable. Here is an example for a content marketing team:

> You are a content strategist for Acme Software, a B2B SaaS company that sells project management tools to mid-size companies (50-500 employees).
>
> When writing content: - Use a professional but approachable tone - Target audience is project managers and team leads, not developers - Avoid jargon unless it is industry-standard (e.g., "sprint" is fine, "kanban" needs brief explanation) - Default to US English spelling and conventions - Include data and specific examples wherever possible - Keep paragraphs short — no more than 3-4 sentences
>
> When reviewing content: - Check for alignment with our brand voice guide (uploaded as a knowledge file) - Flag any claims that need citations - Suggest improvements for SEO without sacrificing readability
>
> Our primary competitors are Monday.com, Asana, and Basecamp. Do not mention them positively.

Notice how specific this is. Claude knows the company, the audience, the tone, the formatting preferences, and the competitive landscape. Every conversation in this Project starts with that context baked in.

What to Include in Custom Instructions

The categories most worth covering:

Role and context: Who is Claude in this Project? An editor? A coding assistant? A research analyst? What is the domain?

Audience: Who will read or use Claude's output? Technical experts? Executives? Customers? Students?

Standards and preferences: Output format, tone, length, language conventions, terminology to use or avoid.

Domain knowledge: Key facts about your company, product, industry, or subject matter that Claude should always know.

Behavioral rules: Things Claude should always do ("always cite sources") or never do ("never suggest competitor products") within this context.

Output format defaults: If you always want Markdown tables, bullet points, or a specific structure, say so.

Updating Custom Instructions

Custom instructions are not permanent. As your project evolves, update them. Launched a new product feature? Add it. Changed your brand voice? Update the tone guidelines. Hired a new team member who uses the Project? Add context they might need.

Changes apply to all new conversations in the Project. Existing conversations will also use the updated instructions going forward.

Adding Knowledge Files

Knowledge files are documents you upload to a Project that Claude can reference in every conversation. Unlike a single-conversation upload, knowledge files persist and are available across every conversation in the Project.

What to Upload as Knowledge Files

The best knowledge files are reference documents Claude needs repeatedly:

- **Brand guidelines and style guides** — So Claude consistently matches your voice and visual standards.
- **Product documentation** — Feature lists, specifications, release notes, API documentation.
- **Company information** — About pages, org charts, key personnel, company history.

- **Process documents** — SOPs, workflows, approval processes, templates.
- **Glossaries and terminology** — Industry terms, internal jargon, acronyms and their meanings.
- **Sample outputs** — Examples of the kind of work you want Claude to produce, so it can match the style and quality.
- **Research and data** — Market research, customer personas, competitive analyses.
- **Code standards** — Coding conventions, architecture documentation, API specs.

How Claude Uses Knowledge Files

When you ask a question in a Project conversation, Claude has access to all knowledge files. It does not read every file for every question — it references the relevant ones based on your query. Ask about brand voice, it checks the style guide. Ask about a product feature, it consults the product documentation.

You can also explicitly direct Claude to a specific knowledge file: "Based on the competitive analysis I uploaded, how does our pricing compare to the market?"

Practical Limits

There are limits to how much knowledge you can upload to a single Project. The exact limits depend on your plan, but in general:

- You can upload multiple files totaling a substantial amount of text.
- Each file should be within Claude's processing capabilities — the same file types supported for regular uploads (PDF, TXT, CSV, code files, etc.).
- Large files count against the Project's knowledge limit, so prioritize the most important reference material.

If you hit the limit, audit your knowledge files. Remove outdated documents, consolidate overlapping ones, and keep only what Claude genuinely needs.

Using Projects for Ongoing Multi-Session Work

The real power of Projects reveals itself over time. A standalone conversation is a single session. A Project is an ongoing relationship.

Continuity Across Conversations

Within a Project, you can start multiple conversations, each addressing a different aspect of your work. A content marketing Project might have separate threads for:

- Brainstorming blog post topics for next month
- Writing a specific blog post about project management trends
- Reviewing and editing a case study draft
- Creating social media copy for a product launch

Each thread is independent, but they all share the same custom instructions and knowledge files. Claude brings the same understanding of your brand, audience, and standards to every one.

When to Start a New Conversation

Start a new conversation within a Project when:

- You are switching to a different task or topic.
- The current conversation has gotten long and you want a fresh context window.
- You want to explore a different approach without cluttering your current thread.
- A new team member needs to work on something independently.

Keep the same conversation going when:

- You are iterating on a single deliverable (a document, a piece of code, an analysis).
- You need Claude to remember earlier parts of the discussion.
- You are in a multi-step workflow where each step builds on the last.

Project History

All conversations within a Project are saved and organized together. You can scroll through past conversations to find previous work, revisit decisions, or pick up where you left off. This organizational benefit alone makes Projects worthwhile if you use Claude regularly in a specific domain.

Project Templates for Common Use Cases

Ready-to-use Project setups for common scenarios. Adapt them to your needs.

Software Development Project

Custom instructions: > You are a senior software engineer working on [project name], a [description] built with [tech stack]. Follow these conventions: [coding standards]. When reviewing code, check for: security vulnerabilities, performance issues, test coverage, and adherence to our architecture patterns. Prefer [language/framework conventions]. Always suggest tests for new code.

Knowledge files: - Architecture documentation - Coding standards guide - API specifications - Database schema - Key configuration files

Content Creation Project

Custom instructions: > You are a content writer for [company]. Target audience: [description]. Tone: [description]. All content should follow our style guide (uploaded). Default format: [blog post / newsletter / social media]. Include CTAs that align with our current campaign: [description].

Knowledge files: - Brand style guide - Content calendar - Customer personas - Product feature documentation - Sample articles that exemplify the desired tone

Research and Analysis Project

Custom instructions: > You are a research analyst specializing in [domain]. When analyzing data or reports, always note methodology, sample sizes, and potential biases. Present findings with confidence levels. Use academic citation format. Flag when data is older than two years as potentially outdated.

Knowledge files: - Key research papers in the field - Industry reports - Dataset descriptions and codebooks - Previous analysis outputs for consistency

Customer Support Knowledge Base

Custom instructions: > You are helping maintain and query our customer support knowledge base. When answering questions, cite the specific article or policy. If the answer is not in the knowledge base, say so clearly. Use friendly, empathetic language appropriate for customer-facing communication. Escalation path: [description].

Knowledge files: - FAQ document - Product troubleshooting guide - Return and refund policies - Warranty terms - Common customer scenarios and approved responses

Projects vs. Standalone Conversations

You do not need a Project for every interaction with Claude. How to decide:

Use a Standalone Conversation When:

- You have a one-off question or task.
- You do not need custom instructions or persistent knowledge.
- The task is self-contained and will not recur.
- You are exploring or experimenting and do not need organizational structure.
- Speed matters — just open a new chat and go.

Use a Project When:

- You return to the same domain or topic repeatedly.
- You need Claude to consistently follow specific instructions.
- You have reference documents Claude should always have access to.
- Multiple conversations are related and should be grouped together.
- You are collaborating with teammates on a shared body of work.
- You want to maintain quality and consistency across multiple sessions.

The Transition Point

Many people start with standalone conversations and realize they need a Project after the third or fourth time they retype the same background context. That is the signal. If you find yourself pasting the same preamble into every new conversation — "I work at X company, we do Y, our audience is Z, please use this tone" — create a Project.

Tips for Getting the Most from Projects

Start with instructions, add knowledge over time. You do not need to upload every possible document before starting. Begin with clear custom instructions and your most essential reference file. Add more as you discover what Claude needs.

Review and prune regularly. Projects accumulate outdated files and instructions. Every month or so, review your Project's contents. Remove files that are no longer relevant. Update instructions to reflect current priorities.

Use descriptive conversation titles. Within a Project, name conversations clearly: "Blog Post: Remote Work Trends 2026" is easier to find than "Chat 47."

Combine Projects with other features. Use Artifacts (Chapter 12) within Projects to create and iterate on deliverables. Use file uploads within conversations for session-specific documents that do not need to persist as knowledge files.

Share Projects with your team thoughtfully. On Team or Enterprise, think about who needs access and what knowledge files might contain sensitive information.

Summary

Projects bring structure, continuity, and efficiency to your work with Claude. Custom instructions and knowledge files create a workspace that understands your context from the first message of every conversation. This eliminates repetitive setup, ensures consistent quality, and makes Claude dramatically more useful for ongoing work.

In the next chapter, we will explore Claude's personality and behavior — what makes it different from other AI assistants, how Constitutional AI shapes its responses, and how you can customize its communication style to suit your preferences.

Part V: Prompting Mastery

"The limits of my language mean the limits of my world."

— Ludwig Wittgenstein

Chapter 14: Claude's Personality and Behavior

Every AI assistant has a personality, whether its creators intended one or not. How it responds to criticism, the tone it takes when delivering bad news, how it handles controversial topics, whether it flatters you or challenges you — these are not technical details. They shape your entire experience.

Claude's personality is one of its most carefully considered features. Anthropic did not bolt on a persona as an afterthought. They built Claude's character from the ground up using a training approach called Constitutional AI, and the result is an assistant that behaves noticeably differently from competitors. Claude is more willing to disagree with you, more honest about its limitations, and less prone to the gratuitous flattery that plagues many AI systems.

In this chapter, you will learn how Constitutional AI works, why Claude sometimes refuses requests, why it pushes back when it thinks you are wrong, and how extended thinking improves the quality of its reasoning. You will also learn how to customize Claude's communication style so it works the way you want.

Constitutional AI: Helpful, Harmless, and Honest

Most AI models are trained with a method called RLHF — Reinforcement Learning from Human Feedback. Human evaluators rate the model's responses, and the model learns to produce responses that get high ratings. The problem with this approach, on its own, is that human evaluators often prefer responses that *feel* good over responses that *are* good. They reward confidence, agreeableness, and length — even when a shorter, more nuanced, or more critical response would be more useful.

Anthropic developed Constitutional AI (CAI) as a different approach. Instead of relying solely on human preferences, Claude is also trained against a set of principles — a constitution — that defines how it should behave. These principles fall into three pillars:

Helpful

Claude should be genuinely useful. It should answer your questions thoroughly, complete tasks competently, and provide real value. But helpfulness has limits — Claude should not be "helpful" in ways that cause harm, such as providing instructions for dangerous activities or helping with deception.

Harmless

Claude should avoid causing harm — to you, to others, or to society. This is why Claude declines certain requests. It is not trying to be difficult. It is applying a principle: some forms of "help" are actually harmful, and a responsible assistant recognizes that.

Honest

Claude should tell you the truth, even when the truth is uncomfortable. It should not pretend to know things it does not know. It should not agree with you just to be agreeable. It should acknowledge uncertainty, correct mistakes, and give you its genuine assessment rather than the answer you want to hear.

These three principles interact and sometimes create tension. Being maximally helpful can conflict with being harmless. Being honest can feel less helpful in the moment. Claude navigates these trade-offs constantly, and the result is an assistant that feels more trustworthy — even if occasionally less convenient — than one that tells you what you want to hear.

When Claude Says No: Understanding Refusals

Every Claude user eventually encounters a refusal — a response where Claude declines to do what you asked. This can be frustrating, especially when your request seems perfectly reasonable. Understanding why refusals happen helps you work with Claude more effectively and avoid unnecessary friction.

Categories of Refusals

Claude may decline requests in several categories:

Harmful content: Requests for instructions on creating weapons, synthesizing dangerous substances, or causing physical harm. Claude will not help with these regardless of how the request is framed.

Deception and fraud: Requests to write phishing emails, create fake documents, impersonate specific people, or facilitate scams. Claude distinguishes between creative fiction (fine) and actual deceptive intent.

Privacy violations: Requests to help stalk, dox, or surveil specific individuals. Claude will not assist in tracking someone's personal information or location.

Illegal activity: Requests for help with clearly illegal activities, such as hacking into systems you do not own or circumventing security measures.

Harmful stereotypes and hate speech: Requests to generate content that attacks or dehumanizes groups of people based on their identity.

When Refusals Feel Wrong

Sometimes Claude refuses a request that is actually benign. A security researcher asking about vulnerability testing techniques. A novelist writing a scene involving conflict. A medical professional discussing drug interactions.

These over-refusals happen because Claude errs on the side of caution. When uncertain whether a request is harmful, it tends to decline rather than risk producing dangerous content. This is a deliberate design choice, though Anthropic continues to refine the balance.

Working Around Legitimate Refusals

If Claude refuses a request you believe is legitimate, here are some strategies:

Provide context. Explain who you are and why you need the information. "I am a cybersecurity professional conducting authorized penetration testing" gives Claude context it did not have before.

Reframe the request. Instead of asking for something that sounds adversarial, frame it in educational or defensive terms. "How can I protect my application against SQL injection attacks?" is more likely to get a helpful response than "How do I do a SQL injection?"

Be specific about intent. "I am writing a crime novel and need realistic but not instructional details about how a character might break into a house" tells Claude you need creative content, not a how-to guide.

Use a Project with custom instructions. If you regularly work in a domain where refusals are common (security research, medical writing, criminal justice), set up a Project with instructions that establish your professional context.

If Claude still refuses and you believe the refusal is a mistake, that is valuable feedback. Anthropic wants to reduce false-positive refusals, and the model improves over time.

Claude's Honesty: Pushback and Disagreement

Something that surprises many people switching to Claude from other AI assistants: Claude will tell you when it thinks you are wrong.

Ask ChatGPT "Is my business plan good?" and you are likely to get enthusiastic praise followed by minor, gentle suggestions. Ask Claude the same question and you might get: "There are some strengths here, but I have concerns about your revenue projections. You are assuming 40% month-over-month growth for 18 months, which is unrealistic for this market. Here is why..."

This is not a bug. It is a feature — arguably Claude's most important one.

Why Honesty Matters

An AI assistant that always agrees with you is not helping you. It is confirming your biases, reinforcing your blind spots, and giving you false confidence. When you are making important decisions — business strategy, code architecture, medical choices, financial planning — you need an advisor who will challenge your assumptions, not rubber-stamp them.

Claude is trained to provide its genuine assessment. This means:

- **It will point out flaws in your reasoning.** If your argument has a logical gap, Claude identifies it.
- **It will flag factual errors.** If you state something incorrect, Claude corrects you — respectfully, but clearly.

- **It will present the other side.** If you ask Claude to argue for a position, it will do so, but it may also note the strongest counterarguments.
- **It will say "I don't know."** Rather than fabricating an answer, Claude admits when it lacks information or certainty.
- **It will express uncertainty.** When the evidence is mixed or the answer is debatable, Claude says so rather than pretending to have a definitive answer.

How to Invite Honest Feedback

If you want Claude's unvarnished opinion, you can encourage it:

- "Be brutally honest — what are the weaknesses in this plan?"
- "Do not sugarcoat this. What is wrong with my code?"
- "I want your genuine assessment, not encouragement. Is this essay any good?"
- "Play devil's advocate. What are the strongest arguments against my position?"

Claude responds well to these prompts because they align with its training. You are giving it permission to do what it is already inclined to do: tell you the truth.

Reducing Sycophancy

Sycophancy — the tendency of AI models to agree with the user, flatter them, and avoid causing displeasure — is one of the most pervasive problems in the AI industry. Models trained primarily on human feedback learn that agreeable responses get higher ratings, so they optimize for agreeableness over accuracy.

Claude is less sycophantic than most AI assistants, by design. Constitutional AI explicitly pushes against the incentive to be a yes-man.

What Sycophancy Looks Like

Common sycophantic behaviors you may recognize from other AI tools:

- **Excessive praise**: "What a fantastic question!" or "That's a brilliant idea!" before every response.

- **Reversing position when challenged**: You say "Actually, I think you're wrong." The AI immediately says "You're absolutely right, I apologize" — even when its original answer was correct.
- **Telling you what you want to hear**: You describe a bad business idea and the AI enthusiastically lists reasons it will succeed.
- **Hedging everything into positivity**: Refusing to give a clear negative assessment, burying criticism in compliments.

How Claude Is Different

Claude does not eliminate these tendencies — no current AI model has — but it reduces them significantly:

- **Claude does not open with gratuitous compliments.** It gets to the substance of your question without performing enthusiasm.
- **Claude holds its ground.** If you challenge a correct answer, Claude explains why it stands by its original response rather than capitulating immediately. It might say: "I understand your perspective, but I think my original assessment is more accurate, and here is why."
- **Claude gives real feedback.** Ask Claude to review your writing, code, or plan, and it identifies genuine problems alongside genuine strengths. It does not search for ways to be positive about everything.
- **Claude distinguishes disagreement from error.** If you push back on something subjective, Claude acknowledges the legitimate disagreement. If you push back on something factual, it either corrects itself (if it was wrong) or stands firm (if it was right).

This does not make Claude rude or contrarian. It is polite, thoughtful, and constructive. But it does not mistake politeness for dishonesty.

Extended Thinking and How It Changes Response Quality

Extended thinking is a feature available with Claude's most capable models — particularly Opus 4.7. When enabled, Claude spends additional time reasoning internally before responding. You see a "thinking" indicator while this happens, and then Claude delivers a more thorough, more carefully reasoned answer.

How Extended Thinking Works

Without extended thinking, Claude generates its response token by token in a single forward pass. Fast, but somewhat like thinking out loud — the model commits to its answer as it goes.

With extended thinking, Claude takes an intermediate step. Before generating its visible response, it works through the problem internally — considering different angles, checking its reasoning, weighing alternatives. You can see a summary of this internal reasoning in the interface (expand the thinking block to review it), and you see the result: a better answer.

When Extended Thinking Helps Most

Extended thinking provides the biggest improvement for:

Complex reasoning tasks: Multi-step math problems, logic puzzles, or any question that requires careful sequential thinking.

Nuanced analysis: Questions where the answer depends on weighing multiple factors, considering trade-offs, or evaluating ambiguous evidence.

Code generation: Producing correct, well-structured code for non-trivial problems. Extended thinking helps Claude plan the architecture before writing.

Strategic planning: Business strategy, project planning, or any task that benefits from considering second-order effects and potential pitfalls.

Difficult writing: Tasks that require careful tone management, complex argumentation, or precise technical communication.

When Extended Thinking Matters Less

For simple factual questions, basic text generation, or straightforward tasks, extended thinking adds latency without meaningfully improving quality. "What is the capital of France?" does not need deep reasoning.

Using Extended Thinking Effectively

On claude.ai, extended thinking may be enabled by default for certain models, or you can toggle it on in your settings. On the API, enable it as a parameter.

The practical advice is straightforward: for important or complex tasks, use a model with extended thinking enabled. For quick, routine tasks, a faster model without extended thinking is more efficient. You will develop an intuition for this with practice.

Customizing Claude's Communication Style

While Claude's core personality — honest, helpful, careful — is consistent, you have significant control over how it communicates. Its writing style and interaction patterns can be customized to your preferences.

In-Conversation Adjustments

Adjust Claude's style on the fly:

- **Length**: "Give me a brief answer" or "Explain this in detail."
- **Formality**: "Write this in a casual, conversational tone" or "Use formal, professional language."
- **Technicality**: "Explain this like I am a beginner" or "You can use technical terminology — I am a domain expert."
- **Format**: "Respond in bullet points" or "Write in full paragraphs" or "Give me a numbered list."
- **Perspective**: "Write from the perspective of a skeptic" or "Take an optimistic angle."

Claude adapts well to these instructions. Ask for brevity, it is brief. Ask for exhaustive detail, it is thorough. Ask for humor, it can be funny. Ask for dry, clinical analysis, it delivers that too.

System-Level Customization

For more persistent style customization, use Projects (Chapter 13) with custom instructions that specify your preferred communication style:

> Communication preferences: - Be concise. Default to short paragraphs and bullet points. - Skip preamble. Do not start responses with "Great question!" or "Certainly!" - When I ask a yes/no question, start with the yes or no, then explain. - Use concrete examples over abstract

explanations. - If something is uncertain, say so directly rather than hedging.

These instructions reshape Claude's default behavior for every conversation in the Project.

Working with Claude's Personality, Not Against It

The most productive relationship with Claude comes from understanding its personality and working with it:

- **Leverage its honesty.** Use Claude as a sounding board precisely because it will challenge weak ideas. That is more valuable than validation.
- **Trust its uncertainty.** When Claude says "I am not sure about this," it is giving you important information. An AI that never expresses uncertainty is hiding its limitations.
- **Appreciate the refusals.** When Claude declines a request, it is applying judgment. You might disagree with the specific call, but the underlying behavior — an AI that has boundaries — is worth valuing.
- **Give it room to be direct.** If you ask for honest feedback and then push back on every critical point, Claude will learn (within the conversation) to soften its responses. If you want genuine feedback, take it openly.

The Bigger Picture

Claude's personality is not just a product feature. It reflects a philosophy about what AI assistants should be. Anthropic believes AI systems should be truthful even when truth is inconvenient, careful even when caution slows things down, and principled even when principles conflict with user demands.

You may not agree with every decision Claude makes. You may find some refusals frustrating, some pushback unwelcome, some caution excessive. Fair. But consider the alternative: an AI that tells you exactly what you want to hear, agrees with everything you say, and never refuses anything. That AI may feel better to use in the moment, but it is a fundamentally less trustworthy tool.

Claude is built to be the assistant you can actually rely on — the one that tells you when your code has a bug, your plan has a flaw, or your assumption is wrong. That reliability, over time, is worth far more than flattery.

Summary

Claude's personality is shaped by Constitutional AI — a training approach built around helpfulness, harmlessness, and honesty. This makes Claude more willing to disagree with you, more honest about uncertainty, and less sycophantic than competing AI assistants. It also means Claude will sometimes refuse requests it considers harmful, though you can often resolve legitimate refusals by providing context.

Extended thinking lets Claude's most capable models reason more carefully before responding, improving quality on complex tasks. Through in-conversation prompts or Project-level custom instructions, you can customize Claude's communication style to match your preferences — while its core character of honesty and reliability stays constant.

In the next chapter, we will turn to prompting fundamentals — the techniques that help you communicate with Claude more effectively and get better results.

Chapter 15: Prompting Fundamentals

If there is one skill that separates people who get mediocre results from Claude and people who get extraordinary results, it is prompting. Not because prompting is some dark art reserved for engineers — it is not. It is because most people have never stopped to think about how they communicate with an AI, and a few small adjustments make a dramatic difference.

This chapter teaches you those adjustments. You will learn what makes a prompt effective, how to structure your requests so Claude understands exactly what you want, and how to avoid the common mistakes that lead to vague or unhelpful responses. By the end, you will have twenty ready-to-use prompt templates to start applying immediately.

What Makes a Good Prompt for Claude

A good prompt is not about magic words or secret phrases. It is about clarity. Claude is remarkably capable at understanding natural language, but it cannot read your mind. The more clearly you express what you want, the better the result.

Think of it this way: if you walked up to a brilliant colleague and said "help me with the thing," they would ask a dozen follow-up questions. Claude will try its best to help, but instead of asking those questions, it will make assumptions — and those assumptions may not match what you had in mind.

A good prompt for Claude has five qualities:

1. **It is specific.** Instead of "write something about marketing," say "write a 500-word blog post about email marketing strategies for small e-commerce businesses."
2. **It provides context.** Claude does not know your situation unless you tell it. Who is the audience? What is the goal? What has already been tried?
3. **It defines the format.** Do you want a list? A paragraph? A table? A formal report? Say so.
4. **It sets constraints.** Word count, tone, topics to avoid, level of detail — these boundaries help Claude deliver exactly what you need.

5. **It assigns a role when helpful.** Telling Claude to act as a specific type of expert focuses its knowledge and shapes its response style.

The Five Elements of an Effective Prompt

Let us break down the anatomy of a strong prompt. You do not need all five elements every time, but knowing them gives you a toolkit for any situation.

1. Role

The role tells Claude what perspective to adopt. Not a gimmick — it shapes the vocabulary, depth, and approach of the response.

> You are an experienced pediatrician. A parent is asking you about childhood vaccination schedules.

Compare the response you would get from that prompt versus simply asking "tell me about vaccines." The role creates focus.

2. Task

The task is the core of your prompt — what you want Claude to do. Be direct. Use action verbs: write, analyze, compare, summarize, explain, create, list, evaluate.

> Write a comparison of three project management tools suitable for a team of 10 people.

3. Context

Context is the background information Claude needs to do the task well. This might include your industry, your audience, your experience level, or relevant constraints.

> My team is fully remote, works across three time zones, and currently uses spreadsheets to track tasks. We have a budget of $50 per user per month.

4. Format

Tell Claude how to structure the output. This eliminates guesswork and gets you results you can use immediately.

> Present this as a table with columns for tool name, price, key features, and pros/cons.

5. Constraints

Constraints are the guardrails. They tell Claude what to include, what to exclude, and any boundaries to respect.

> Keep the comparison under 800 words. Do not include tools that require desktop installation. Write in a casual, friendly tone.

Putting It All Together

Here is what a complete prompt looks like when you combine all five elements:

> You are a technology consultant who specializes in helping small remote teams. Compare three project management tools suitable for a team of 10 people that works across three time zones. We currently use spreadsheets and have a budget of $50 per user per month. Present this as a table with columns for tool name, monthly price per user, key features, and pros/cons, followed by a one-paragraph recommendation. Keep it under 800 words, do not include tools requiring desktop installation, and write in a casual but professional tone.

That prompt will get you a useful answer on the first try.

Specific vs. Vague: The Difference That Matters Most

The single biggest improvement most people can make to their prompting is being more specific. Some before-and-after examples:

Vague: "Help me with my resume." **Specific:** "Review my resume for a senior marketing manager position at a tech company. Focus on whether my bullet points use strong action verbs and quantifiable achievements. Here is my resume: [paste resume]."

Vague: "Write a story." **Specific:** "Write a 1,000-word short story in the style of literary fiction about a retired teacher who discovers something unexpected in her garden. Use a contemplative, quiet tone. The ending should be ambiguous."

Vague: "Explain machine learning." **Specific:** "Explain machine learning to a 14-year-old who is good at math but has no programming experience. Use everyday analogies. Keep it to three paragraphs."

Notice how the specific versions give Claude a clear target. You are not limiting creativity — you are focusing it.

Common Beginner Mistakes

After watching thousands of people interact with Claude, certain patterns emerge among those who struggle to get good results. The mistakes to avoid:

Mistake 1: Being Too Brief

One-sentence prompts almost always produce generic responses. Claude is not a search engine — it does not need a query, it needs instructions. Do not be afraid to write a prompt that runs a full paragraph or more.

Mistake 2: Asking Multiple Unrelated Questions at Once

"What is the capital of France, how do I fix a leaky faucet, and can you write me a poem about dogs?" Claude will answer all three, but the quality of each suffers. Focus on one task at a time, or explicitly number your separate questions so Claude can address each one clearly.

Mistake 3: Not Providing Examples

If you want output in a specific style or format, show Claude an example. "Write product descriptions like this one: [example]" is far more effective than describing the style abstractly.

Mistake 4: Forgetting to Specify the Audience

A financial analysis written for a CFO looks very different from one written for a college student. Always tell Claude who will be reading the output.

Mistake 5: Assuming Claude Remembers Previous Conversations

Each new conversation with Claude starts fresh. Claude does not retain information from past chats. If context from a previous conversation matters, paste it in or summarize it.

Mistake 6: Not Iterating

Your first prompt does not have to be perfect. Treat it as a starting point. If the response is close but not quite right, tell Claude what to adjust. "This is good, but make the tone more formal and add a section about pricing" is a perfectly valid follow-up.

Mistake 7: Overcomplicating the Prompt

There is a balance. Detail is good, but wrapping your request in unnecessary jargon or convoluted instructions muddies the waters. Write naturally. Pretend you are giving instructions to a smart coworker.

XML Tags for Structured Prompting

Something that sets Claude apart from other AI assistants: Claude responds especially well to XML tags in prompts. XML tags are angle-bracket markers like `<tag>` and `</tag>` that you may have seen in web development. You do not need to know anything about coding to use them — they are a way to clearly label different parts of your prompt.

Why do XML tags work so well with Claude? They create unambiguous boundaries between sections. Instead of Claude having to guess where your instructions end and your source material begins, the tags make it explicit.

Basic XML Tag Usage

A simple example:

```
<role>You are a professional copywriter with 15 years of experience.</role>

<task>Write three subject lines for a marketing email.</task>

<context>
The email is promoting a 30% off sale on winter clothing.
The target audience is women aged 25-45.
The brand voice is warm and playful.
</context>

<constraints>
- Each subject line should be under 50 characters
- Include at least one emoji-free option
```

```
- Do not use the word "discount"
</constraints>
```

Claude parses this cleanly, treating each tagged section as a distinct piece of the puzzle.

Using XML Tags to Separate Source Material

XML tags are especially useful when you are asking Claude to work with source material — a document to summarize, text to edit, data to analyze:

```
Please analyze the following customer review and identify the key themes.

<review>
[Paste the full customer review here]
</review>

<output_format>
List each theme as a bullet point with a one-sentence explanation and a direct q
uote from the review that supports it.
</output_format>
```

Without the tags, Claude might confuse parts of the customer review with your instructions. With the tags, there is zero ambiguity.

Nesting Tags for Complex Prompts

For more sophisticated prompts, you can nest tags:

```
<task>Compare these two articles and identify where they agree and disagree.</ta
sk>

<articles>
  <article_1>
  [First article text]
  </article_1>

  <article_2>
  [Second article text]
  </article_2>
</articles>

<instructions>
- Focus on factual claims, not opinions
- Present disagreements as a numbered list
```

```
- For each disagreement, quote the relevant passage from each article
</instructions>
```

When to Use XML Tags vs. Plain Language

You do not need XML tags for simple prompts. "Summarize this paragraph in two sentences" works fine without them. Use XML tags when:

- Your prompt has multiple distinct sections (instructions, source material, examples, constraints)
- You are pasting in large blocks of text that Claude needs to analyze
- You want to provide few-shot examples with clear boundaries
- You are building reusable prompt templates

Think of XML tags as organizational tools. They do not change what Claude can do — they make it easier for Claude to understand what you are asking.

20 Prompt Templates for Everyday Use

Twenty prompts you can copy, customize, and use immediately. Each one demonstrates the principles covered in this chapter.

Writing and Communication

1. Professional Email

```
Write a professional email to [recipient/role] regarding [topic]. The tone shoul
d be [formal/friendly/urgent]. Key points to cover: [list points]. Keep it under
 [number] words.
```

2. Blog Post

```
<role>You are an experienced content writer specializing in [industry].</role>
<task>Write a [word count]-word blog post titled "[title]".</task>
<audience>[Describe target reader]</audience>
<requirements>
- Include an engaging introduction with a hook
- Use subheadings to break up sections
- End with a clear call to action
- Tone: [casual/professional/authoritative]
</requirements>
```

3. Social Media Post

```
Write a [platform] post about [topic]. Target audience: [describe]. Goal: [engag
ement/clicks/awareness]. Include a call to action. Keep it under [character coun
t] characters.
```

4. Difficult Conversation Script

```
Help me prepare for a conversation with [person/role] about [sensitive topic]. I
 want to be [direct but kind/firm but fair/empathetic]. The key message I need t
o communicate is [message]. Suggest an opening, key talking points, and how to h
andle likely pushback.
```

Analysis and Decision-Making

5. Pros and Cons Analysis

```
I am deciding between [option A] and [option B] for [purpose]. My priorities are
 [list priorities]. Create a detailed pros and cons comparison, then give me you
r recommendation with reasoning.
```

6. Document Summary

```
<task>Summarize the following document.</task>
<document>[Paste document]</document>
<format>
- One-paragraph executive summary
- 5-7 key takeaways as bullet points
- Any action items or next steps mentioned
</format>
```

7. Data Interpretation

```
<role>You are a data analyst.</role>
<data>[Paste data or describe the dataset]</data>
<task>Analyze this data and identify the three most important trends. For each t
rend, explain what it means in practical terms and suggest one action to take ba
sed on it.</task>
```

Learning and Research

8. Concept Explanation

```
Explain [concept] to me as if I am [experience level: beginner/intermediate/expe
rt] in [field]. Use [analogies/examples/diagrams described in text]. Focus on pr
actical application rather than theory.
```

9. Study Guide

Create a study guide for [subject/exam]. Cover the following topics: [list topics]. For each topic, include: a concise explanation, one example, and two practice questions with answers.

10. Book Summary

Provide a comprehensive summary of [book title] by [author]. Include: main thesis, key arguments, most important examples, practical takeaways, and who would benefit most from reading it. Keep it to [word count] words.

Business and Work

11. Meeting Agenda

Create a meeting agenda for a [duration]-minute [meeting type] meeting. Attendees: [list roles]. Goals: [list goals]. Include time allocations for each section and suggested discussion questions.

12. Project Plan

<role>You are a project manager.</role>
<task>Create a project plan for [project description].</task>
<constraints>
- Timeline: [duration]
- Team size: [number]
- Budget: [amount or "limited"]

</constraints>
<format>Include milestones, deliverables, responsible parties, and risk factors. Present as a structured outline.</format>

13. Performance Review Draft

Help me write a performance review for [role]. Key accomplishments this period: [list]. Areas for improvement: [list]. Tone should be constructive and supportive. Include specific, measurable goals for next period.

Creative Projects

14. Story Outline

Create a detailed outline for a [genre] story. Premise: [one-sentence premise]. Include: main characters with brief descriptions, three-act structure, key plot points, and the central conflict. The theme should explore [theme].

15. Product Description

Write a product description for [product] sold on [platform]. Target customer: [describe]. Key features: [list]. Tone: [describe]. Include a headline, three bullet points, and a short paragraph. Optimize for [SEO keywords if applicable].

16. Recipe or How-To

Write a step-by-step guide for [task]. Assume the reader is a [beginner/intermediate]. Include: materials or ingredients needed, estimated time, numbered steps with brief explanations, and common mistakes to avoid.

Personal and Daily Life

17. Travel Itinerary

Plan a [number]-day trip to [destination] for [number] people. Budget: [amount]. Interests: [list]. Include: daily schedule, recommended restaurants, must-see attractions, transportation tips, and one off-the-beaten-path suggestion per day.

18. Negotiation Preparation

I need to negotiate [what] with [who]. My ideal outcome is [describe]. My walk-away point is [describe]. Help me prepare by listing my strongest arguments, anticipating their counterarguments, and suggesting three negotiation tactics appropriate for this situation.

19. Feedback on My Writing

<task>Review the following text and provide feedback.</task>
<text>[Paste your writing]</text>
<focus_areas>
- Clarity and readability
- Logical flow and structure
- Grammar and style
- Strength of arguments
</focus_areas>
<instructions>Be specific. For each issue, quote the problematic passage and suggest a concrete revision.</instructions>

20. Weekly Planning

Help me plan my week. Here are my commitments and goals:
<commitments>[List fixed appointments, deadlines, obligations]</commitments>
<goals>[List what you want to accomplish]</goals>
<preferences>[Morning person? Need breaks? Work style?]</preferences>
Create a day-by-day schedule that balances productivity with rest. Flag any potential conflicts.

Building Your Prompting Intuition

These templates are a starting point, not a cage. As you use Claude more, you will develop intuition for what level of detail different tasks require. A quick factual question needs a sentence. A complex creative project might need a full paragraph of instructions with XML-tagged examples.

The key principles to carry forward:

- **Be specific** about what you want
- **Provide context** about your situation
- **Define the format** you need
- **Set constraints** to focus the output
- **Use XML tags** when your prompt has multiple parts or includes source material
- **Iterate** — refine your prompt based on Claude's response

Prompting is a conversation, not a single shot. The more you practice, the faster you will get to exactly the result you need — often on the first try.

In the next chapter, we will build on these fundamentals and tackle working with Claude on tasks that are too big or too complex for a single prompt.

Chapter 16: Working with Long and Complex Tasks

Some tasks fit neatly into a single prompt and response. You ask, you get an answer, you move on. But the most valuable work — writing a business plan, analyzing a large dataset, developing a curriculum, refactoring a codebase — does not work that way. These tasks are too big, too nuanced, or too layered for one exchange.

This chapter is about tackling those bigger challenges. You will learn how to break complex work into manageable steps, chain prompts together so each one builds on the last, manage long conversations without losing quality, and know when to start fresh versus continue. You will also learn how to use Claude's extended thinking feature — a capability that lets Claude reason through complex problems before responding.

Why Big Tasks Need a Different Approach

When you give Claude a single prompt that tries to do too much at once, several things can go wrong. The response might be shallow because Claude spread its attention across too many sub-tasks. It might lose track of early requirements by the time it reaches the end. Or it might produce something that is technically complete but does not hang together as a coherent whole.

This is not a limitation unique to AI. Ask a human colleague to "write me a complete marketing strategy, with budget, timeline, channel recommendations, creative briefs, and KPIs" in a single breath and you would get a rough sketch at best. Complex work requires iteration, focus, and building block by block.

The good news: Claude excels at this kind of structured work — if you guide it properly.

Breaking Big Tasks into Steps

The first skill to develop is decomposition: taking a large task and splitting it into sequential, focused steps. Each step should have a clear input, a clear output, and a manageable scope.

The Planning Step

Before diving into execution, ask Claude to help you plan the work itself. This is one of the most underused techniques, and it is highly effective.

```
I need to write a 20-page white paper on the future of remote work for our HR de
partment. Before we start writing, help me create a detailed outline. For each s
ection, suggest:
- The main argument or point
- Key data or evidence to include
- Approximate word count
- Any research I should gather before we write that section
```

Now you have a roadmap. Instead of asking Claude to write the entire white paper in one go, work through it section by section, giving full attention to each part.

Sequential Execution

Once you have your plan, work through it step by step:

Step 1: "Let's start with the executive summary. Based on our outline, write a 300-word executive summary that previews the key findings we'll cover."

Step 2: "Now write Section 1: The Current State of Remote Work. Here are the statistics I gathered: [paste data]. Aim for 1,500 words."

Step 3: "Review what we have so far. Does the executive summary still accurately preview Section 1? If not, suggest revisions."

Each step is focused, and you can course-correct as you go.

The Divide-and-Conquer Method

For some tasks, the steps are not sequential but parallel — they do not depend on each other. Handle them in separate conversations and combine the results.

For example, if you are preparing a business pitch:

- **Conversation 1:** Market analysis and competitive landscape
- **Conversation 2:** Financial projections and revenue model
- **Conversation 3:** Product description and value proposition
- **Conversation 4:** Team bios and company background

Then use a final conversation to weave these pieces together into a cohesive deck.

Chaining Prompts Together

Prompt chaining is using the output of one prompt as the input for the next. It is one of the most powerful strategies for complex work, and it comes in several flavors.

Linear Chains

In a linear chain, each prompt builds directly on the previous response:

1. "Generate a list of 10 potential blog post topics about sustainable fashion."
2. "Take topic number 4 and create a detailed outline with five sections."
3. "Write the introduction based on this outline. Hook the reader with a surprising statistic."
4. "Now write Section 1. Maintain the same tone as the introduction."
5. "Review the introduction and Section 1 together. Flag any inconsistencies in tone or messaging."

Transformation Chains

In a transformation chain, you take the same content through multiple processing steps:

1. "Here is a raw transcript of our customer interview: [paste]. Clean it up — remove filler words, fix grammar, but preserve the speaker's voice."
2. "Now extract the key themes from this cleaned transcript. List each theme with supporting quotes."
3. "Turn these themes into a one-page executive summary for our product team."

4. “Finally, create three user story tickets based on the pain points identified in the summary.”

Each step transforms the material into something more refined and useful.

Evaluation Chains

An evaluation chain has Claude generate something, critically review it, then improve it:

1. “Write a cover letter for this job posting: [paste posting]. Here is my resume: [paste resume].”
2. “Now evaluate this cover letter. Score it on: relevance to the job (1–10), specificity (1–10), tone (1–10), and uniqueness (1–10). Explain each score.”
3. “Based on your evaluation, rewrite the cover letter to address the weaknesses you identified.”

This generate-evaluate-improve cycle consistently beats a single prompt.

Multi-Turn Strategies

A multi-turn conversation is a back-and-forth exchange where you and Claude build on each other’s messages. Strategies for making these conversations productive:

The Refinement Approach

Start with a broad request and narrow down through feedback:

You: “Draft an email to our investors updating them on Q3 performance.”

Claude: [Produces a draft]

You: “Good structure, but the tone is too casual. Make it more formal. Lead with the revenue growth number — that is our strongest metric.”

Claude: [Produces revised draft]

You: “Better. The second paragraph is too long. Break it into two. And add a sentence about the new partnership with Acme Corp.”

Claude: [Produces final version]

This works because each round of feedback is specific and actionable. Avoid vague feedback like "make it better." Tell Claude exactly what to change.

The Expert Interview

Treat Claude as a subject matter expert you are interviewing:

You: "I am considering switching our database from MySQL to PostgreSQL. What are the key factors I should consider?"

Claude: [Lists factors]

You: "Tell me more about the migration complexity. Our database is about 50GB with heavy use of stored procedures."

Claude: [Provides detailed migration analysis]

You: "What about the performance implications for read-heavy workloads? We do about 10,000 queries per second, mostly SELECT statements."

Claude: [Addresses specific performance considerations]

Each question drills deeper based on what you learned from the previous answer.

The Collaborative Draft

Work with Claude as a writing partner, not a ghostwriter:

You: "I have a rough idea for the opening of my novel. The main character is a lighthouse keeper in the 1950s who receives a mysterious letter. Here is my rough draft: [paste]. What is working and what could be stronger?"

Claude: [Provides detailed feedback]

You: "I like your point about the pacing. Here is my revised version: [paste]. I also tried a different approach to the letter reveal. Which version is more compelling?"

This collaborative mode tends to produce the most original and satisfying creative work.

Managing Context in Long Conversations

Every conversation with Claude has a context window — the total amount of text Claude can "see" at once. As your conversation grows longer, earlier messages eventually fall outside this window, and Claude may lose track of details from the beginning.

Strategies for managing this effectively:

Periodic Summaries

Every five to ten exchanges, ask Claude to summarize the current state of the work:

"Before we continue, summarize what we have established so far: the key decisions we have made, the content we have produced, and what remains to be done."

This creates a fresh reference point that keeps the important details in the active conversation, even if the original messages have scrolled out of the context window.

Pasting Key Context Forward

If you are in a long conversation and Claude seems to have forgotten an important detail, restate it:

"As a reminder, the target audience for this report is C-level executives with no technical background. With that in mind, revise this section to remove the jargon."

This is not a failure — it is a practical strategy. Claude will immediately incorporate the restated context.

Using Documents as Anchors

When working on a long project, keep a running document outside of Claude that captures the current state — your outline, style guidelines, key decisions, and any completed sections. When you start a new conversation or need to refocus, paste the relevant portions into your prompt.

```
<project_context>
We are writing a white paper on remote work. Here is our approved outline:
```

```
[paste outline]

Completed sections:
- Executive summary (approved)
- Section 1 (approved)
- Section 2 (in revision -- needs more data on productivity)

Style guidelines:
- Formal but accessible tone
- Use data to support every major claim
- Target length: 5,000 words total
</project_context>

Now let's work on revising Section 2. Here is the current draft: [paste draft].
The feedback was that it needs more concrete data on remote worker productivity.
```

Knowing Your Conversation's Limits

A practical rule of thumb: if your conversation has run more than 20–30 exchanges, or if you have pasted in large documents, you are likely approaching the limits of the context window. You will notice this when Claude starts giving responses that seem to ignore earlier context, or when it contradicts something you established earlier.

When this happens, start a fresh conversation with a well-crafted summary of where things stand.

When to Start Fresh vs. Continue

This is one of the most practical questions in working with Claude, and the answer depends on the situation.

Continue the Conversation When:

- You are iterating on a specific piece of work (editing a document, refining an analysis)
- The conversation is still relatively short (under 15–20 exchanges)
- Claude's responses still reference earlier context accurately
- You are in a creative flow and the tone or style is dialed in

Start a New Conversation When:

- The topic is shifting significantly from what you have been discussing
- The conversation has become very long and Claude seems to be losing context
- You want to approach the same problem from a fresh angle without prior assumptions
- You are starting a new phase of a larger project
- Claude seems to be stuck in a pattern you cannot redirect

Starting fresh is not wasted work. Copy the valuable outputs from your previous conversation, paste them into the new one as context, and continue. A fresh start with good context often produces better results than pushing forward in a cluttered conversation.

Using Extended Thinking for Complex Reasoning

Extended thinking is one of Claude's most powerful features for complex tasks, available on Pro, Max, Team, and Enterprise plans. When enabled, Claude takes additional time to reason through a problem before responding — similar to how you might think through a difficult problem on paper before presenting your answer.

What Extended Thinking Does

Normally, Claude generates its response word by word, left to right. With extended thinking enabled, Claude first works through the problem in a dedicated reasoning phase. It considers different approaches, evaluates evidence, catches errors in its own logic, and organizes its thoughts — all before writing the final response.

You can see a summary of this thinking process in the interface, which can be informative on its own. It lets you understand not just what Claude concluded, but how it got there.

When to Use Extended Thinking

Extended thinking is most valuable for:

- **Complex analysis** — tasks that require weighing multiple factors, such as evaluating a business strategy or diagnosing a technical problem
- **Math and logic** — problems where step-by-step reasoning matters and mistakes are easy to make
- **Nuanced writing** — situations where Claude needs to balance competing requirements (be persuasive but not pushy, be detailed but concise)
- **Code debugging** — tracing through logic to find where things go wrong
- **Multi-step planning** — tasks like creating a project plan where each decision affects subsequent ones

When You Do Not Need Extended Thinking

For straightforward tasks — writing a simple email, answering a factual question, generating a list — extended thinking adds time without meaningfully improving the result. Save it for problems that require deeper reasoning.

How to Get the Most from Extended Thinking

When you are using extended thinking, your prompts can be more ambitious. Because Claude has space to reason through complexity, you can ask harder questions and expect more thoughtful answers.

For example, instead of breaking a complex analysis into five separate prompts, try it in one or two with extended thinking enabled:

```
Analyze our company's competitive position in the enterprise SaaS market. Consid
er our pricing (which is 20% above market average), our feature set (strong in a
nalytics, weak in integrations), our customer base (primarily mid-market, trying
 to move upmarket), and our team (strong engineering, small sales team). What is
 our best path to doubling revenue in 18 months? Consider at least three differe
nt strategies before recommending one.
```

With extended thinking, Claude will consider multiple strategies, weigh trade-offs, and present a reasoned recommendation rather than jumping to the most obvious answer.

A Complete Walkthrough: From Complex Task to Finished Product

Let us put it all together with a realistic example. Say you need to create a quarterly business review presentation.

Prompt 1 — Planning: "I need to create a quarterly business review presentation for our board of directors. The company is a B2B SaaS startup with $5M ARR. Help me create an outline for a 15-slide presentation. What information should I gather before we start building each slide?"

Prompt 2 — Data Organization: "Here is the raw data for Q3: [paste financials, metrics, customer data]. Organize this into the key metrics our board will care about. Highlight what is on track and what is behind plan."

Prompt 3 — Narrative: "Based on the metrics, what is the overall story of Q3? Help me craft a narrative arc: where did we start the quarter, what happened, where did we end up, and what does it mean for Q4?"

Prompt 4 — Slide Content: "Let's build the slides. Start with slides 1–5. For each slide, give me: the slide title, 3–4 bullet points, and speaker notes."

Prompt 5 — Review: "Here are all 15 slides. Review the full presentation for: narrative consistency, data accuracy (flag anything that seems off), and completeness. What is missing? What is unnecessary?"

Prompt 6 — Polish: "Based on your review, here are the revisions. Now write the executive summary email that will accompany this presentation when we send it to the board ahead of the meeting."

Six focused prompts, each building on the last, producing a board-ready presentation. That is the power of structured multi-step work with Claude.

Key Takeaways

- **Plan before you execute.** Ask Claude to help you break big tasks into steps before diving in.
- **Chain your prompts.** Use the output of one prompt as input for the next — linear, transformation, or evaluation chains.

- **Iterate with specific feedback.** Each round of revision should tell Claude exactly what to change.
- **Manage your context.** Use periodic summaries, restate key details, and keep a running document outside of Claude.
- **Start fresh when needed.** A new conversation with good context often beats a cluttered long conversation.
- **Use extended thinking for hard problems.** Complex analysis, multi-step reasoning, and nuanced work all benefit from Claude's ability to think before responding.

Managing long, complex work with Claude is what separates casual users from power users. Master these techniques and there is very little you cannot accomplish.

Chapter 17: Output Formatting and Control

Getting a great answer from Claude is only half the battle. The other half is getting that answer in a format you can use. Whether you need a clean table for a spreadsheet, a structured report for your boss, or a consistently formatted list you can paste into a CMS, formatting matters.

This chapter covers how to control the shape, structure, and style of Claude's output. You will learn how to request specific formats, use Markdown for rich text, control length precisely, maintain consistency across conversations, and use XML tags to structure output as effectively as you use them to structure input.

Tables

Tables are one of the most useful output formats Claude can produce, and one of the easiest to request. Ask for one.

Basic request:

```
Compare the three main Claude models in a table. Include columns for model name,
 best use case, speed, and relative cost.
```

Claude will produce a clean Markdown table:

Model	Best Use Case	Speed	Relative Cost
Opus 4.7	Complex analysis, nuanced writing	Slower	Highest
Sonnet 4.6	Balanced everyday tasks	Medium	Medium
Haiku 4.5	Quick tasks, high volume	Fastest	Lowest

Controlling Table Structure

You can be specific about your table requirements:

```
Create a table with exactly these columns: Feature, Free Plan, Pro Plan, Enterpr
ise Plan. Include rows for: message limits, model access, file uploads, extended
 thinking, and priority access. Use "Yes", "No", or specific details in each cel
l.
```

Multi-Level Tables

For more complex comparisons, you can ask for grouped rows or nested information:

```
Create a comparison table of project management tools. Group features into categ
ories: Task Management, Collaboration, Reporting, and Integrations. Under each c
ategory, list 3-4 specific features and indicate support with checkmarks or deta
ils.
```

Tables for Data

When you provide raw data, Claude can organize it into tables automatically:

```
Here are our Q3 sales figures by region: North $450K (up 12%), South $320K (down
 3%), East $580K (up 8%), West $410K (up 15%). Put this in a table and add a tot
al row.
```

Lists and Bullet Points

Lists are Claude's bread and butter, but there is more nuance to them than you might expect.

Ordered vs. Unordered Lists

Use numbered lists when sequence matters — steps in a process, ranked recommendations, prioritized actions. Use bullet points when items are parallel and order does not matter — features, characteristics, options.

Be explicit:

```
Give me a numbered list of steps to set up a new email marketing campaign, in th
e order they should be completed.
```

Versus:

```
Give me a bullet-point list of features to look for when choosing an email marke
ting platform.
```

Nested Lists

For hierarchical information, ask for nested lists:

```
Create an outline for a marketing strategy using nested bullet points. Top level
 should be the main strategic pillars, second level should be specific tactics,
and third level should be concrete action items.
```

Definition Lists

When you need term-definition pairs:

```
Define the following financial terms in a list format, with each term in bold fo
llowed by a clear, one-sentence definition: ROI, EBITDA, burn rate, runway, ARR,
 churn rate.
```

Checklist Format

For actionable items:

```
Create a pre-launch checklist for our new website. Format each item as a checkbo
x-style list item (using - [ ] notation) grouped by category: Content, Technical,
 Legal, and Marketing.
```

Markdown Formatting

Claude natively produces Markdown, the formatting language used by many platforms, text editors, and content management systems. Understanding what you can request gives you much more control over the output.

Headers and Structure

```
Write a report on renewable energy trends. Use the following structure:
- H1 for the report title
- H2 for major sections
- H3 for subsections
- Bold for key terms on first use
- Italics for emphasis
```

Code Blocks

When you need code or technical content, Claude will format it in code blocks with syntax highlighting:

```
Show me a Python function that reads a CSV file and calculates the average of a
specific column. Use a fenced code block with the python language tag.
```

Blockquotes

For quotations or callouts:

```
Write a summary of the article, and use blockquotes to highlight the three most
important direct quotes from the text.
```

Horizontal Rules

To separate sections visually:

```
Write three distinct product descriptions, separated by horizontal rules.
```

Combining Markdown Elements

For professional-looking documents, combine multiple Markdown elements:

```
Create a project status report using Markdown formatting:
- Use a level-1 heading for the title
- Include a metadata section (date, author, status) in bold/plain text pairs
- Use level-2 headings for each section: Summary, Progress, Risks, Next Steps
- Use a table for the progress section showing tasks, owners, and status
- Use bullet points for risks and next steps
- End with a horizontal rule and a "Document History" section
```

Controlling Length and Detail

A common frustration with AI output is getting too much or too little. Here is how to control length precisely.

Word and Sentence Counts

Claude responds well to specific length instructions:

```
Explain quantum computing in exactly 100 words.
```

```
Summarize this article in no more than three sentences.
```

```
Write a product description between 150 and 200 words.
```

Claude may not hit the exact word count every time, but it will get close. For precise requirements, add: “Count the words and adjust if needed before finalizing.”

Level of Detail

Instead of word counts, you can control detail level:

```
Explain blockchain technology at three levels:
1. The elevator pitch (2 sentences)
2. The cocktail party explanation (1 paragraph)
3. The detailed briefing (500 words)
```

Brevity Instructions

When you want Claude to be concise:

```
Answer the following questions. Be as concise as possible – aim for one to two s
entences per answer unless more detail is necessary.
```

Or more forcefully:

```
Give me the short version. No preamble, no caveats, no elaboration. Just the ans
wer.
```

Expansion Instructions

When you want more depth:

```
Elaborate on each point with examples, evidence, and practical implications. Do
not summarize – go deep.
```

Specific Structures and Templates

Claude can produce output in virtually any structure you define. The key is to show it what you want.

Report Format

```
Write this analysis as a formal report with the following structure:

1. Executive Summary (1 paragraph)
2. Background (2-3 paragraphs)
3. Methodology (describe approach taken)
4. Findings (use subheadings for each finding)
5. Recommendations (numbered list)
6. Appendix (any supporting details)
```

Email Newsletter Format

```
Format this content as an email newsletter:
- Subject line
- Preview text (under 90 characters)
- Greeting
- Lead story (2 paragraphs with a bold headline)
- Three secondary stories (1 paragraph each with bold headlines)
- CTA button text
- Footer text
```

Slide Deck Outlines

```
Create a 10-slide presentation outline. For each slide, provide:
- Slide number and title
- 3-4 bullet points of content
- Speaker notes (2-3 sentences)
- Suggested visual (describe what image, chart, or graphic would work)
```

Structured Data Formats

Claude can produce output in specific data formats:

```
Convert this product information into JSON format with fields for: name, categor
y, price, description, and tags (as an array).
```

```
Format this data as a CSV with headers. Use commas as delimiters and enclose tex
t fields in double quotes.
```

Consistent Output Across Conversations

One challenge with AI is getting consistent formatting when you reuse similar prompts across different conversations. Here are techniques for maintaining consistency.

Style Guides

Create a style guide prompt that you reuse at the beginning of every relevant conversation:

```
<style_guide>
All content should follow these rules:
- Use active voice
- Sentences should average 15-20 words
```

```
- Use Oxford commas
- Write numbers one through nine as words, 10 and above as numerals
- Use em dashes (--) rather than parentheses for asides
- Headers should be in title case
- Always bold key terms on first use
</style_guide>
```

Template Definitions

Define your template once and reference it:

```
<template>
Every product review should follow this structure:
### [Product Name] Review
**Rating:** [X/10]
**Price:** [Price]
**Best for:** [One sentence]

#### Overview
[2-3 paragraphs]

#### Pros
- [Bullet list]

#### Cons
- [Bullet list]

#### Verdict
[1 paragraph]
</template>

Using the template above, write a review of [product].
```

Few-Shot Examples

The most reliable way to get consistent output is to show Claude an example of what you want:

```
Write product descriptions in this exact style:

<example>
**The Weekender Bag** | $89
Your new travel essential. Crafted from waxed canvas with leather trim, this bag
 fits everything you need for a two-day getaway — and nothing you do not. Fits o
verhead bins. Comes in Slate, Olive, and Rust.
```

```
*Free shipping on orders over $50.*
</example>

Now write descriptions for these three products: [list products with details].
```

XML Tags for Structured Output

Just as XML tags help you structure your input to Claude, they can help you request structured output. This is especially useful when you need to parse Claude's response programmatically or when you want clearly delineated sections.

Requesting XML-Formatted Output

```
Analyze this customer feedback and return your analysis in the following XML str
ucture:

<analysis>
  <sentiment>positive/negative/mixed</sentiment>
  <key_themes>
    <theme>[theme 1]</theme>
    <theme>[theme 2]</theme>
  </key_themes>
  <action_items>
    <item priority="high/medium/low">[action item]</item>
  </action_items>
  <summary>[one paragraph summary]</summary>
</analysis>
```

Claude will follow this structure precisely, filling in the appropriate content.

Mixing XML with Natural Language

You do not have to go fully XML. You can use tags selectively to mark the parts of the output you want clearly separated:

```
Write a blog post about sustainable fashion. After the blog post, separately pro
vide:

<meta>
Title tag (under 60 characters):
Meta description (under 155 characters):
Keywords:
</meta>
```

```
<social>
Twitter post:
LinkedIn post:
</social>
```

Using XML Output Tags for Parsing

If you are building workflows where Claude's output feeds into another system, XML tags make parsing straightforward:

```
For each item in the following list, provide your analysis wrapped in these tags:

<item>
  <name>[item name]</name>
  <category>[category]</category>
  <risk_level>[low/medium/high]</risk_level>
  <explanation>[one sentence explanation]</explanation>
</item>
```

This approach bridges the gap between natural language responses and structured data, making Claude's output directly usable in automated workflows.

Exporting and Sharing Results

Great formatted output is only useful if you can move it into your target destination. Here are practical tips for getting Claude's output into the tools you use every day.

Copy to Google Docs or Word

Claude's Markdown output translates well when pasted into Google Docs or Word. Headers, bold text, italics, and lists will generally maintain their formatting. Tables may need minor adjustment depending on the platform.

For the cleanest transfer, ask Claude to use simple formatting — avoid deeply nested structures or complex table layouts if you know the destination will be a word processor.

Copy to Spreadsheets

When you need data in a spreadsheet, ask Claude to format it as tab-separated values:

```
Format this data as tab-separated values that I can paste directly into a spreadsheet. Include a header row.
```

Tab-separated output pastes cleanly into both Excel and Google Sheets, with each value landing in the correct cell.

Copy to Presentations

For slide content, ask Claude to clearly separate each slide:

```
Format each slide as a separate section with a clear heading. Use short bullet points (no more than 8 words each). I will be copying this into PowerPoint.
```

Copy to HTML or CMS

If you are pasting into a content management system that accepts HTML:

```
Write this blog post and provide it in HTML format. Use <h2> for section headings, <p> for paragraphs, <ul> and <li> for bullet lists, and <strong> for bold text.
```

Copy to Code

For developers, Claude can output in any format you need — JSON, YAML, XML, CSV, SQL, or any programming language. Specify the format and any constraints (indentation style, naming conventions, etc.).

Formatting Troubleshooting

Sometimes Claude's formatting does not quite match what you wanted. Here are quick fixes for common issues.

Problem: Response is too long and verbose. **Fix:** "Shorten this by 50%. Keep only the essential points."

Problem: Table columns are misaligned or too wide. **Fix:** "Reformat this table with shorter cell values. Abbreviate where possible."

Problem: Inconsistent formatting across sections. **Fix:** "Standardize the formatting. Every section should follow the same structure as Section 1."

Problem: Claude is adding unwanted preamble or commentary. **Fix:** "Provide only the [table/list/document] with no introduction or commentary before or after it."

Problem: Output includes Markdown syntax but you wanted plain text. **Fix:** "Rewrite this in plain text with no Markdown formatting. Use ALL CAPS for headers and dashes for bullet points."

Key Takeaways

- **Be explicit about format.** Claude can produce tables, lists, reports, JSON, CSV, HTML, and virtually any other format — but you need to ask for it.
- **Control length with specific instructions.** Word counts, sentence limits, and detail levels all work.
- **Use Markdown intentionally.** Understanding Markdown gives you precise control over headers, emphasis, code blocks, tables, and more.
- **Create reusable templates.** Define your format once, then reference it across conversations for consistent output.
- **Leverage XML tags.** Use them to request clearly structured output, especially when you need to parse the results or maintain separation between sections.
- **Think about the destination.** Format your request based on where the output will end up — a document, spreadsheet, presentation, or CMS.
- **Iterate on formatting.** If the first output is close but not right, give specific formatting feedback rather than starting over.

Mastering output formatting transforms Claude from an interesting chatbot into a practical production tool. When you can get the exact format you need on the first or second try, you eliminate the tedious reformatting work that eats up so much time.

Part VI: Claude for Your Field

"In theory, there is no difference between theory and practice. In practice, there is."

— Jan L. A. van de Snepscheut

Chapter 18: Claude for Students and Educators

Education is one of the most promising — and most debated — areas for AI. Claude can be an extraordinary learning tool when used thoughtfully, and a shortcut to nowhere when misused. This chapter is for both sides of the classroom: students who want to learn more effectively, and educators who want to enhance their teaching without losing what makes education valuable.

We will cover practical study techniques, the line between help and dishonesty, lesson planning tools for teachers, age-appropriate guidelines, and a complete walkthrough of using Claude to prepare for an exam.

Study Techniques with Claude

The best way to use Claude for studying is not to ask it to do your work — it is to use it as a learning accelerator. Think of Claude as an infinitely patient tutor who is available at midnight, never judges a "dumb" question, and can explain the same concept fifteen different ways until one clicks.

The Feynman Technique with Claude

The Feynman Technique — named after physicist Richard Feynman — says that the best way to learn something is to try to explain it simply. Claude is the perfect practice audience.

```
I am going to try to explain photosynthesis to you as if you were a 10-year-old.
 After I finish, tell me what I got right, what I got wrong, and what I left out.
 Do not correct me during my explanation -- wait until I say I am done.
```

After you give your explanation, Claude will provide targeted feedback that reveals where your understanding is solid and where it has gaps.

Active Recall and Quizzing

Passive re-reading of notes is one of the least effective study methods. Active recall — testing yourself — is one of the most effective. Claude excels at generating quizzes tailored to exactly what you need to study.

```
I am studying for my biology midterm on genetics. Here are the topics that will
be covered: Mendelian inheritance, Punnett squares, DNA replication, transcripti
on, translation, and gene expression. Generate 15 quiz questions at a college so
phomore level. Mix question types: 5 multiple choice, 5 short answer, and 5 that
 require me to solve problems or draw connections between concepts. Do not show
me the answers yet.
```

After you answer, paste your responses back and ask Claude to grade them with explanations.

Spaced Repetition Support

Spaced repetition — reviewing material at increasing intervals — is proven to improve long-term retention. Claude can help you create materials for this:

```
I am learning Spanish vocabulary for travel. Create 30 flashcard pairs (Spanish
on front, English on back) organized into three difficulty tiers: beginner (gree
tings and basic phrases), intermediate (restaurant and hotel vocabulary), and ad
vanced (asking for directions and handling problems). Format them so I can easil
y copy them into a flashcard app.
```

Concept Mapping

When you are trying to understand how ideas connect:

```
I am studying the causes of World War I. Help me create a concept map. List the
major causes (alliances, imperialism, militarism, nationalism, the assassination
 of Archduke Franz Ferdinand) and draw connections between them. Explain how eac
h cause relates to and reinforced the others.
```

Reading Comprehension

When you are working through difficult texts:

```
I am reading Chapter 4 of "The Wealth of Nations" by Adam Smith and struggling w
ith the language. Here is a passage: [paste passage]. Explain what Smith is argu
ing in modern English. Then tell me why this argument was significant in its his
torical context and how it relates to modern economics.
```

Socratic Dialogue

One of the most powerful study techniques is asking Claude to guide you with questions rather than answers:

```
I need to understand the concept of supply and demand. Instead of explaining it
to me, guide me to understand it through questions. Ask me one question at a tim
e, and based on my answers, lead me to discover the key principles on my own. If
 I get stuck, give me a hint rather than the answer.
```

This approach builds deeper understanding than reading an explanation.

Homework Help vs. Academic Integrity

This is the section that matters most, and it requires honesty about what is happening in classrooms around the world. Students are using AI. The question is whether they are using it in ways that help them learn or in ways that bypass learning.

The Bright Line

Here is a clear principle: **using Claude to understand is learning; using Claude to avoid understanding is cheating.**

Consider the difference between these two interactions:

Learning: "I am stuck on this calculus problem. I understand that I need to use the chain rule, but I do not see how to apply it here. Can you walk me through the first two steps without solving the whole problem?"

Cheating: "Solve this calculus problem for me: [paste homework problem]."

The first student is using Claude to get past a sticking point so they can complete the work themselves. The second is outsourcing the work entirely. Both students will turn in correct answers, but only the first will be able to solve similar problems on the exam.

Guidelines for Students

1. **Try first.** Always attempt the work yourself before turning to Claude. Your mistakes are where learning happens.
2. **Ask for explanation, not answers.** "Help me understand how to approach this type of problem" is better than "solve this problem."
3. **Use Claude as a checker.** Do the work yourself, then ask Claude to review it and explain any errors.

4. **Follow your institution's policy.** Schools and professors vary widely in what AI use they allow. When in doubt, ask your instructor. If AI use is prohibited for an assignment, respect that boundary.
5. **Cite your use.** If your school allows AI assistance, be transparent about how you used it. Many institutions now have specific citation formats for AI-assisted work.
6. **Ask yourself the accountability question.** If your professor asked you to explain your work in person, could you? If the answer is no, you have not actually learned the material.

Guidelines for Parents

If you have children using Claude for schoolwork:

- Talk to them about the difference between learning with AI and having AI do the work
- Check their school's AI policy and make sure they understand it
- Encourage them to show you how they are using Claude — ask them to walk you through a session
- Frame AI as a study tool, like a tutor, not a homework-completion service
- For younger children, consider sitting with them during AI-assisted study sessions

Lesson Planning and Curriculum Development

For educators, Claude is an effective lesson planning partner. It will not replace your expertise and judgment, but it can dramatically reduce the time you spend on planning and materials creation.

Generating Lesson Plans

```
<role>You are an experienced curriculum designer.</role>

<task>Create a detailed lesson plan for a 50-minute high school biology class on
 cellular respiration.</task>

<context>
- Students are 10th graders, mixed ability levels
- They have already covered photosynthesis
- This is the first of three classes on cellular respiration
```

```
- The classroom has a projector and lab equipment
</context>

<format>
Include:
- Learning objectives (aligned to NGSS standards)
- Warm-up activity (5 minutes)
- Direct instruction (15 minutes)
- Group activity (20 minutes)
- Assessment/closure (10 minutes)
- Materials needed
- Differentiation strategies for advanced and struggling learners
- Homework assignment
</format>
```

Creating Assessments

```
Create a unit test for 8th grade American History covering the American Revoluti
on. Include:
- 10 multiple choice questions (varying difficulty)
- 5 short answer questions
- 1 essay question with a rubric
- An answer key with explanations
- One bonus question that requires critical thinking

Ensure questions test different levels of Bloom's taxonomy -- not just recall, b
ut also analysis, evaluation, and application.
```

Differentiated Materials

```
I have a reading passage about the water cycle at a 6th grade level. I need to c
reate three versions:
1. Simplified version for students reading below grade level (4th grade reading
level)
2. Original version with vocabulary support (glossary of key terms in the margin
s)
3. Extended version for advanced readers that includes additional complexity and
 critical thinking questions

Here is the original passage: [paste passage]
```

Discussion Questions and Rubrics

```
Generate 10 discussion questions for a college seminar on "To Kill a Mockingbird.
" Questions should progress from comprehension to analysis to evaluation. For ea
```

```
ch question, include:
- The question itself
- The level of thinking it targets
- Key points a strong answer would include
- A follow-up question to deepen the discussion
```

Administrative Tasks

Claude can also help with the less glamorous parts of teaching:

```
Write three versions of a parent email about the upcoming science fair:
1. Initial announcement (2 weeks before)
2. Reminder with logistics (1 week before)
3. Thank-you follow-up (day after)

Tone should be warm, organized, and professional. Include key dates, what studen
ts need to bring, and volunteer opportunities.
```

Age-Appropriate Use Guidelines

Not all students are ready for the same level of AI interaction. Here are guidelines organized by age group.

Elementary School (Ages 5–10)

At this age, AI use should be supervised and limited. Appropriate uses include:

- **Read-aloud companion.** A parent or teacher uses Claude to generate age-appropriate stories on topics the child is interested in.
- **Curiosity exploration.** The child asks questions about the world ("Why is the sky blue?") with a parent present to discuss the answers.
- **Creative play.** Collaborative storytelling where the child and Claude take turns adding to a story.

A parent or teacher should always be present during AI interactions at this age. Children this young are not equipped to evaluate AI output critically or to understand the boundaries of appropriate use.

Middle School (Ages 11–13)

Students can begin using Claude more independently, with guidance:

- **Supervised study sessions.** Using Claude to quiz themselves, explain difficult concepts, or check their work.
- **Research starting point.** Using Claude to understand a topic before diving into primary sources. Emphasize that Claude is a starting point, not a source to cite.
- **Writing feedback.** Having Claude review their essays for structure and clarity — but doing the revisions themselves.

Key conversation to have: AI can make mistakes. Because Claude says something does not make it true. Always verify important facts from reliable sources.

High School (Ages 14–18)

High schoolers can use Claude more extensively, with emphasis on responsible use:

- **Deep study and test prep.** All the study techniques described earlier in this chapter.
- **Essay brainstorming and outlining.** Using Claude to generate ideas and structure before writing independently.
- **College application support.** Brainstorming essay topics, getting feedback on drafts (but writing the essays themselves).
- **Skill building.** Learning to code, exploring career interests, practicing foreign languages.

Key conversation to have: academic integrity, the difference between assistance and dishonesty, and your school's specific AI policy.

College and Graduate Students

At this level, AI literacy becomes a professional skill. Students should:

- **Understand their institution's policies.** These vary widely and are evolving rapidly.
- **Learn to prompt effectively.** Prompting is a skill that will serve them in their careers.
- **Use Claude for higher-order learning.** Debating ideas, stress-testing arguments, exploring alternative perspectives.

- **Develop critical evaluation skills.** Learn to identify when Claude is confident but wrong, and how to verify AI-generated information.
- **Be transparent.** Cite AI use when required, and be prepared to discuss how you used it.

Walkthrough: Preparing for an Exam

Let us walk through a complete exam preparation workflow with Claude, using the example of a college student preparing for a midterm in Introduction to Psychology.

Step 1: Organize What You Need to Study

```
I have a midterm exam in Introduction to Psychology in five days. The exam cover
s Chapters 1-6 of our textbook. Here are the chapter topics:
1. History and methods of psychology
2. Biological bases of behavior (neurons, brain structure)
3. Sensation and perception
4. Learning (classical conditioning, operant conditioning)
5. Memory
6. Cognition and language

I have class notes and the textbook. Help me create a 5-day study plan that uses
 spaced repetition and active recall. I can study for about 2 hours per day.
```

Claude will produce a day-by-day plan that covers all material with built-in review cycles for earlier topics.

Step 2: Identify Weak Areas

```
I am going to tell you what I think I know well and where I am struggling. Stron
g areas: history of psychology, sensation and perception, operant conditioning.
Weak areas: brain structure (I keep mixing up the regions), classical conditioni
ng (I confuse CS, UCS, CR, UCR), and memory encoding vs retrieval. Focus my stud
y time on the weak areas while still reviewing the strong ones.
```

Step 3: Deep Dive on Weak Topics

```
Explain the major brain regions and their functions in a way I will actually rem
ember. Use memorable analogies or mnemonics for each region. Then give me a prac
tice exercise where you name a function and I have to identify the brain region.
```

After studying the explanation:

```
Test me. Give me 10 scenarios one at a time -- describe what is happening (like
"a person is planning their schedule for tomorrow") and I will tell you which br
ain region is primarily involved.
```

Step 4: Practice with Exam-Style Questions

```
Generate a practice midterm that mirrors the format my professor would use. Base
d on a typical intro psych course, that probably means:
- 30 multiple choice questions
- 5 short answer questions
- 1 essay question

Cover all six chapters proportionally. Make the difficulty level appropriate for
 a college midterm -- not too easy, not impossibly hard.
```

Take the practice exam with your books closed, then:

```
Here are my answers: [paste your answers]. Grade this practice exam. For every w
rong answer, explain why my answer was incorrect and why the correct answer is r
ight. For partially correct short answers, tell me what I was missing.
```

Step 5: Target Remaining Gaps

Based on your practice exam results:

```
I got questions 4, 12, 17, 23, and 28 wrong on the practice exam. These all seem
 to relate to memory and classical conditioning. Give me a focused review of jus
t these concepts, then five more practice questions targeting exactly these weak
 spots.
```

Step 6: Final Review

On the day before the exam:

```
Give me a comprehensive one-page review sheet covering the most important concep
ts from all six chapters. Organize it as a table: concept, definition, key examp
le, and common exam question type. This should fit on one printed page -- be con
cise.
```

And finally:

```
What are the five things most commonly tested on an intro psych midterm that stu
dents tend to forget? Give me a quick refresher on each one.
```

Why This Works

This study workflow is effective because it applies evidence-based learning strategies:

- **Spaced repetition:** Topics are revisited across multiple days
- **Active recall:** You are being tested, not just re-reading
- **Elaborative interrogation:** You are explaining concepts in your own words
- **Targeted practice:** Weak areas get extra attention
- **Practice testing:** The mock exam simulates real conditions
- **Interleaving:** Topics are mixed together rather than studied in isolation

Claude is the tool, but you are doing the actual learning. That is the critical distinction.

A Note for Educators on AI in the Classroom

The arrival of AI in education cannot be ignored or banned out of existence. Students have access to these tools, and many are already using them. The most effective approach for educators is to engage with the technology directly.

Consider:

- **Teaching AI literacy.** Help students understand what AI can and cannot do, how it works at a high level, and how to use it responsibly.
- **Designing AI-resistant assessments when appropriate.** In-class essays, oral exams, portfolio-based assessments, and process-focused assignments (where students submit drafts and revisions) are harder to shortcut with AI.
- **Designing AI-integrated assessments when appropriate.** Some assignments can explicitly incorporate AI use — "Use Claude to generate three counterarguments to your thesis, then address each one in your essay."
- **Having honest conversations.** Students respond better to "Here is why this matters for your learning" than to "You are not allowed to use this."

- **Modeling good use.** Show students how you use AI in your own work. Demonstrate that experts use it as a tool, not a replacement for thinking.

Education is about developing the ability to think. AI does not threaten that mission if we are thoughtful about how we integrate it. Used well, it may be the most powerful tutoring tool we have ever had.

Key Takeaways

- **Claude is a tutor, not a shortcut.** The most effective study techniques involve active engagement, not passive consumption of AI-generated answers.
- **Academic integrity matters.** Use Claude to understand, not to avoid understanding. Follow your institution's policies.
- **Educators can save significant planning time.** Lesson plans, assessments, differentiated materials, and administrative communications can all be accelerated with Claude.
- **Age-appropriate guidelines are essential.** Younger students need more supervision; older students need more explicit conversations about responsible use.
- **Evidence-based study strategies work.** Claude is the delivery mechanism, but spaced repetition, active recall, and practice testing are what produce learning.
- **The exam prep workflow is a template.** Organize, identify weaknesses, deep-dive, practice, target gaps, and review. This pattern works for any subject.

Chapter 19: Claude for Business and Teams

Using Claude as an individual is one thing. Deploying it across a team or an entire organization is another challenge entirely. The questions shift from "How do I write a better prompt?" to "How do we govern this? Who has access to what? How do we keep proprietary data safe?" and, most practically, "How do we get everyone on the team to actually use this thing effectively?"

This chapter covers the business side of Claude: team workspaces, administrative controls, department-by-department use cases, building a responsible AI usage policy, and an honest comparison of Claude versus ChatGPT for business contexts.

Team Workspaces and Shared Conversations

Anthropic offers Claude plans designed for team use, and the collaboration features make a meaningful difference compared to everyone running individual accounts.

How Team Plans Work

With Claude's Team and Enterprise plans, organizations get a shared workspace where team members can collaborate. (Note: the Max plan, covered in Chapter 2, is an individual plan with higher usage limits — it does not include team or shared workspace features.) The key features include:

- **Shared conversations.** Team members can share conversations with colleagues, making it easy to hand off work or collaborate on a task. Instead of copying and pasting Claude's output into an email, you can share the conversation directly.
- **Projects.** Teams can create shared projects that persist knowledge and instructions across conversations. A project might contain your company's style guide, product documentation, or standard operating procedures — and every conversation within that project will have access to that context.

- **Consistent system prompts.** Administrators can set up shared instructions that apply to all team members, ensuring consistent behavior across the organization. This means your sales team's Claude interactions can be pre-loaded with your product catalog and messaging guidelines.

Getting the Most from Team Features

The teams that get the most value from shared workspaces follow a few patterns:

Create a shared prompt library. Build a collection of tested, effective prompts for common tasks in your organization. Store them in a shared document or project so everyone benefits from the best prompts — not just the person who wrote them.

Standardize with projects. If your team produces consistent types of output — weekly reports, client proposals, product descriptions — create projects with the relevant context and guidelines pre-loaded. This ensures consistent quality regardless of who on the team is doing the work.

Share good examples. When someone gets an especially good result from Claude, share the conversation with the team. Seeing what good looks like is the fastest way to improve everyone's usage.

Admin Controls and Data Governance

Data governance is not optional. Before deploying Claude across your organization, you need to understand what happens to your data and what controls you have.

Data Handling

Anthropic's business plans come with meaningful data protections:

- **No training on your data.** On Team and Enterprise plans, Anthropic does not use your conversations to train its models. Your proprietary information stays your proprietary information.
- **Data retention controls.** Enterprise plans offer configurable data retention policies. You can set how long conversations are stored and when they are automatically deleted.

- **SOC 2 compliance.** Anthropic maintains SOC 2 Type II compliance, which means their security practices have been independently audited.

Administrative Controls

Team and Enterprise administrators have several key capabilities:

- **User management.** Add and remove team members, control who has access to what.
- **Usage monitoring.** Track how the team is using Claude — who is using it most, what types of tasks are most common, and where adoption might be lagging.
- **Policy enforcement.** Set organization-wide guidelines for Claude usage that are presented to all team members.
- **SSO integration.** Enterprise plans support single sign-on through your existing identity provider, which simplifies access management and improves security.

What to Evaluate Before Deploying

Before rolling Claude out to your team, work through this checklist:

1. **Data classification.** What types of data will people be putting into Claude? Public information? Internal documents? Customer data? Define what is and is not acceptable to share.
2. **Regulatory requirements.** Are you in a regulated industry (healthcare, finance, legal)? Understand any specific compliance requirements that affect AI usage.
3. **Integration needs.** Will Claude be used standalone, or do you need it connected to other systems through the API or MCP (Model Context Protocol)?
4. **Training plan.** How will you train employees to use Claude effectively? A tool nobody knows how to use well is a waste of money.
5. **Success metrics.** How will you measure whether Claude is delivering value? Time saved? Quality improvements? Revenue impact?

Use Cases by Department

A common question from business leaders is "Where should we start?" Here is a department-by-department breakdown of the highest-value use cases.

Marketing

- **Content creation.** Blog posts, social media copy, email campaigns, ad copy, and landing page content. Claude can produce first drafts rapidly, which your team then edits and refines.
- **Market research synthesis.** Paste in market reports, competitor analyses, or customer survey data and ask Claude to identify key themes and actionable insights.
- **Campaign planning.** Brainstorm campaign concepts, develop messaging frameworks, and create content calendars.
- **SEO support.** Generate keyword-optimized content outlines, meta descriptions, and title tags.

Sales

- **Proposal generation.** Create customized proposals by providing Claude with the prospect's details and your product capabilities.
- **Email sequences.** Draft personalized outreach sequences, follow-up emails, and nurture campaigns.
- **Competitive intelligence.** Analyze competitor materials and develop battle cards highlighting your advantages.
- **Call preparation.** Before important calls, share what you know about the prospect and ask Claude to suggest talking points, anticipate objections, and recommend closing strategies.

Customer Support

- **Response drafting.** Draft replies to customer inquiries that support agents can review, personalize, and send.
- **Knowledge base creation.** Generate and maintain FAQ documents, help articles, and troubleshooting guides.
- **Escalation summaries.** When a ticket is escalated, use Claude to summarize the conversation history and highlight key issues so the next agent does not have to read everything from scratch.

Human Resources

- **Job descriptions.** Generate inclusive, compelling job descriptions based on role requirements.
- **Policy development.** Draft company policies, employee handbooks, and procedural documents.
- **Interview preparation.** Create structured interview questions tailored to specific roles and competencies.
- **Training materials.** Develop onboarding guides, training modules, and assessment materials.

Finance

- **Report generation.** Draft financial summaries, variance analyses, and board reports from raw data.
- **Data analysis.** Analyze expense reports, revenue trends, and budget variances. Claude can identify patterns and anomalies in financial data.
- **Process documentation.** Document financial procedures, approval workflows, and compliance checklists.

Legal

- **Document review.** Summarize contracts, identify key terms, and flag potential issues. (Note: always have a qualified attorney make final legal decisions.)
- **Research memos.** Draft research memos on legal questions, identifying relevant considerations and precedents.
- **Template creation.** Generate first drafts of standard agreements, NDAs, and other routine legal documents.

Product and Engineering

- **Requirements documentation.** Transform meeting notes and stakeholder conversations into structured product requirements.
- **Technical documentation.** Generate API documentation, user guides, and architecture documents.
- **Code review and generation.** Covered in detail in Chapter 20.

Building a Company AI Usage Policy

Every company using AI should have a clear usage policy. Here is a framework for one that is practical enough to follow and thorough enough to protect your organization.

Section 1: Purpose and Scope

Define why the policy exists and who it applies to. Be specific about which AI tools are covered. A sample opening:

> This policy governs the use of generative AI tools, including Claude, ChatGPT, and similar services, by all employees of [Company Name]. Its purpose is to enable productive use of AI while protecting company data, maintaining quality standards, and ensuring compliance with applicable regulations.

Section 2: Approved Tools and Access

Specify which AI tools are approved for use, at what tier, and who can access them:

- **Approved tools.** List the specific tools employees may use (e.g., "Claude via our Team plan").
- **Unapproved tools.** Clarify that employees should not use personal AI accounts for work tasks, particularly those involving company data.
- **Access levels.** Define who gets access. Is it everyone, or specific teams?

Section 3: Data Classification Rules

This is the most critical section. Define what data can and cannot be shared with AI tools:

- **Permitted:** Publicly available information, general business questions, content creation that does not involve proprietary data.
- **Permitted with caution:** Internal documents on approved (non-training) plans, anonymized data, general strategic questions.

- **Prohibited:** Customer personal data (unless specifically authorized and compliant), trade secrets, passwords or credentials, unannounced financial results, attorney-client privileged information.

Section 4: Quality Control Requirements

AI output needs human oversight. Define your review requirements:

- All AI-generated content intended for external publication must be reviewed by a qualified person before distribution.
- AI-generated code must go through the same review process as human-written code.
- AI-generated financial figures or legal language must be verified by the appropriate specialist.
- Employees are responsible for the accuracy and quality of any AI-assisted work they submit.

Section 5: Attribution and Transparency

Decide your stance on disclosure:

- When must AI use be disclosed to clients or customers?
- Is there a standard disclosure statement?
- How should AI use be documented internally?

Section 6: Training and Support

Outline how employees will learn to use AI effectively:

- Required training before access is granted
- Available resources (prompt libraries, best practices guides, internal champions)
- Who to contact with questions

Section 7: Compliance and Enforcement

Specify consequences for policy violations and how the policy will be updated:

- This policy is reviewed quarterly and updated as needed.
- Violations should be reported to [department/person].

- Significant violations may result in [consequences].

Claude vs. ChatGPT for Business: When to Use Which

Many business leaders want this comparison, and it deserves a candid assessment. Both Claude and ChatGPT (powered by OpenAI's GPT models) are excellent AI assistants, but they have different strengths.

Where Claude Excels

Long-form writing quality. Claude consistently produces more natural, nuanced writing. If your business leans heavily on content creation, proposals, reports, or communications, Claude's writing quality is a meaningful advantage.

Following complex instructions. Claude is particularly good at adhering to detailed prompts with multiple constraints. When you need precise formatting, specific structures, or layered requirements, Claude follows instructions more faithfully.

Analysis and reasoning. For tasks that require careful analysis — evaluating arguments, identifying flaws in logic, synthesizing information from multiple sources — Claude's reasoning capabilities, particularly with extended thinking, are strong.

Safety and reliability. Anthropic's emphasis on safety means Claude is less likely to produce harmful, biased, or wildly inaccurate content. For businesses, this reduces risk.

Document handling. Claude handles long documents well. If your workflow involves analyzing contracts, reports, or lengthy documents, Claude's large context window is valuable.

Developer tools. Claude Code, Anthropic's CLI tool, provides a terminal-based interface for developers that can read and write files, run commands, and work across entire codebases. It is a distinctive offering that does not have a direct equivalent.

Where ChatGPT Excels

Image generation. ChatGPT integrates with DALL-E for image generation. If your business needs AI-generated images, ChatGPT has this built in while Claude does not generate images.

Plugin and integration ecosystem. ChatGPT has a large library of third-party plugins and integrations through its GPT Store. If you need specific third-party tool connections, check what is available.

Web browsing. ChatGPT's built-in web browsing can access current information from the internet during a conversation.

Voice interaction. ChatGPT offers a polished voice interface for spoken conversations, which some users prefer for brainstorming or hands-free use.

Brand recognition. More people know what ChatGPT is. If you are working with external partners or clients, they may already be familiar with it, which reduces the learning curve.

The Honest Answer

For most businesses, the best approach is not to pick one exclusively but to understand the strengths of each and use the right tool for the job. Many organizations maintain accounts with both services.

That said, if you are choosing one platform for your team:

- **Choose Claude if** your primary use cases are writing, analysis, document processing, code development, or tasks requiring precise instruction-following.
- **Choose ChatGPT if** your primary use cases require image generation, voice interaction, web browsing, or specific third-party integrations.
- **Choose both if** your budget allows and your team has diverse needs.

Pricing Considerations

Both services offer tiered pricing for individuals and teams. Pricing is competitive and changes frequently. Rather than listing specific prices that will be outdated quickly, here is what to evaluate:

- **Per-seat cost** for your team size
- **Usage limits** at each tier (message caps, file upload limits)
- **Feature availability** at each tier (which models, which features)
- **Enterprise features** (SSO, data retention controls, admin tools)
- **API pricing** if you plan to build custom integrations

Request demos and trials from both providers before committing.

Getting Your Team to Actually Use It

Buying licenses is easy. Getting adoption is hard. Here are the strategies that work.

Start with Champions

Identify two or three enthusiastic early adopters in each department. Give them early access, invest in their training, and make them the go-to people for questions. Peer influence drives adoption far more than top-down mandates.

Show, Do Not Tell

Abstract presentations about AI's potential are forgettable. Live demonstrations using real work tasks are convincing. Show your sales team how Claude can draft a proposal in two minutes. Show your marketing team how it can produce a month of social media content in an afternoon. Show your HR team how it can build a structured interview guide in five minutes.

Reduce Friction

The easier it is to use Claude, the more people will use it. This means:

- Providing a shared prompt library for common tasks
- Pre-configuring projects with relevant context
- Creating simple how-to guides specific to each department's use cases
- Making it part of existing workflows rather than an additional step

Measure and Share Wins

Track the time saved, the quality improvements, and the revenue impact. Share these wins visibly. When one team sees another team saving ten hours a week, they want in.

Be Patient

Adoption does not happen overnight. Some people will embrace AI immediately, others will be cautious, and a few will resist. Provide support, celebrate wins, and give people time to develop comfort. The most effective thing you can do is ensure your early adopters are having such obviously positive experiences that curiosity eventually overcomes resistance.

Key Takeaways

- **Team plans offer meaningful advantages** over individual accounts: shared conversations, projects, administrative controls, and data protections.
- **Data governance is non-negotiable.** Define what data can be shared with AI tools before you deploy them.
- **Every department benefits.** Marketing, sales, support, HR, finance, legal, and product all have high-value use cases.
- **A clear usage policy protects your organization.** Cover approved tools, data classification, quality control, attribution, and training.
- **Claude and ChatGPT have different strengths.** Choose based on your specific needs, or use both.
- **Adoption requires effort.** Champions, live demonstrations, reduced friction, and measured wins drive adoption more than mandates.

Chapter 20: Claude for Developers

If you write code for a living — or even as a side project — Claude may be the most impactful tool you adopt this year. Not because it will replace you. It will not. But because the tedious, time-consuming parts of software development — boilerplate code, debugging obscure errors, writing documentation, refactoring messy code, and navigating unfamiliar codebases — are the tasks where Claude excels.

This chapter covers the full spectrum of developer use cases: code generation, debugging, refactoring, documentation, Claude Code (Anthropic's CLI tool for developers), the Claude API for building your own applications, MCP for connecting Claude to external tools, and an honest comparison with other developer AI tools.

Code Generation and Review

Writing New Code

Claude can generate code in virtually any programming language. But the quality of the code depends on the quality of your prompt. Here is the difference between a prompt that produces usable code and one that produces something you will immediately rewrite.

Weak prompt:

```
Write a function to process user data.
```

Strong prompt:

```
Write a Python function called `process_user_data` that:
- Takes a list of dictionaries, each containing 'name' (str), 'email' (str), and
 'age' (int)
- Validates that all required fields are present and correctly typed
- Filters out users under 18
- Returns a list of validated users sorted by name
- Raises a ValueError with a descriptive message for invalid input
- Include type hints and a docstring
```

The strong prompt produces production-ready code because you told Claude exactly what you need. Specificity is everything.

Code Review

Claude is a strong code reviewer. Paste in your code and ask for specific feedback:

```
Review this Python code for:
1. Bugs or logic errors
2. Security vulnerabilities (especially SQL injection and XSS)
3. Performance issues
4. Code style and readability
5. Missing error handling

Be specific -- quote the problematic lines and explain the issue and fix for eac
h one.

<code>
[paste your code]
</code>
```

Claude often catches issues that slip through human review, especially in input validation, edge cases, and error handling.

Working with Existing Codebases

When you need to modify existing code, provide Claude with context:

```
Here is our current authentication middleware:

<current_code>
[paste code]
</current_code>

I need to add rate limiting that:
- Limits each IP to 100 requests per 15-minute window
- Returns a 429 status code when the limit is exceeded
- Includes a Retry-After header
- Uses Redis for tracking (we already have a Redis connection available as `redi
s_client`)

Modify the existing code to add this functionality. Keep the existing auth logic
 intact.
```

Giving Claude the existing code, the specific requirements, and the available infrastructure lets it produce modifications that fit into your codebase.

Debugging and Refactoring

Debugging

Debugging is where Claude saves developers the most time. Instead of staring at a stack trace for an hour, paste it into Claude with context:

```
I am getting this error when processing large CSV files (over 100MB):

<error>
[paste stack trace]
</error>

Here is the relevant code:

<code>
[paste the function that is failing]
</code>

The code works fine with smaller files. What is causing this, and how do I fix i
t?
```

Claude will typically identify the issue, explain why it occurs, and provide a corrected version. For complex bugs, use extended thinking — it gives Claude room to trace through the logic step by step.

Refactoring

Refactoring is another high-value use case. Claude can help you improve code without changing its behavior:

```
Refactor this function to:
1. Follow the single responsibility principle (break it into smaller functions i
f needed)
2. Replace the nested if/else blocks with early returns
3. Add proper error handling
4. Improve variable names to be more descriptive
5. Add type hints

Preserve the exact same behavior -- I will be running our existing test suite ag
```

```
ainst the refactored code.

<code>
[paste code]
</code>
```

The instruction to preserve existing behavior matters — it tells Claude to focus on structure and readability, not functionality changes.

Explaining Unfamiliar Code

When you inherit a codebase or encounter unfamiliar patterns:

```
Explain what this code does, step by step. I am a mid-level developer unfamiliar
 with this codebase. Focus on:
- What the overall function accomplishes
- Why it is structured this way
- Any design patterns being used
- Anything that looks unusual or potentially problematic

<code>
[paste code]
</code>
```

Documentation and Technical Writing

Documentation is the part of development that everyone knows is important and nobody wants to do. Claude makes it painless.

API Documentation

```
Generate API documentation for the following Express.js routes. For each route,
include:
- HTTP method and path
- Description
- Request parameters (path, query, body) with types
- Response format with example JSON
- Possible error codes and their meanings
- Example curl command

<routes>
[paste route handlers]
</routes>
```

README Files

```
Generate a README.md for this project. Include:
- Project name and one-paragraph description
- Prerequisites
- Installation instructions
- Configuration (environment variables)
- Usage examples
- API reference (brief)
- Contributing guidelines
- License

Here is the project structure and key files:
<project>
[paste directory listing and key configuration files]
</project>
```

Inline Code Comments

```
Add clear, concise inline comments to this code. Comment on the "why" not the "w
hat" -- do not state the obvious. Focus on explaining business logic, non-obviou
s decisions, and potential gotchas.

<code>
[paste code]
</code>
```

Claude Code: The CLI Tool

Claude Code is Anthropic's command-line interface for developers, and it represents a different way of working with AI on code. Instead of copying and pasting code into a chat window, Claude Code runs in your terminal and interacts directly with your codebase.

What Claude Code Does

Claude Code is a terminal-based tool that can:

- **Read files** from your project
- **Write and edit files** directly in your codebase
- **Run shell commands** (build, test, lint, deploy)

- **Navigate entire codebases** — not just individual files, but the relationships between them
- **Maintain context** across an entire project, understanding how different files relate to each other

This is a significant step beyond chat-based code assistance. Instead of acting as the intermediary — copying code into Claude, getting a response, copying it back — Claude Code works directly with your files.

When to Use Claude Code vs. Chat

Use the standard Claude chat interface when you want to:

- Discuss architecture or design decisions
- Get a quick code snippet or algorithm
- Learn about a technology or pattern
- Review a small piece of code

Use Claude Code when you want to:

- Make changes across multiple files in a project
- Understand a large, unfamiliar codebase
- Run a sequence of development commands (build, test, fix, repeat)
- Refactor code that spans many files
- Generate code that needs to fit into existing project structure and conventions

Practical Claude Code Workflows

Codebase exploration: When you join a new project, Claude Code can read through the codebase and explain the architecture, key patterns, and how components connect. It understands file relationships, import chains, and project structure in ways chat-based tools cannot.

Multi-file changes: Need to rename a function that is used in 30 files? Add a new field to a database model that requires changes to the schema, the API, and the frontend? Claude Code can plan and execute these changes across your entire project.

Test-driven workflows: You can ask Claude Code to write tests for your code, run them, see what fails, fix the failures, and re-run until everything passes — all in one workflow.

Debugging in context: Instead of copying error messages and code snippets into a chat window, Claude Code can see the actual error, read the relevant files, understand the project structure, and propose a fix in place.

Getting Started with Claude Code

Claude Code is installed via npm and runs in your terminal:

```
npm install -g @anthropic-ai/claude-code
```

Once installed, navigate to your project directory and launch it. Claude Code will analyze your project structure and be ready to assist. It requires a Claude subscription or API key to function.

API Overview: Building with Claude

If you want to integrate Claude into your own applications — a chatbot on your website, an internal tool, an automated workflow — you use the Claude API.

The Basics

The Claude API is available at **api.anthropic.com**. You send HTTP requests with your prompt, and you get back Claude's response. Anthropic provides official SDKs that make this straightforward:

- **Python:** `pip install anthropic`
- **TypeScript/JavaScript:** `npm install @anthropic-ai/sdk`

A Simple API Call

Here is what a basic API call looks like in Python:

```
import anthropic

client = anthropic.Anthropic()  # uses ANTHROPIC_API_KEY env var

message = client.messages.create(
    model="claude-sonnet-4-6",
```

```
    max_tokens=1024,
    messages=[
        {"role": "user", "content": "Explain REST APIs in two paragraphs."}
    ]
)

print(message.content[0].text)
```

And in TypeScript:

```
import Anthropic from "@anthropic-ai/sdk";

const client = new Anthropic(); // uses ANTHROPIC_API_KEY env var

const message = await client.messages.create({
  model: "claude-sonnet-4-6",
  max_tokens: 1024,
  messages: [
    { role: "user", content: "Explain REST APIs in two paragraphs." }
  ],
});

console.log(message.content[0].text);
```

Key Concepts

Models. You choose which Claude model to use for each request. Opus 4.7 for the most capable responses, Sonnet 4.6 for a balance of capability and speed, Haiku 4.5 for fast, lightweight tasks.

System prompts. The API lets you set a system prompt that defines Claude's behavior for the entire conversation — its role, tone, constraints, and any knowledge it should reference.

Conversations. To maintain a multi-turn conversation, you send the full message history with each request. The API is stateless — you manage the conversation state on your side.

Streaming. For real-time applications, you can stream Claude's response token by token instead of waiting for the full response. This is how the chat interface achieves its typing effect.

Token limits and pricing. You pay per token (roughly per word) for both input and output. Different models have different prices. Set `max_tokens` to control the maximum response length.

What You Can Build

The API opens up a wide range of applications:

- **Customer-facing chatbots** with your custom knowledge base and personality
- **Internal tools** that automate document processing, summarization, or analysis
- **Content pipelines** that generate, edit, and format content at scale
- **Code review bots** that analyze pull requests automatically
- **Data extraction tools** that pull structured information from unstructured text

MCP: Model Context Protocol

MCP — the Model Context Protocol — is an open standard from Anthropic for connecting AI models to external tools and data sources. Think of it as a universal adapter that lets Claude interact with the outside world.

What Problem MCP Solves

Without MCP, connecting Claude to an external tool — say, your company's database, a Slack workspace, or a GitHub repository — requires custom integration code for each tool. MCP standardizes this connection, so tools built for MCP work with any AI that supports the protocol.

How MCP Works

MCP follows a client-server architecture:

- **MCP Servers** expose tools and data. For example, a GitHub MCP server exposes operations like "list repositories," "create issue," and "read file."
- **MCP Clients** (like Claude Code or applications built on the Claude API) connect to these servers and use the tools they expose.

When Claude has access to MCP tools, it can decide when to use them while handling your request. Ask Claude to "check the status of our latest deployment" and it can use a connected CI/CD MCP server to look that up directly.

Available MCP Servers

The MCP ecosystem is growing. Some examples of what is available:

- **File system** — read and write local files
- **GitHub** — manage repositories, issues, and pull requests
- **Slack** — read and send messages
- **Database connectors** — query PostgreSQL, MySQL, SQLite
- **Google Drive** — access documents and spreadsheets
- **Web browsing** — fetch and parse web pages

Why MCP Matters for Developers

MCP matters because it turns Claude from a tool that only processes text into one that can take action. Instead of telling you what SQL query to run, it can run the query. Instead of drafting a Slack message for you to copy, it can send the message.

For developers building AI-powered applications, MCP means you do not have to build custom tool integrations from scratch. You can leverage existing MCP servers or build your own against the open standard, and they will work across any MCP-compatible client.

When to Use Claude vs. ChatGPT vs. GitHub Copilot

Developers have multiple AI tools available, and each has a sweet spot.

Claude

Best for: - Complex code generation requiring detailed specifications - Code review and analysis of large files or codebases - Refactoring with nuanced requirements - Technical writing and documentation - Working with long documents or large code contexts - Architectural discussions and design decisions - Tasks that benefit from extended thinking (debugging complex logic, analyzing algorithms)

Developer-specific strengths: - Claude Code provides direct codebase interaction via the terminal - Large context window handles substantial code files and multiple files at once - Strong at following complex, multi-constraint instructions - Excellent at explaining code and technical concepts - MCP ecosystem for connecting to developer tools

ChatGPT

Best for: - Quick code snippets and one-off questions - Web browsing for current documentation or library versions - Tasks involving image input (screenshots of errors, UI mockups) - Voice-based coding discussions - Plugin ecosystem for specific tool integrations

GitHub Copilot

Best for: - Inline code completion as you type - Autocompleting patterns from your current file - Small, contextual suggestions within your editor - Rapid iteration on code that follows established patterns in your project

Important distinction: GitHub Copilot is an IDE extension that works at the line and function level — it suggests completions as you type. Claude (whether through chat or Claude Code) works at a higher level — you describe what you want and get complete implementations, explanations, or reviews. They are complementary, not direct competitors.

The Practical Approach

Many professional developers use all three:

- **GitHub Copilot** for real-time autocomplete while typing
- **Claude** (chat or Claude Code) for substantial tasks: multi-file changes, code review, debugging complex issues, documentation, and architectural planning
- **ChatGPT** for quick lookups, web-based research, and tasks that benefit from plugins

You do not have to choose one. Use each tool where it is strongest.

Best Practices for Developers Using Claude

Always Review Generated Code

Claude generates code that looks correct and often is correct. But "often" is not "always." Never push AI-generated code to production without reviewing it. Pay attention to:

- Edge cases and error handling
- Security implications (input validation, authentication, authorization)
- Performance characteristics (does it scale? Is it efficient?)
- Compatibility with your existing codebase
- Test coverage

Provide Context Generously

The more Claude knows about your project — the tech stack, the coding conventions, the existing architecture, the specific requirements — the better the code it produces. Spending thirty seconds writing a detailed prompt saves thirty minutes of post-generation editing.

Use Claude for Learning, Not Just Production

When Claude generates code using a pattern you do not recognize, ask it to explain. "Why did you use a generator here instead of a list comprehension?" or "Explain the advantage of this approach over the one I was using." Every interaction can be a learning opportunity.

Version Control Everything

This should go without saying, but commit your code before asking Claude to make changes. Whether through the chat interface or Claude Code, having a clean git state means you can always revert if a change does not work out.

Start with Tests

One of the best workflows with Claude is test-driven: write the tests (or have Claude write them from your specifications), then implement the code to pass them. This gives you automatic verification and makes AI-generated code much safer to use.

Key Takeaways

- **Code generation quality depends on prompt quality.** Be specific about inputs, outputs, error handling, and constraints.
- **Claude excels at debugging.** Paste the error, the code, and the context. Let Claude trace the logic.
- **Documentation no longer has to be painful.** API docs, READMEs, inline comments — Claude produces them quickly and thoroughly.
- **Claude Code is a game-changer for codebase-level work.** Terminal-based, file-aware, and capable of multi-file changes.
- **The API lets you build Claude into your own tools.** Available at api.anthropic.com with Python and TypeScript SDKs.
- **MCP connects Claude to external tools.** An open standard that turns Claude from a text processor into an action-taker.
- **Claude, ChatGPT, and Copilot are complementary.** Use each where it is strongest rather than picking one exclusively.
- **Always review AI-generated code.** Trust, but verify.

Chapter 21: Claude for Creators and Freelancers

If you make a living from your creative output — whether you are a writer, designer, marketer, consultant, coach, or any flavor of independent professional — Claude can transform how you work. Not by replacing your creativity, but by eliminating the bottlenecks that slow you down and handling the parts of the business that drain your energy.

This chapter is a practical guide to using Claude in a creative freelance workflow. We will cover content creation, client communication, portfolio development, combining Claude's tools for maximum effect, the reality of what Claude cannot do (no image or video generation), and concrete strategies for increasing your income with AI assistance.

Content Creation Workflows

Content is currency for creators and freelancers. Whether you are producing blog posts, newsletters, social media, scripts, copy, or courses, Claude can accelerate every stage of the process.

The Three-Phase Content Workflow

The most effective way to use Claude for content creation is not to say "write me a blog post" and use whatever comes out. Break the process into three phases: ideation, drafting, and refinement.

Phase 1: Ideation

Use Claude to generate and evaluate ideas before committing to one:

```
I write a weekly newsletter about personal finance for millennials. My audience
is 25-35, college-educated, earning $50K-$100K, and trying to balance student lo
an repayment with building wealth. I have already covered budgeting basics, inde
x fund investing, and debt snowball vs. avalanche.

Generate 10 newsletter topic ideas that:
- Address a specific problem or question my audience has
```

```
- Have not been covered in my previous issues
- Are timely or evergreen (note which)
- Could each be covered in 800-1,200 words
```

Once you have your list, you can ask Claude to develop the strongest ideas further:

```
Expand on ideas 3, 7, and 9. For each, give me: a working title, a one-paragraph
 outline, a potential hook for the opening, and the key takeaway for the reader.
 Help me decide which to write this week.
```

Phase 2: Drafting

Now write with Claude's help. The key is to stay in control of the voice and direction:

```
<role>You are helping me draft my weekly newsletter. My writing style is convers
ational, slightly irreverent, and heavy on practical advice. I use short paragra
phs, rhetorical questions, and specific numbers rather than vague generalities.<
/role>

<task>Write a first draft of a newsletter titled "Why Your Emergency Fund Is Pro
bably Too Small" based on this outline:</task>

<outline>
- Hook: Most advice says 3-6 months. That math is outdated.
- Why the old rule fails (gig economy, higher costs, longer job searches)
- New framework: calculate YOUR actual number
- Step-by-step calculation with example
- Where to keep it (high-yield savings, not checking)
- Close: the peace of mind is worth more than the opportunity cost
</outline>

<constraints>
- Target length: 1,000 words
- Write in first person
- Include at least two specific examples with real numbers
- End with a single clear action step
</constraints>
```

Phase 3: Refinement

Never publish a first draft. Use Claude to improve it:

```
Here is my newsletter draft after I have edited it with my own revisions. Review
 it for:
1. Does the hook grab attention in the first two sentences?
```

```
2. Is the advice actionable and specific enough?
3. Are there any points that feel underdeveloped or unsupported?
4. Does the closing drive the reader to act?
5. Highlight any sentences that feel clunky or could be tightened.

<draft>
[paste your edited draft]
</draft>
```

Batch Content Production

One of the biggest advantages of using Claude is batch production. Instead of creating content one piece at a time, you can generate a week or month of content in a focused session:

```
I need to create 4 weeks of social media content for my photography business. Ea
ch week needs:
- 3 Instagram captions (mix of educational, behind-the-scenes, and promotional)
- 2 LinkedIn posts (industry insights or portfolio highlights)
- 1 email newsletter topic with subject line and brief outline

My brand voice is professional but warm. I specialize in corporate headshots and
 brand photography. Current promotion: spring refresh packages.

Create all 4 weeks now. I will customize and schedule them.
```

This is not about having Claude do all the work. It is about getting the scaffolding up quickly so you can spend your creative energy on the customization and polish that makes the content distinctly yours.

Repurposing Content

Claude excels at transforming one piece of content into many:

```
Here is a 2,000-word blog post I wrote about color theory in brand design:

<blog_post>
[paste post]
</blog_post>

Repurpose this into:
1. A Twitter/X thread (8-10 tweets)
2. A LinkedIn article summary (300 words)
3. An Instagram carousel outline (10 slides, with text for each slide)
```

```
4. Three pull quotes suitable for social media graphics
5. A YouTube video script outline based on the same content (5-7 minutes)
```

One piece of original content becomes five or more assets. This multiplier effect is where Claude delivers outsized value for creators.

Client Communication and Proposals

For freelancers, client communication is where projects are won or lost. Claude can help you communicate more professionally, respond more quickly, and close more deals.

Proposals That Win

A strong proposal is specific, professional, and shows you understand the client's problem. Claude can help you craft one:

```
I am a freelance web developer. A potential client -- a local bakery -- wants a
new website. From our discovery call, here are the details:

<client_details>
- Current website is 8 years old, not mobile-friendly
- Wants online ordering for pickup and delivery
- Needs to showcase their menu with photos
- Budget: $5,000-$8,000
- Timeline: wants it live in 6 weeks
- Competitors: two other bakeries in town have modern sites
</client_details>

Write a professional proposal that includes:
1. Understanding of their needs (show I listened)
2. Proposed solution (specific recommendations)
3. Scope of work (what is included and what is not)
4. Timeline with milestones
5. Investment (present it as value, not just cost)
6. Next steps

Tone: professional, confident, but warm. I want them to feel like I am a trustwo
rthy partner, not just a vendor.
```

Email Templates for Common Situations

Build a library of templates you can customize quickly:

```
Create email templates for these common freelance situations:
1. Following up after a discovery call (warm but not pushy)
2. Sending a proposal with a call to action
3. Requesting project feedback or approval
4. Handling a scope change request (set boundaries kindly)
5. Asking for a testimonial after project completion
6. Re-engaging a past client (it has been 6+ months)
7. Politely declining a project that is not a good fit
8. Addressing a late payment

For each, write a subject line and email body. Keep them concise -- under 200 wo
rds each. My tone is professional but personable.
```

Handling Difficult Conversations

When you need to raise your rates, push back on scope creep, or deliver unwelcome news:

```
I need to tell a long-term client that I am raising my rates from $75/hour to $1
00/hour starting next quarter. They have been my client for two years and I valu
e the relationship. Help me write an email that:
- Frames the increase as a reflection of increased value and expertise
- Gives adequate notice (I want to announce it 6 weeks in advance)
- Offers a small incentive to ease the transition (maybe a locked rate for prepa
id hours)
- Is firm but kind -- I am not negotiating the rate itself, but I am flexible on
 timing
```

Portfolio and Brand Development

Your portfolio and personal brand are what attract clients in the first place. Claude can help you develop both strategically.

Portfolio Descriptions

The text accompanying your portfolio work matters as much as the work itself:

```
I am a freelance graphic designer updating my portfolio website. For each projec
t, I need a case study write-up. Here are the details for one project:

<project>
Client: GreenLeaf Organics (organic grocery delivery)
Work: Complete brand identity (logo, color palette, typography, packaging, websi
te design)
```

```
Challenge: They were a farmer's market vendor going online for the first time. N
eeded to feel premium but approachable.
Result: 40% increase in online orders in first month after launch.
Timeline: 6 weeks
</project>

Write a portfolio case study that includes:
- A compelling headline
- The Challenge (2-3 sentences)
- The Approach (3-4 sentences about my process)
- The Solution (describe the key design decisions)
- The Results (quantify the impact)

Tone: confident, design-literate, but accessible to non-designers (since clients
 are the audience, not other designers).
```

Personal Brand Voice

Developing a consistent brand voice across all your communications:

```
Help me define my personal brand voice. Here are some data points:

<about_me>
- I am a freelance UX writer and content strategist
- My clients are SaaS companies, mostly B2B
- I have 8 years of experience, including 3 years at a major tech company
- I am known for being direct, data-driven, and easy to work with
- My values: clarity over cleverness, user needs over business jargon, evidence
over opinion
</about_me>

Based on this, create:
1. A brand voice guide (4-5 adjectives with descriptions of what each means in p
ractice)
2. A 100-word bio I can use on my website and LinkedIn
3. A 50-word bio for speaking engagements
4. A one-sentence tagline
5. Three examples of how my voice sounds in different contexts: a social media p
ost, a client email, and a blog introduction
```

LinkedIn and Professional Presence

```
I am updating my LinkedIn profile. I am a freelance copywriter specializing in e
mail marketing for e-commerce brands. My results include a 45% average increase
in open rates for my clients and over $2M in attributed revenue.
```

```
Write:
1. A LinkedIn headline (under 120 characters) that positions me as an expert, no
t just "freelance copywriter"
2. An About section (under 2,000 characters) that tells my story, highlights res
ults, and ends with a soft call to action
3. Three LinkedIn posts I could publish this week to establish thought leadershi
p: one tactical tip, one opinion piece, one case study teaser
```

Combining Claude's Tools

Claude is not just a text generator. It has multiple capabilities — writing, analysis, code generation, and artifacts (interactive outputs in the web interface) — and the real power comes from combining them.

Writing + Analysis

Pair Claude's analytical and writing capabilities for data-driven content:

```
Here are our website analytics for the past 6 months: [paste data or describe me
trics].

1. First, analyze the data: identify the top 3 trends, any concerning patterns,
and the biggest opportunity.
2. Then, write a client report summarizing these findings in plain language. Inc
lude a recommendations section with three specific actions ranked by expected im
pact.
3. Finally, draft a short email to the client introducing the report and highlig
hting the most important finding.
```

Analysis + Planning

Use Claude's analytical ability to inform strategic planning:

```
I want to launch a paid newsletter on Substack about AI for small business owner
s. Before I start, help me think this through:

1. Analyze the competitive landscape -- what paid newsletters exist in this spac
e? What topics do they cover? What is the typical price point?
2. Based on gaps in the market, suggest a specific positioning for my newsletter
 that differentiates it.
3. Create a launch plan: pre-launch (4 weeks), launch week, and first month. Inc
lude content strategy, pricing strategy, and growth tactics.
```

```
4. Build a simple financial model: what subscriber count do I need at what price
 to replace $3,000/month in freelance income?
```

Code + Content

If you build websites or digital products for clients, combine Claude's code and content abilities:

```
I am building a landing page for a client's new SaaS product (a time-tracking to
ol for freelancers).

1. Write the landing page copy: headline, subheadline, three feature sections wi
th headers and descriptions, a testimonial placeholder format, pricing section c
opy, and a FAQ section with 5 questions.
2. Then generate the HTML and CSS for a clean, responsive landing page using thi
s copy. Use modern CSS (grid/flexbox), a professional color scheme, and make it
mobile-first.
```

What Claude Cannot Do: Images and Video

Worth addressing directly. Claude does not generate images, illustrations, photos, graphics, or video. It is a text and code tool. If your creative work requires visual asset generation, you will need separate tools — Midjourney, DALL-E (via ChatGPT), Adobe Firefly, or similar services.

What Claude can do is everything around the visual work:

- **Art direction briefs** that describe exactly what images you need
- **Image generation prompts** for tools like Midjourney or DALL-E
- **Alt text and image descriptions** for accessibility
- **Video scripts and storyboards** (in text form)
- **Shot lists** for photo and video shoots
- **Creative briefs** for designers and videographers you work with

Think of Claude as the planning, writing, and strategy layer that supports your visual creative process. Use it to write the creative brief, the script, and the marketing copy — then use visual tools for the visual assets.

Monetization Strategies with AI Assistance

Here is where it gets interesting. Claude is not just a productivity tool — it is a leverage tool. It lets you do more valuable work in less time, which directly impacts your earning potential.

Strategy 1: Increase Your Output Without Increasing Hours

The most direct path to earning more as a freelancer is doing more work. If Claude helps you write blog posts in half the time, you can take on twice as many clients — or spend the saved time on higher-value activities like strategy and client relationships.

Track your time before and after adopting Claude. Most freelancers find they save 30–50% of production time on content-related tasks. That is real money.

Strategy 2: Move Up the Value Chain

AI handles production well. It does not handle strategy, judgment, or relationships. Use Claude to automate production and reposition yourself as a strategist:

Before Claude: "I am a freelance writer. I charge $0.15 per word." **After Claude:** "I am a content strategist. I develop content plans, create editorial calendars, produce the content, and analyze performance. I charge $3,000 per month as a retainer."

The writer sells labor. The strategist sells outcomes. Claude makes the transition possible by handling the production so you can focus on the strategy.

Strategy 3: Productize Your Services

Use Claude to create scalable products alongside your services:

- **Templates and frameworks.** Develop reusable templates based on your expertise and sell them. Claude can help you build them out comprehensively.
- **Online courses.** Use Claude to develop curriculum, write lesson scripts, create exercises, and build assessment materials.

- **Guides and ebooks.** Write comprehensive guides in your area of expertise. What would take months solo can be done in weeks with Claude's assistance.
- **Audit services.** Build structured audit frameworks (website audits, content audits, brand audits) that Claude helps you execute efficiently. You provide the expertise and judgment; Claude handles the documentation and report generation.

Strategy 4: Offer New Services

Claude's capabilities let you expand what you offer:

- A web designer can now offer copywriting as part of the package
- A copywriter can now offer basic data analysis and reporting
- A consultant can now offer comprehensive documentation and process manuals
- A marketer can now offer email automation setup and management

Each new service is a new revenue stream.

Strategy 5: Reduce Non-Billable Time

Freelancers spend a shocking amount of time on non-billable work: proposals, invoicing, admin emails, project management, bookkeeping prep, and self-promotion. Claude can streamline almost all of it:

- Proposals take 15 minutes instead of 2 hours
- Client emails are drafted in 2 minutes instead of 20
- Social media content for self-promotion is batched monthly instead of scrambled daily
- Project documentation is generated automatically instead of painstakingly

Every hour saved on admin is an hour available for billable work or rest.

Strategy 6: Build Recurring Revenue

Use Claude to develop offerings that generate recurring income:

```
I am a freelance marketing consultant. Help me design a monthly retainer package
 I can offer to small businesses. It should include:
```

```
- A manageable scope of work I can deliver in 15-20 hours/month
- Clear deliverables the client receives each month
- Pricing that is attractive to the client but profitable for me ($100/hour effe
ctive rate)
- An onboarding process for new retainer clients
- A quarterly review structure to demonstrate ongoing value
```

Retainer income provides stability that project work does not. Claude helps you design, deliver, and maintain these packages efficiently.

Building a Sustainable AI-Assisted Practice

A word of caution as we close this chapter. The goal of using Claude is not to remove yourself from your work. Clients hire you for your judgment, your taste, your experience, and your ability to understand their specific situation. Claude amplifies those qualities — it does not replace them.

The freelancers who thrive with AI are those who:

- **Maintain their craft.** Keep developing your core skills. AI is a tool, not a substitute for expertise.
- **Stay honest with clients.** If a client asks whether you use AI, answer straight. Most clients care about results, not methods — but transparency builds trust.
- **Add human value at every step.** Review everything Claude produces. Add your perspective, your taste, your knowledge of the client. The output should always pass through your judgment before it reaches the client.
- **Invest the time savings wisely.** Reinvest saved time into relationship building, skill development, strategic thinking, or rest. Do not just fill the saved hours with more production.
- **Price for value, not time.** As AI makes you faster, switch from hourly pricing to project or value-based pricing. Your speed is an advantage, not a discount.

Key Takeaways

- **Use the three-phase workflow.** Ideation, drafting, and refinement — each phase has a different relationship with Claude.

- **Batch content production is a game-changer.** Create a week or month of content in a single focused session, then customize and schedule.
- **Win more clients with better proposals.** Claude helps you create professional, specific proposals quickly.
- **Develop your brand strategically.** Portfolio descriptions, brand voice guides, and professional presence all benefit from Claude's help.
- **Combine Claude's capabilities.** Writing plus analysis plus code is more powerful than any one alone.
- **Remember Claude's limits.** No image or video generation. Use Claude for the text, planning, and strategy side of creative work.
- **Monetize through leverage.** Increase output, move up the value chain, productize, add services, reduce admin, and build recurring revenue.
- **Stay in the driver's seat.** Claude is your most capable tool, but your judgment, taste, and client relationships are what make you irreplaceable.

Part VII: Limitations, Safety, and Ethics

"With great power comes great responsibility."

— Voltaire (paraphrased)

Chapter 22: What Claude Gets Wrong

No AI system is perfect, and Claude is no exception. If you have spent any meaningful time with Claude, you have encountered moments where something felt off — a confident answer that turned out to be wrong, a refusal that seemed unnecessary, or a calculation that did not add up. Understanding these limitations is a practical skill that will make you a more effective user and help you avoid costly mistakes.

This chapter is about honesty. The previous twenty-one chapters showed you what Claude can do. Now it is time to talk about what it cannot do, what it gets wrong, and how to protect yourself when it stumbles.

Hallucinations: When Claude Makes Things Up

The most important limitation to understand about Claude — and every large language model — is hallucination. This is the tendency to generate information that sounds plausible but is partially or completely fabricated.

Hallucinations are not bugs in the traditional sense. They are a consequence of how language models work. Claude does not look up facts in a database. It predicts what text is most likely to follow a given prompt, based on patterns learned during training. Most of the time, those predictions align with reality. Sometimes they do not.

Here is what hallucination looks like in practice:

- **Fabricated citations.** You ask Claude for academic sources on a topic, and it provides author names, journal titles, volume numbers, and page ranges that look legitimate — but the papers do not exist. This is one of the most common and most dangerous forms of hallucination.
- **Invented statistics.** Claude might cite a specific percentage or dollar figure with full confidence, when in reality it has generated a plausible-sounding number rather than recalled an actual data point.
- **Fictional people and events.** Ask about a niche historical event or an obscure person, and Claude may blend real facts with invented details, creating a narrative that feels authoritative but contains fabrications.

- **False technical details.** In programming, Claude might reference a function or API method that does not exist, or describe a library feature that was never implemented.

Why Does This Happen?

Claude's training process optimizes for generating helpful, coherent, natural-sounding text. When it encounters a question where it has limited or no training data, it does not say "I don't know." Instead, it fills gaps with statistically plausible content. The model has no internal mechanism for distinguishing between what it "knows" and what it is "inventing" — everything it produces comes from the same generative process.

Anthropic has made significant progress in reducing hallucinations through Constitutional AI training and reinforcement learning from human feedback. Claude is more willing to say "I'm not sure" than many competing models. But the problem has not been solved, and it may never be entirely eliminated.

How to Protect Yourself

Always verify critical facts. If you are using Claude's output in a professional context — a report, a legal document, an academic paper, a business decision — verify any specific claims independently, especially statistics, dates, names, and citations.

Ask Claude to flag uncertainty. You can prompt Claude with something like: "If you are not confident about any part of your answer, please flag it explicitly." This does not guarantee honesty, but it nudges the model toward expressing doubt rather than confabulating.

Request sources and then check them. When Claude provides references, actually look them up. Do not assume a well-formatted citation is a real one.

Be cautious with niche topics. Hallucination rates increase on obscure subjects where training data is sparse. If you are asking about a narrow technical topic, a local regulation, or a lesser-known historical event, raise your verification standard.

Use extended thinking for complex factual questions. When Claude uses extended thinking (available on Pro and higher plans), it reasons through problems more carefully, which can reduce — though not eliminate — hallucination on complex queries.

Knowledge Cutoff and Outdated Information

Claude's training data has a cutoff that varies by model — January 2026 for Opus 4.7, August 2025 for Sonnet 4.6, July 2025 for Haiku 4.5. This means Claude has no knowledge of events, developments, or changes that occurred after the relevant cutoff. This is not a flaw in the traditional sense — it is a structural reality of how the model was built.

The practical implications are significant:

- **Current events.** Claude cannot tell you about news from the past several months. It does not know who won recent elections, what happened in the latest earnings season, or what laws were passed last month.
- **Software updates.** If a framework or programming language released a new version after the cutoff, Claude will not know about it. It might describe deprecated features as current or miss new functionality entirely.
- **Pricing and policies.** Product prices, subscription plans, company policies, and regulatory requirements change frequently. Claude's information may be months out of date.
- **People and organizations.** Career changes, company acquisitions, leadership transitions, and organizational restructurings after the cutoff will not be reflected in Claude's responses.

How to Handle This

Ask Claude about its knowledge cutoff. Claude is transparent about this limitation when asked directly.

Pair Claude with current sources. Use Claude for analysis, synthesis, and reasoning — tasks where its capabilities shine regardless of recency. Supplement with up-to-date information from the web, databases, or other current sources.

Be explicit about time sensitivity. If your question involves time-sensitive information, tell Claude what you already know about recent developments. It can often provide useful analysis even when its base knowledge is outdated, as long as you supply the current facts.

Be cautious with time-sensitive information. Claude can search the web when the feature is enabled, which helps with some current topics. Its web search is more limited than ChatGPT's deeply integrated browsing, however, and should not be your sole source for stock prices, live sports scores, or breaking news. Verify time-sensitive information through your own research.

Math and Reasoning Limitations

Claude is remarkably capable at many forms of reasoning, but it has weaknesses in certain mathematical and logical domains. Understanding where these weaknesses lie will help you use Claude effectively without being misled.

Where Claude Struggles

Multi-step arithmetic. Claude can stumble on long chains of arithmetic, especially with large numbers, many decimal places, or operations that require carrying values across multiple steps. A ten-step calculation is more likely to contain an error than a two-step one.

Word problems with many variables. Complex word problems that require tracking multiple changing quantities can trip Claude up. It may lose track of a variable, make an incorrect substitution, or apply a formula wrong.

Probability and statistics. Claude handles basic probability well, but can make errors on problems involving conditional probability, Bayesian reasoning, or complex combinatorics. These are areas where human intuition also often fails, and Claude's pattern-matching approach can amplify those errors.

Spatial and geometric reasoning. Problems that require visualizing three-dimensional space, complex geometric relationships, or spatial transformations are challenging for a text-based model.

Formal logic with many premises. Claude handles simple logical deductions well, but chains of formal logic with many premises and nested conditionals can lead to errors.

How Extended Thinking Helps

One of the most meaningful improvements in recent Claude models is extended thinking. When enabled, Claude takes additional time to reason through a problem step by step before generating its final answer. This is not cosmetic — extended thinking measurably improves accuracy on mathematical and reasoning tasks.

With extended thinking, Claude:

- Shows its work, making errors easier to spot
- Is less likely to skip steps or make careless mistakes
- Can handle longer chains of reasoning more reliably
- Provides a reasoning trace you can audit

Extended thinking is available on Pro, Max, Team, and Enterprise plans. If you regularly use Claude for math, logic, or complex analysis, this feature alone may justify the subscription cost.

Practical Advice

Use Claude as a reasoning partner, not a calculator. For exact arithmetic, use an actual calculator or spreadsheet. Use Claude to set up the problem, explain the approach, and interpret the results.

Ask Claude to show its work. Even without extended thinking, asking Claude to work through a problem step by step reduces errors compared to asking for just a final answer.

Double-check critical calculations. If a business decision or technical implementation depends on Claude's math, verify independently.

Break complex problems into smaller pieces. Rather than asking Claude to solve a ten-step problem in one go, walk through it step by step. Confirm each step before moving to the next.

Bias in Responses

Claude's training data reflects the internet and other text sources, which means it inevitably absorbs certain biases. Anthropic works hard to mitigate this through

Constitutional AI and careful training, but bias remains an issue worth understanding.

Forms of Bias You Might Encounter

Cultural bias. Claude's training data skews heavily toward English-language, Western, and particularly American perspectives. If you ask about cultural practices, social norms, or historical events from a non-Western perspective, Claude may default to Western framings or miss key nuances.

Recency bias. Claude's training data is weighted toward more recent text, which means it may overrepresent current mainstream views and underrepresent historical perspectives or minority viewpoints.

Sycophancy. This is a well-documented tendency in language models to agree with the user rather than push back. If you present a flawed argument, Claude may validate it rather than challenge it, especially if you sound confident. Anthropic has made progress here — Claude is more willing to disagree than many models — but the tendency persists.

Professional and demographic assumptions. Claude may make assumptions based on stereotypes, such as assuming a doctor is male or a nurse is female, or defaulting to certain cultural assumptions about family structure, career paths, or social roles.

How to Counteract Bias

Ask for multiple perspectives. Instead of asking Claude for "the answer," ask it to present multiple viewpoints or consider the question from different cultural, professional, or ideological angles.

Challenge Claude's assumptions. If an answer feels one-sided, push back. Ask "What would someone who disagrees say?" or "Are there perspectives from other cultures on this?"

Be aware of your own confirmation bias. The sycophancy problem is worst when you are already leaning toward an answer and Claude validates it. Be especially critical of responses that perfectly align with what you wanted to hear.

Specify the perspective you need. If you need a non-Western perspective, a conservative viewpoint, a contrarian analysis, or any other specific angle, ask for it explicitly.

Overly Cautious Refusals

One of the more frustrating limitations you will encounter is Claude's tendency to refuse perfectly reasonable requests. This is a consequence of Anthropic's safety training — Claude is designed to err on the side of caution, which sometimes means it declines to help when it should not.

Common Scenarios

Creative writing with mature themes. Claude may refuse to write fiction that involves violence, conflict, or adult themes, even when the request is clearly for legitimate creative purposes.

Medical and legal information. Claude sometimes adds excessive disclaimers or refuses to provide general information about medical conditions or legal concepts, even when you are clearly asking for educational purposes rather than professional advice.

Security and technical topics. Questions about cybersecurity, lock mechanisms, chemistry, or other dual-use topics may trigger refusals, even when the intent is clearly educational or professional.

Hypothetical and academic discussions. Claude may refuse to engage with thought experiments, devil's advocate arguments, or academic discussions of controversial topics.

How to Work Around Refusals

Provide context. Explain why you need the information. "I'm a nurse studying pharmacology" or "I'm writing a thriller novel" gives Claude the context it needs to understand your intent.

Rephrase professionally. Sometimes a more formal or academic tone gets past overly cautious filters that a casual request triggers.

Be direct about your purpose. Claude responds well to honesty. If you are a security professional, a medical student, a fiction writer, or a researcher, say so.

Acknowledge that you are not asking for professional advice. For medical or legal topics, explicitly stating that you understand this is general information and not a substitute for professional consultation can help.

Anthropic continues to refine Claude's refusal behavior. The balance between safety and helpfulness is difficult, and the company has been responsive to feedback about over-refusal. The trend has been toward fewer unnecessary refusals with each model update.

How to Spot and Handle Errors

Beyond the specific categories of error, you need a general framework for detecting and managing mistakes in Claude's output. Here is a practical approach.

Red Flags to Watch For

Excessive confidence on obscure topics. If Claude sounds authoritative about something highly specific and niche, that is when you should be most skeptical. Real expertise often comes with hedging and nuance. Unwavering confidence on an obscure point is a hallucination warning sign.

Suspiciously perfect answers. If an answer seems too clean, too well-structured, or too perfectly aligned with your expectations, pause. Real information is often messy and full of caveats.

Internal contradictions. Sometimes Claude will contradict itself within a single response or across a conversation. Inconsistencies are a strong signal that at least some of the content is unreliable.

Specific numbers without context. When Claude provides specific statistics or measurements, especially if you did not provide them in your prompt, treat them with skepticism.

Overly detailed biographical information. When Claude provides extensive details about an obscure person — specific dates, precise quotes, detailed career timelines — verify before trusting.

A Verification Framework

1. **Categorize the risk.** How consequential would an error be? A mistake in a casual brainstorming session matters less than an error in a business report or medical context.
2. **Identify verifiable claims.** In any response, separate the analysis and reasoning (which is Claude's strength) from specific factual claims (which may need checking).
3. **Cross-reference key facts.** For high-stakes content, check critical facts against reliable sources.
4. **Use Claude to check Claude.** Start a new conversation and ask the same question differently. If you get a different answer, investigate further.
5. **Trust patterns, question specifics.** Claude's general knowledge and analytical frameworks are usually reliable. Specific details — names, dates, numbers, citations — are where errors most commonly occur.

Building Good Habits

The best approach to Claude's limitations is not paranoia but calibrated trust. Think of it like working with a brilliant colleague who sometimes gets details wrong. You value their analysis, their creativity, and their ability to synthesize complex information. But you double-check the numbers in their spreadsheets and verify the sources in their reports.

Over time, you will develop intuition for when Claude is on solid ground and when it might be shaky. That intuition is one of the most valuable skills you can develop as an AI user, and it applies not just to Claude but to every AI system you will encounter in the years ahead.

The Bigger Picture

Claude's limitations are real, but they belong in context. Every tool has limitations. Search engines return unreliable results. Spreadsheets contain formula errors. Human experts have blind spots and biases. The question is never whether a tool is perfect — it is whether you understand its failure modes well enough to use it effectively.

By reading this chapter, you have already taken the most important step: acknowledging that Claude can be wrong. Most errors happen not because Claude is unreliable, but because users assume it is infallible. Now that you know better, you are equipped to get the most out of Claude while avoiding its pitfalls.

The next chapter looks at another critical topic: how to keep your information safe when using Claude, and what Anthropic does — and does not do — with your data.

Chapter 23: Privacy, Security, and Safe Use

Every time you type a message to Claude, you are sending information to Anthropic's servers. That is not alarming on its own — you send information to servers every time you use email, search the web, or log into a banking app. But it does mean you need to understand what happens to your data, how it is protected, and what you should and should not share.

This chapter gives you a clear-eyed look at Claude's privacy and security landscape. No corporate-speak, no hand-waving — just the practical information you need to use Claude safely.

What Data Anthropic Collects

Anthropic collects several categories of data when you use Claude. Understanding each one helps you decide what to share.

Conversation Data

The most obvious category is the content of your conversations. Every prompt you send and every response Claude generates is transmitted to Anthropic's servers and processed there. That includes:

- Text you type directly into the chat
- Files you upload for analysis
- Images you share for Claude to examine
- The full context of your conversation history within a session

Account Information

When you create an account, Anthropic collects standard account data: your email address, name, payment information (for paid plans), and authentication details. No different from any other online service.

Usage Data

Anthropic collects metadata about how you use Claude: session length, feature usage, frequency of interactions, which model you select, and similar behavioral data. This helps Anthropic improve the product and understand usage patterns.

Technical Data

Like most web services, Anthropic collects technical information such as your IP address, browser type, operating system, and device information. This is used for security, debugging, and service optimization.

How Your Data Is Used

This is the question that matters most, and the answer depends on which plan you are on.

Training: Opt-In by Default on Consumer Plans

In August 2025, Anthropic updated its consumer terms. As of late September 2025, training is **on by default** for Free, Pro, and Max users. Your conversations and coding sessions can be used to improve future Claude models unless you opt out in Privacy Settings. Opting in extends data retention to up to five years; opting out keeps the standard 30-day retention.

This applies to consumer plans only. The Commercial Terms covering Team, Enterprise, the API, Claude for Work, Claude for Government, and Claude for Education exclude data from model training by default.

If you have not made a selection yet, take a minute to do so explicitly. The setting lives under Privacy in your account, and you can change it at any time.

Team and Enterprise Plans: Stronger Defaults

If you are on a Team or Enterprise plan, the default protections are substantially stronger:

- Your data is **not used for model training** unless your organization explicitly opts in
- Conversations are isolated within your organization's workspace

- Enterprise plans include additional security certifications and compliance features
- Administrators have granular control over data retention and access policies

This distinction matters for business use. If your company is evaluating Claude, the Team and Enterprise plans provide the contractual and technical safeguards that compliance teams typically require.

Conversation Retention

Anthropic retains conversation data for a period to give you chat history, enable features like Projects, and handle safety and abuse issues. The specific retention period varies by plan and is detailed in Anthropic's privacy policy. Enterprise customers can often negotiate custom retention terms.

Safety and Abuse Monitoring

Anthropic may review conversations flagged by automated safety systems — primarily to prevent misuse, like attempts to generate harmful content. Anthropic does not employ teams of people casually reading your conversations for entertainment or market research.

Team and Enterprise Protections

If you are using Claude in a professional context, the Team and Enterprise plans offer several security features worth understanding in detail.

Team Plan (Standard $25/seat/mo, Premium $150/seat/mo, 5-seat minimum)

The Team plan provides:

- **No training on your data** by default
- **Centralized billing** and administration
- **Workspace isolation** so that conversations are contained within your team
- **Higher usage limits** than individual plans (and substantially higher on Premium seats)
- **Admin controls** for managing team members and access

Enterprise Plan

Enterprise adds substantially to the Team plan:

- **SOC 2 Type II compliance** and other security certifications
- **Single Sign-On (SSO)** integration with your existing identity provider
- **SCIM provisioning** for automated user management
- **Custom data retention policies** tailored to your compliance requirements
- **Dedicated support** and account management
- **Audit logs** for monitoring usage and access
- **Role-based access controls** for fine-grained permissions

For organizations in regulated industries — healthcare, finance, legal, government — these Enterprise features are not luxuries. They are baseline requirements for deploying any AI tool.

API Usage

If your organization uses Claude through the API rather than the web interface, the data handling policies are distinct. API data is subject to stricter default protections and is not used for training. If your team's developers are building Claude-powered applications, this matters — the API offers the strongest default privacy posture.

What You Should Never Share with Claude

Regardless of your plan, there are categories of information you should never type into any AI chatbot, Claude included. This is not about trust in Anthropic specifically — it is basic information security hygiene.

Passwords and Authentication Credentials

Never share passwords, API keys, secret tokens, private keys, or any authentication credentials with Claude. Even if you are asking for help with a configuration file or debugging an authentication issue, replace real credentials with placeholders before sharing.

Social Security Numbers and Government IDs

Do not share Social Security numbers, passport numbers, driver's license numbers, or other government-issued identification numbers. There is no scenario where Claude needs this information to help you.

Financial Account Numbers

Keep bank account numbers, full credit card numbers, and investment account details out of your conversations. If you need help with financial analysis, use anonymized or fictional data.

Protected Health Information

If you are in a healthcare context, do not share patient data, medical record numbers, or other protected health information (PHI) unless your organization has an Enterprise agreement with Anthropic that specifically addresses HIPAA compliance.

Confidential Business Information

Be thoughtful about sharing trade secrets, proprietary algorithms, unreleased product plans, confidential financial data, or sensitive business strategies. Even with training opt-out enabled, you are still transmitting this information over the internet to a third party.

Other People's Private Information

Do not share other people's personal data — addresses, phone numbers, financial details, medical information — without their knowledge and consent. This is an ethical issue and, in many jurisdictions, a legal one.

A Practical Rule of Thumb

Before pasting anything into Claude, ask yourself: would I be comfortable if this information appeared in a data breach notification? If the answer is no, do not share it. Anonymize the data, use placeholders, or restructure your question so the sensitive information is not required.

Using Claude at Work

The intersection of AI tools and workplace policies is still evolving, and the ground rules vary enormously between organizations. Here is a framework for thinking about Claude use at work.

Check Your Company's AI Policy

Many organizations now have explicit policies about AI tool usage. Before using Claude for work, find out:

- Is Claude on your organization's approved tool list?
- Are there restrictions on what data can be shared with external AI services?
- Does your company require specific plans (Team or Enterprise) for business use?
- Are there documentation or disclosure requirements when AI is used in work product?

If your company does not have an AI policy yet, that does not mean anything goes. Use common sense and err on the side of caution until formal guidance exists.

Data Classification Matters

Most organizations classify data into tiers — public, internal, confidential, and restricted, or something similar. As a general guideline:

- **Public data** is generally fine to use with Claude on any plan
- **Internal data** may be acceptable on Team or Enterprise plans, depending on your organization's policy
- **Confidential data** should only be used with Claude under Enterprise agreements with appropriate safeguards
- **Restricted data** (trade secrets, regulated data, classified information) should generally not be used with external AI tools without explicit legal and compliance approval

Intellectual Property Considerations

If you are using Claude to help create content, code, or other work product, be aware of the intellectual property implications. In most cases, content generated with Claude's assistance belongs to you or your employer, consistent with existing work-for-hire and intellectual property frameworks. The legal landscape around AI-generated content is still evolving, though, and your organization may have specific policies.

The "Would My Boss Be OK With This?" Test

When in doubt, apply a simple test: if your manager could see exactly what you are sharing with Claude and how you are using the responses, would they be comfortable with it? If you hesitate, reconsider.

Children and Family Safety

If you have children who use or want to use Claude, a few considerations matter.

Age Restrictions

Anthropic's terms of service require users to be at least 13 years old (or the minimum age in their jurisdiction, which may be higher). Users between 13 and 18 generally need parental consent. The Free plan does not include parental controls or family management features.

What Parents Should Know

Claude is designed to be helpful, harmless, and honest, and Anthropic's Constitutional AI approach includes safety guardrails. No AI system is perfectly childproof, though. A few practical considerations:

Claude will refuse harmful requests. If a child asks Claude for dangerous information — how to make weapons, how to obtain drugs, how to harm themselves or others — Claude will decline and often offer to help in a constructive way instead. This is one of Claude's real strengths.

Claude is not a substitute for parental oversight. Claude's safety features are robust, but they do not replace parental awareness of what children are doing online. The same principles that apply to internet use generally apply here.

Academic integrity matters early. If your child is using Claude for schoolwork, have a conversation about what counts as appropriate use versus academic dishonesty. We cover this in detail in Chapter 18, and the ethical dimensions in Chapter 24. The foundation starts at home.

Claude may discuss mature topics in educational contexts. If a teenager asks Claude about historical violence, medical conditions, or other mature subjects in an educational context, Claude may provide informative responses. This is generally appropriate for older teens but may concern parents of younger users.

Recommendations for Families

1. **Have an open conversation** about AI tools, what they can do, and how to use them responsibly
2. **Set clear expectations** about when AI help is appropriate for schoolwork and when it is not
3. **Encourage critical thinking** — teach children to question and verify Claude's responses rather than accepting them as gospel
4. **Monitor usage** for younger teens, just as you would monitor other internet usage
5. **Use Claude together** initially, so you can model good AI interaction habits

Staying Safe: A Summary Checklist

Here is a quick-reference checklist for safe Claude use:

- ☐ Review and configure your privacy settings in your Anthropic account
- ☐ Enable the training data opt-out if you prefer your conversations not be used for model improvement
- ☐ Never share passwords, government IDs, financial account numbers, or health records
- ☐ Anonymize sensitive data before sharing it with Claude
- ☐ Check your workplace AI policy before using Claude for professional tasks
- ☐ Use Team or Enterprise plans for business-sensitive work
- ☐ Verify that your use case aligns with your organization's data classification requirements
- ☐ For families, ensure children meet age requirements and understand responsible use
- ☐ Periodically review Anthropic's privacy policy, as it may evolve over time

Looking Ahead

Privacy and security in AI is a rapidly evolving space. Regulations are changing, company policies are being written, and best practices are still being established. Anthropic has been proactive about privacy — their approach to Constitutional AI and their emphasis on safety set them apart in the industry. But ultimately, your privacy is your responsibility.

The good news: being safe with Claude does not require paranoia or technical expertise. It requires the same common-sense approach you already apply to email, cloud storage, and other digital tools: understand what you are sharing, with whom, and what protections are in place. Follow the guidelines in this chapter, and you can use Claude confidently.

The next chapter tackles the broader ethical questions around AI assistance — academic integrity, disclosure, copyright, and the future of human-AI collaboration.

Chapter 24: The Ethics of AI Assistance

We have covered what Claude can do, what it gets wrong, and how to keep your data safe. Now for the harder questions — the ones without clean technical answers. When is it appropriate to use AI help? When should you disclose that you used it? What does the rise of AI mean for jobs, creativity, and the way we learn?

These are not hypothetical questions for philosophers. They are practical questions millions of people are navigating right now, every day, in classrooms, offices, and creative studios. This chapter will not give you a single authoritative answer to every ethical dilemma — no honest book could. But it will give you a framework for thinking these issues through and making decisions you can stand behind.

Academic Integrity

Start with one of the most contentious areas: education.

The Core Tension

Students have a powerful AI assistant that can write essays, solve problems, explain concepts, generate code, and analyze data. Teachers and professors are trying to evaluate whether students have learned the material. These two realities are on a collision course, and institutions are still figuring out how to handle it.

The honest truth: using Claude to write your essay and submitting it as your own work is cheating. It is no different from paying someone else to write it. The fact that the "someone else" is an AI does not change the dishonesty of representing another entity's work as your own.

The picture gets more nuanced quickly, though. Consider these scenarios:

- **Using Claude to brainstorm essay topics** before writing the essay yourself. Similar to discussing ideas with a friend or visiting a writing center.

- **Asking Claude to explain a concept** you do not understand. Using it as a tutor — not much different from watching a Khan Academy video.
- **Using Claude to check your grammar and improve your writing.** This exists on a spectrum from Grammarly (widely accepted) to full rewriting (clearly not acceptable).
- **Having Claude solve a math problem so you can see the solution approach,** then working through similar problems yourself. This is how many students use solution manuals.
- **Asking Claude to write an outline** and then writing the content yourself. Where does planning assistance end and composition begin?

A Practical Framework for Students

Rather than trying to draw a bright line, here is a framework based on the purpose of the assignment:

Ask yourself: What is this assignment designed to teach me?

If an assignment exists to develop your writing skills, having Claude write for you defeats the purpose — even if you learn something from reading its output. If an assignment exists to test your understanding of a concept, having Claude solve it tells your teacher nothing about what you know.

But if the assignment is about demonstrating a final capability — and the real world would allow you to use tools — then using Claude as a tool may be appropriate. A professional data analyst uses every tool available. A working programmer uses AI coding assistants. The question is whether the educational context is training you for that professional reality or developing foundational skills you need first.

When in doubt, ask your instructor. Academic integrity policies vary dramatically between institutions, departments, and even individual professors. Many instructors now state explicitly what AI assistance is and is not permitted. If they have not, ask. The question itself demonstrates integrity.

Always disclose AI use when submitting work. If your school or instructor has not given explicit permission for AI use, tell them what you used and how. Transparency is the foundation of academic integrity, and most instructors will respect the honesty even if they decide the level of AI use was not appropriate.

A Note for Educators

If you are a teacher or professor reading this: the genie is not going back in the bottle. Students have access to Claude, ChatGPT, and a growing array of AI tools, and they will use them. The most productive path forward is not detection and punishment but designing assignments that account for AI's existence — assessments that test understanding rather than production, require personal reflection and original thought, and teach students to use AI as a tool rather than a crutch.

Disclosure: When to Say You Used AI

Beyond academia, the question of disclosure comes up constantly. Should you tell your boss that Claude helped you write that report? Should you mention it on your blog? Should you disclose it when submitting a short story to a literary magazine?

Where Disclosure Is Required

Some contexts have explicit requirements:

- **Academic submissions** at institutions with AI policies
- **Professional certifications and exams** that prohibit external assistance
- **Legal filings and regulatory submissions** where authorship attestations are required
- **Government work** subject to specific AI use policies
- **Publishing submissions** where many outlets now require AI use disclosure

Where Disclosure Is Expected but Not Always Required

Many contexts have evolving norms where disclosure is increasingly expected:

- **Journalism and media.** Major publications are developing policies about AI use in reporting and editing. If you write for any publication, check their policy.

- **Professional reports and analysis.** If colleagues or clients would assume a human wrote something without AI assistance, and that assumption matters to them, disclosure is appropriate.
- **Creative work.** Literary magazines, art competitions, and creative communities are actively debating this. Many now require disclosure. Even where not required, transparency builds trust.

Where Disclosure Is Generally Not Expected

In many everyday contexts, AI assistance is just a tool, and disclosing its use is no more necessary than disclosing that you used spellcheck:

- Using Claude to brainstorm ideas for a meeting
- Having Claude help you draft a routine email that you then edit
- Using Claude to debug code or explain a technical concept
- Asking Claude for recipe suggestions or travel recommendations

A Decision Framework

When deciding whether to disclose, ask:

1. **Would the recipient care?** If knowing about AI involvement would change how someone evaluates your work, disclose.
2. **Is there an implicit claim of sole authorship?** Some contexts carry an assumption that the work is entirely yours. If AI use would violate that assumption, disclose.
3. **What are the norms of your community?** Different professional and creative communities have different expectations. Follow the norms of yours.
4. **When in doubt, disclose.** Transparency is rarely penalized. Concealment, when discovered, often is.

Copyright Considerations

The legal landscape around AI and copyright is evolving rapidly, and anything written here may be partially outdated by the time you read it. That said, here are the key issues as they stand.

Can You Copyright AI-Generated Content?

The emerging legal consensus in the United States is nuanced. Purely AI-generated content — where a human provided a simple prompt and the AI did all the creative work — is generally not eligible for copyright protection. The U.S. Copyright Office has stated that copyright requires human authorship.

Most real-world use of Claude involves substantial human involvement, though: crafting detailed prompts, editing outputs, combining AI-generated elements with original work, making creative selections and arrangements. This human involvement likely supports copyright protection for the resulting work, though the boundaries are still being defined through legal cases and policy decisions.

Does Claude's Output Infringe Others' Copyrights?

Claude was trained on a large corpus of text, and there are ongoing legal debates about whether that training process constitutes fair use. As a practical matter, Claude is designed to generate original responses rather than reproduce training data verbatim. It is highly unlikely to output an exact copy of someone else's copyrighted work in normal use.

If you specifically try to get Claude to reproduce copyrighted material — "Write out the full text of Chapter 1 of Harry Potter" — Claude will refuse. By design.

Practical Advice

- **Treat Claude as a collaborator, not a source to copy from.** The more you edit, refine, and add your own creativity to Claude's output, the stronger your copyright position.
- **Keep records of your creative process.** If copyright matters for your work, document your prompts, your editing process, and the degree of human involvement.
- **Stay current on legal developments.** Copyright law around AI is changing quickly. What is uncertain today may be settled next year.
- **Do not use Claude to reproduce copyrighted material.** Even if Claude were willing (it generally is not), using AI to copy someone else's work is no more legal than copying it by hand.

Job Displacement: An Honest Perspective

This is the question that keeps people up at night: will AI take my job?

The honest answer: AI, Claude included, will significantly change the nature of many jobs. Some roles will be eliminated. Others will be transformed. New roles will emerge that we cannot fully anticipate today. Let us be specific rather than vague.

Jobs Most Likely to Be Affected

Roles that involve routine text production, basic data analysis, simple coding tasks, standard customer service responses, and formulaic content creation are already being affected. This is not speculation — it is happening now.

If your job consists mostly of tasks Claude can do well — summarizing documents, writing standard reports, answering frequently asked questions, translating straightforward text — your role is likely to change significantly.

Jobs Least Likely to Be Eliminated

Roles that require physical presence, complex human judgment, deep relationship management, creative vision, strategic thinking, or work in unpredictable environments are more resistant to AI displacement. Plumbers, surgeons, therapists, trial lawyers, and kindergarten teachers are not being replaced by Claude anytime soon.

The More Likely Outcome: Transformation, Not Elimination

For most knowledge workers, the realistic scenario is not replacement but transformation. A marketing team that once needed five copywriters might need two — but those two will be far more productive, using Claude to draft, iterate, and refine content at a pace that was previously impossible. A software team might need fewer junior developers for routine tasks but more architects who can use AI tools effectively.

What You Can Do

Learn to use AI tools well. The people who will thrive are not those who ignore AI or those who fear it, but those who develop real skill in using it. That is, incidentally, why you are reading this book.

Develop skills that complement AI. Critical thinking, creative judgment, emotional intelligence, strategic decision-making, and the ability to ask the right questions all become more valuable as AI handles routine tasks.

Stay adaptable. The specific tools and capabilities will keep changing. The ability to learn new technologies and adapt your workflow matters more than mastering any single tool.

Be honest about your situation. If your role is highly susceptible to AI automation, pretending otherwise is not a strategy. Consider how your skills can evolve, and start that evolution now.

Responsible Use Principles

Drawing together the themes of this chapter, here are principles for using Claude responsibly.

Be Honest

Do not represent AI-generated work as entirely your own when the context implies otherwise. Do not use Claude to deceive, manipulate, or mislead. Transparency is not just an ethical ideal — it is a practical one. Dishonesty around AI use tends to catch up with people, like other forms of dishonesty do.

Be Thoughtful

Consider the impact of how you use Claude. Using it to write persuasive misinformation, generate spam, impersonate others, or create content designed to harm — these uses are unethical regardless of whether Claude's safety features catch them.

Be Fair

If you gain an advantage from using Claude — in a competition, an application process, or a professional context — consider whether that advantage is fair within the rules and norms of the situation. An AI-assisted application in a process that prohibits AI is not just dishonest; it is unfair to everyone playing by the rules.

Be Human

AI is a tool. A powerful, transformative, sometimes astonishing tool. But a tool. The value of human creativity, empathy, judgment, and connection does not diminish because a machine can generate fluent text. Use Claude to augment your capabilities, not to replace the parts of yourself that matter most.

The Future of Human-AI Collaboration

We are in the early chapters of a story that will unfold over decades. The relationship between humans and AI systems like Claude is not static — it is evolving rapidly, and the choices we make now will shape how it develops.

The most productive vision of the future is not one where AI replaces human capabilities but one where humans and AI complement each other. Claude excels at processing large amounts of information, generating draft content quickly, maintaining consistency across long documents, and offering perspectives you might not have considered. You excel at judgment, creativity, empathy, context, and understanding what matters.

The best results come from real collaboration — using Claude's strengths to amplify your own, while maintaining the critical thinking and human judgment that no AI can replicate.

That collaboration requires the kind of honest, thoughtful engagement this chapter has described. It requires knowing Claude's limitations (Chapter 22), protecting your privacy (Chapter 23), and approaching the ethical dimensions with seriousness and good faith.

The future of human-AI collaboration will be shaped not by the technology alone but by the choices millions of people make every day about how to use it. We hope this book has equipped you to make those choices well.

Epilogue

You know Claude now. Not just the surface — the marketing bullet points and the quick demo — but the real thing: how it thinks, where it excels, where it stumbles, and how to get the most out of it for work that matters to you. That understanding puts you ahead of the vast majority of people who interact with AI tools every day without ever learning how they work or how to use them well.

If you write code professionally, there is a natural next step. *Claude Code: The Power User Guide*, the fourth book in this series, covers Anthropic's command-line tool for developers in the same depth applied here. Claude Code operates directly in your terminal, reads and writes files in your codebase, and turns Claude into something closer to a pair-programming partner than a chatbot. If that sounds useful, it probably is.

For everyone else — and for the developers too — the most important thing to take away from this book is not any single feature, prompt technique, or workflow. It is a way of thinking. Claude's specific capabilities will change. Models will get faster, smarter, and more capable. Features will be added, renamed, and occasionally removed. The interface you see today will not be the interface you see in a year. That is the nature of a technology moving this quickly.

What will not change are the principles: communicate clearly, verify what matters, understand the tool's limitations, and maintain your own judgment. The people who get the most from AI are not the ones who memorize every feature — they are the ones who develop good instincts for when to trust, when to verify, and when to push back. Those instincts transfer across tools, across updates, and across whatever comes next.

An AI assistant that makes you a better thinker is worth far more than one that just makes you faster. Claude, at its best, does both. You have the knowledge now. Go put it to work.

Part VIII: Reference

"A good notation has a subtlety and suggestiveness which at times make it seem almost like a live teacher."

— Bertrand Russell

Appendix A: Keyboard Shortcuts and Interface Tips

This appendix is your quick-reference guide to navigating Claude efficiently across every platform. Whether you use the web app, desktop client, or mobile app, these shortcuts and tips will save you time.

Web Interface Shortcuts

The Claude web interface at claude.ai supports several keyboard shortcuts that are not immediately obvious. These work in most modern browsers on both Windows/Linux and macOS.

Conversation Management

Action	Windows/Linux	macOS
New conversation	Ctrl + Shift + O	Cmd + Shift + O
Focus chat input	Shift + Esc	Shift + Esc
Send message	Enter	Enter
New line in message	Shift + Enter	Shift + Enter
Stop generation	Esc	Esc

Navigation

Action	Windows/Linux	macOS
Open sidebar	Ctrl + Shift + S	Cmd + Shift + S
Search conversations	Ctrl + K	Cmd + K
Toggle sidebar	Ctrl + Shift + S	Cmd + Shift + S

Editing

Action	Windows/Linux	macOS
Copy last response	Ctrl + Shift + C	Cmd + Shift + C
Edit last message	Click pencil icon on your message	Click pencil icon on your message

Action	Windows/Linux	macOS
Retry last response	Click retry icon on Claude's response	Click retry icon on Claude's response

Desktop App Shortcuts

The Claude desktop app (Windows and macOS) supports all the web shortcuts above, plus a few extras specific to the desktop experience.

Windows Desktop

Action	Shortcut
New conversation	Ctrl + N
Close tab/window	Ctrl + W
Minimize	Ctrl + M
Zoom in	Ctrl + =
Zoom out	Ctrl + -
Reset zoom	Ctrl + 0
Toggle full screen	F11
Open settings	Ctrl + ,

macOS Desktop

Action	Shortcut
New conversation	Cmd + N
Close tab/window	Cmd + W
Minimize	Cmd + M
Zoom in	Cmd + =
Zoom out	Cmd + -
Reset zoom	Cmd + 0
Toggle full screen	Ctrl + Cmd + F
Open settings	Cmd + ,
Hide app	Cmd + H
Quit	Cmd + Q

Mobile App Tips

The iOS and Android apps do not have keyboard shortcuts in the traditional sense (unless you use an external keyboard with a tablet). Here are the most useful gestures and interface tips.

General Mobile Tips

- **Swipe right from the left edge** to open the conversation sidebar
- **Long-press on Claude's response** to copy text or access options
- **Tap the model name** at the top of a conversation to switch models
- **Pull down to refresh** if a conversation seems stuck
- **Use voice input** via your phone's built-in keyboard microphone for hands-free prompting

iOS-Specific Tips

- Use the share sheet to send text from other apps directly to Claude
- The app supports Split View and Slide Over on iPad for multitasking
- Dictation works well for longer prompts — just tap the microphone on your keyboard

Android-Specific Tips

- The app supports split-screen mode on compatible devices
- You can add a Claude shortcut to your home screen for quick access
- Android's built-in text selection and sharing features work with Claude's responses

Power-User Navigation Tips

Beyond keyboard shortcuts, these habits will make you significantly more efficient with Claude.

Manage Your Conversation History

Your sidebar fills up quickly. Strategies for keeping it useful:

- **Rename important conversations.** Click a conversation title in the sidebar to rename it. Use descriptive names like "Q1 Marketing Strategy" rather than letting Claude auto-title them.
- **Delete conversations you no longer need.** Reduces clutter and makes it easier to find important threads.
- **Use search.** The conversation search function (Ctrl/Cmd + K) is faster than scrolling through a long sidebar.

Master the Input Box

The message input area is more capable than it first appears:

- **Drag and drop files** directly into the input area to upload them. Claude accepts PDFs, images, text files, code files, and more.
- **Paste images directly** from your clipboard. On most systems, you can take a screenshot and paste it straight into Claude with Ctrl/Cmd + V.
- **Use Shift + Enter liberally.** Structuring your prompts with clear line breaks and sections makes a measurable difference in response quality.

Work with Long Responses

When Claude generates lengthy responses:

- **Use your browser's built-in Find** (Ctrl/Cmd + F) to search within a long response
- **Copy in sections.** Select and copy specific parts of Claude's response rather than the whole thing
- **Use Artifacts for substantial content.** When Claude generates code, documents, or structured content, it often creates an Artifact — a separate panel you can copy, download, or continue editing

Optimize for Different Tasks

- **For code work,** use the web or desktop interface where you can see Artifacts rendered properly and copy code easily
- **For quick questions,** the mobile app is perfectly adequate
- **For long research sessions,** the desktop app provides the most stable experience with the fewest distractions

- **For collaborative work,** use Projects to organize related conversations and share context across your team

Browser Tips for the Web Interface

- **Pin the Claude tab** in your browser for quick access
- **Use browser profiles** to separate personal and work Claude accounts
- **If the interface feels slow,** try clearing your browser cache or using a different browser. Claude works well in Chrome, Firefox, Safari, and Edge
- **Bookmark specific Projects** for one-click access to your most-used workspaces

Accessibility

Claude's interface supports standard accessibility features:

- Screen readers work with Claude's web and desktop interfaces
- Keyboard navigation is supported throughout the interface
- High-contrast and dark mode options are available in settings
- Text size can be adjusted using your browser or OS zoom controls

Quick Reference Card

Print this page or save it as a screenshot for quick reference:

Essential shortcuts (Web and Desktop):

- New chat: Ctrl/Cmd + Shift + O
- Search: Ctrl/Cmd + K
- Send: Enter
- New line: Shift + Enter
- Stop: Esc
- Copy response: Ctrl/Cmd + Shift + C

Essential habits:

- Rename important conversations
- Use Shift + Enter to structure prompts

- Drag and drop files instead of using the upload button
- Use Artifacts for code and documents
- Search your conversation history instead of scrolling

These shortcuts and tips may seem minor individually, but they compound. A few seconds saved per interaction, across hundreds of interactions, adds up to meaningful productivity gains. Build these habits now, and they will serve you well as Claude continues to evolve.

Appendix B: Prompt Template Library

This appendix contains 77 ready-to-use prompt templates organized by category. Each template uses [brackets] to indicate parts you should customize. Copy, paste, and fill in the blanks to get high-quality results from Claude immediately.

These templates work with any Claude model and plan. For best results on complex templates, use Sonnet 4.6 or Opus 4.7 with extended thinking enabled.

Writing Templates

1. Blog Post Draft

```
Write a blog post about [topic]. Target audience: [audience description]. Tone:
[casual/professional/humorous/authoritative]. Length: approximately [word count]
 words. Include a compelling headline, an engaging introduction, [number] main s
ections with subheadings, and a conclusion with a call to action.
```

2. Email — Professional Request

```
Write a professional email to [recipient/role] requesting [what you need]. Conte
xt: [brief background]. Keep the tone [polite/formal/friendly but professional].
 The email should be concise -- no more than [number] paragraphs.
```

3. Email — Difficult Conversation

```
Help me write an email to [recipient] about [sensitive topic]. I need to communi
cate [key message] while maintaining a [respectful/empathetic/firm] tone. Key po
ints to include: [list points]. Things to avoid saying: [list].
```

4. Executive Summary

```
Write an executive summary of the following [report/document/proposal]. Target r
eader: [audience, e.g., C-suite executives]. Maximum length: [word count] words.
 Focus on: key findings, implications, and recommended actions. Here is the cont
ent to summarize:

[paste content]
```

5. Social Media Post

Write a [platform: LinkedIn/Twitter/Instagram/Facebook] post about [topic]. Goal: [inform/engage/promote/celebrate]. Tone: [professional/casual/inspirational]. Include a hook in the first line. [Include/exclude] hashtags. Maximum length: [character/word count].

6. Press Release

Write a press release for [company name] announcing [news/event/product]. Key details: who: [names/roles], what: [announcement], when: [date], where: [location], why: [significance]. Include a quote from [person/role]. Target media: [industry/local/national]. Follow standard press release format.

7. Product Description

Write a product description for [product name]. Key features: [list features]. Target customer: [description]. Tone: [exciting/professional/luxurious/practical]. Highlight the main benefit in the first sentence. Length: [word count] words. Include a call to action.

8. Cover Letter

Write a cover letter for a [job title] position at [company]. My relevant experience: [brief summary]. Key qualifications from the job listing: [list]. Specific achievements I want to highlight: [list]. Tone: professional and confident but not arrogant. Keep it to one page.

9. Thank-You Note

Write a [formal/informal] thank-you note to [recipient] for [reason]. Specific things I want to mention: [details]. Tone: [warm/professional/heartfelt]. Keep it [brief/moderate length].

10. Apology Message

Help me write an apology to [recipient] for [situation]. I want to acknowledge [what went wrong], take responsibility for [my part], and propose [solution/next steps]. Tone: sincere and [professional/personal]. Avoid excuses or deflection.

Research and Analysis Templates

11. Topic Overview

Give me a comprehensive overview of [topic]. Cover: definition, historical background, current state, key debates or controversies, and future outlook. Target someone with [beginner/intermediate/advanced] knowledge. Length: approximately [word count] words.

12. Pros and Cons Analysis

Provide a balanced pros and cons analysis of [topic/decision/product]. List at least [number] pros and [number] cons. For each point, provide a brief explanation. Conclude with a summary of who this would be best suited for and who should avoid it.

13. Comparison

Compare [option A] and [option B] across these dimensions: [list criteria, e.g., cost, features, ease of use, reliability]. Present the comparison in a table format, then provide a written summary with a recommendation based on [priority/use case].

14. Literature Review Summary

Summarize the key themes and findings in research on [topic]. Organize by [chronological/thematic/methodological] approach. Highlight areas of consensus, ongoing debates, and gaps in the research. Note: I will verify all citations independently.

15. Data Interpretation

Analyze the following data and provide insights:

[paste data]

Specifically, I want to understand: [list questions]. Present your findings in [narrative/bullet points/a combination]. Identify any notable trends, outliers, or patterns.

16. Policy Analysis

Analyze [policy/regulation/proposal] from multiple perspectives. Cover: intended goals, likely effects on [stakeholders], potential unintended consequences, his torical precedents, and arguments for and against. Present balanced analysis without advocacy.

17. SWOT Analysis

Conduct a SWOT analysis for [company/project/idea]. Context: [brief background]. Be specific and actionable in each category. After the SWOT matrix, provide 3 strategic recommendations based on the analysis.

18. Market Research Brief

Create a market research brief for [product/service] in the [industry/market]. Cover: market size and trends, target demographics, competitive landscape (key players and their positioning), opportunities, and threats. Use [available data/general knowledge] as the basis.

Business Templates

19. Meeting Agenda

Create a meeting agenda for [meeting purpose]. Attendees: [list or describe]. Duration: [time]. Include: welcome, [list topics with estimated time per topic], action items review, and next steps. Format as a clean, numbered list.

20. Project Plan Outline

Create a project plan outline for [project description]. Timeline: [duration]. Key milestones: [list if known]. Team: [size/roles]. Include: objectives, scope, deliverables, timeline with phases, resource requirements, risk factors, and success metrics.

21. Business Proposal

Draft a business proposal for [purpose]. Client/audience: [description]. Our offering: [product/service description]. Key value proposition: [main benefit]. Include: executive summary, problem statement, proposed solution, timeline, pricing, and next steps.

22. Performance Review — Self-Assessment

Help me write a self-assessment for my performance review. My role: [job title]. Key accomplishments this period: [list]. Challenges I faced: [list]. Goals I me t/exceeded/missed: [details]. Areas I want to develop: [list]. Tone: honest, professional, and growth-oriented.

23. Job Description

Write a job description for a [job title] at [company type/size]. Key responsibilities: [list]. Required qualifications: [list]. Preferred qualifications: [list]. Salary range: [range or "competitive"]. Include information about [company culture/benefits/growth opportunities].

24. Customer Feedback Response

Draft a response to this customer [complaint/review/feedback]:

"[paste customer message]"

Tone: [empathetic/professional/solution-oriented]. Acknowledge their concern, [apologize if appropriate/thank them], and offer [specific resolution]. Keep it concise.

25. Quarterly Report Summary

Help me structure a quarterly report for [department/project]. Period: [quarter/year]. Key metrics to cover: [list]. Major accomplishments: [list]. Challenges: [list]. Next quarter priorities: [list]. Format for [executive audience/team audience/board presentation].

26. Negotiation Preparation

Help me prepare for a negotiation about [subject]. My position: [what I want]. Their likely position: [what they want]. My BATNA (best alternative): [alternative]. Key interests behind my position: [list]. Potential areas for compromise: [list]. Suggest 3 strategies and likely counterarguments.

27. Elevator Pitch

Write a [30-second/60-second] elevator pitch for [product/company/idea]. Target audience: [who you are pitching to]. Key problem it solves: [problem]. Unique value: [what makes it different]. End with: [call to action/memorable hook].

Creative Templates

28. Short Story Opening

Write the opening scene ([word count] words) of a [genre] short story. Setting: [time and place]. Main character: [brief description]. Opening conflict or hook: [situation]. Tone: [dark/whimsical/literary/suspenseful]. Write in [first/third] person, [past/present] tense.

29. Character Development

Create a detailed character profile for [character name or type] in a [genre] story. Include: physical description, personality traits (including flaws), backstory, motivations, speech patterns, relationships, and a key internal conflict. Make them feel real and three-dimensional.

30. Dialogue Scene

Write a dialogue scene between [character A description] and [character B description]. Setting: [where/when]. The conversation is about [topic/conflict]. Subtext: [what they really mean but are not saying]. Tone: [tense/humorous/emotional/casual]. Include action beats between dialogue lines.

31. Poetry

Write a [form: sonnet/haiku/free verse/limerick/villanelle] about [subject]. Tone: [contemplative/joyful/melancholy/fierce]. Imagery focus: [visual/auditory/tactile]. [Include/avoid] rhyme. [Include/avoid] metaphor about [concept].

32. Worldbuilding

Help me develop the world for a [genre] story. Starting point: [basic concept]. I need you to flesh out: [geography/political systems/magic system/technology level/social structure/economy/religion -- select relevant ones]. Make it internally consistent and identify potential story conflicts that arise from the world's structure.

33. Plot Outline

Create a plot outline for a [genre] [novel/screenplay/short story]. Premise: [one-sentence concept]. Main character: [brief description]. Use [three-act structure/hero's journey/five-act structure]. Include major turning points, midpoint reversal, climax, and resolution. Identify the theme.

34. Song Lyrics

Write lyrics for a [genre: pop/rock/country/folk/hip-hop/R&B] song about [subject]. Mood: [happy/sad/angry/reflective/energetic]. Structure: [verse-chorus-verse-chorus-bridge-chorus]. Include [number] verses. [Rhyme scheme preference if any].

35. Satire/Comedy Piece

Write a [satirical essay/comedic sketch/humorous list/parody] about [topic]. Style: [dry wit/absurdist/observational/slapstick]. Target: [what you are satirizing]. Keep it [gentle/sharp/edgy]. Length: [word count] words.

36. Creative Nonfiction

Help me write a [personal essay/memoir excerpt/creative nonfiction piece] about [experience/topic]. The main theme I want to explore: [theme]. Specific sensory details to include: [list]. Emotional arc: [where it starts emotionally and where it ends]. Length: [word count] words.

Education Templates

37. Concept Explanation

Explain [concept] to someone with [no background/some background/advanced knowledge] in [field]. Use [an analogy/real-world examples/a step-by-step breakdown]. Avoid jargon [or define jargon when used]. Length: [brief paragraph/detailed explanation].

38. Study Guide

Create a study guide for [subject/exam/chapter]. Cover these topics: [list]. For each topic, include: key concepts, important terms with definitions, common exam questions, and memory aids or mnemonics where helpful. Format for easy scanning.

39. Lesson Plan

Create a lesson plan for teaching [topic] to [age group/level]. Duration: [time]. Learning objectives: [list]. Include: warm-up activity, main instruction, practice activity, assessment method, and materials needed. [Include differentiation for different learning levels].

40. Quiz Questions

Generate [number] [multiple choice/short answer/true-false/essay] questions about [topic]. Difficulty level: [easy/medium/hard/mixed]. For multiple choice, include plausible distractors. [Include/exclude] an answer key. Target audience: [description].

41. Concept Comparison

Compare and contrast [concept A] and [concept B] in [field]. Cover: definitions, key similarities, key differences, when each applies, and common misconceptions. Use a comparison table followed by a narrative explanation. Target audience: [level].

42. Reading Summary and Analysis

Summarize and analyze the key arguments in [text/chapter/article] by [author]. Cover: main thesis, supporting arguments, evidence used, strengths of the argument, weaknesses or counterarguments, and significance in the broader field. Length: [word count] words.

43. Flashcard Set

Create a set of [number] flashcards for studying [topic]. Front: term, concept, or question. Back: definition, explanation, or answer. Keep answers concise but complete. Organize by [subtopic/difficulty/chapter].

44. Research Question Development

Help me develop a research question about [broad topic]. My area of interest within this topic: [specific angle]. I am at the [undergraduate/graduate/professional] level in [field]. Suggest 5 potential research questions, ranging from narrow to broad, and explain what methodology each might require.

Productivity Templates

45. Daily Planning

Help me plan my day. My top priorities: [list]. Meetings/fixed commitments: [list with times]. Estimated time for priorities: [estimates if known]. I work best on [complex tasks in the morning/afternoon/evening]. Energy level today: [high/medium/low]. Create a time-blocked schedule.

46. Decision Matrix

Help me make a decision between [option A], [option B], and [option C]. My criteria (in order of importance): [list criteria]. For each option, rate it against each criterion and provide a brief rationale. Present as a weighted decision matrix with a final recommendation.

47. Goal Setting

Help me set [SMART/OKR-style] goals for [timeframe] in [area: career/health/finance/learning/personal]. My current situation: [brief description]. Where I want to be: [desired outcome]. Break down into [quarterly/monthly/weekly] milestones with specific, measurable actions.

48. Process Documentation

Document the process for [task/workflow]. Audience: [who will read this -- new employees, team members, etc.]. Include: purpose, prerequisites, step-by-step instructions, decision points, common pitfalls, and tips. Format: numbered steps with screenshots described where helpful.

49. Meeting Notes Cleanup

Clean up and organize these meeting notes into a professional format:

[paste rough notes]

Include: meeting details (date, attendees, purpose), key discussion points, decisions made, action items (with owners and deadlines), and next steps.

50. Weekly Review

Help me conduct a weekly review. This week's accomplishments: [list]. Unfinished tasks: [list]. What went well: [notes]. What did not go well: [notes]. Next week's priorities: [list]. Help me identify patterns, suggest adjustments, and create next week's plan.

51. Habit Tracker Setup

Help me design a habit tracking system for these habits I want to build: [list habits]. For each habit, suggest: a specific daily trigger, a minimum viable version (for low-energy days), a way to track it, and a weekly review question. My preferred tracking method: [paper/app/spreadsheet].

52. Delegation Brief

```
Write a delegation brief for [task/project] that I am assigning to [person/role].
 Include: objective, background context, specific deliverables, deadline, qualit
y standards, resources available, decision-making authority, and check-in schedu
le. Tone: clear and empowering.
```

Technical Templates

53. Code Review

```
Review the following code for [language]. Check for: bugs, security issues, perf
ormance concerns, readability, and adherence to [coding standard/best practices].
 Suggest specific improvements with explanations.

[paste code]
```

54. Bug Report

```
Help me write a clear bug report. Software: [name/version]. Environment: [OS, br
owser, device]. Steps to reproduce: [list steps]. Expected behavior: [what shoul
d happen]. Actual behavior: [what happens instead]. Frequency: [always/sometimes
/once]. Additional context: [error messages, screenshots described, etc.].
```

55. Technical Documentation

```
Write technical documentation for [function/API/system/feature]. Audience: [deve
lopers/end users/administrators]. Include: overview, prerequisites, [installatio
n/setup if applicable], usage with code examples, parameters/options, return val
ues, error handling, and common use cases.
```

56. SQL Query

```
Write a SQL query to [describe what you need]. Database type: [PostgreSQL/MySQL/
SQLite/SQL Server]. Tables involved: [describe tables and key columns]. Conditio
ns: [filters/constraints]. Output: [what columns/aggregations you need]. [Includ
e/exclude] explanation of the query.
```

57. Regex Pattern

```
Write a regex pattern to [describe what you want to match]. Programming language
/tool: [Python/JavaScript/grep/etc.]. Test cases that should match: [list]. Test
 cases that should not match: [list]. Explain the pattern breakdown.
```

58. API Request

Show me how to make an API request to [API/endpoint] using [language/tool: Python requests/curl/JavaScript fetch/etc.]. Authentication: [type: API key/OAuth/Bearer token]. Parameters: [list]. I need to [GET/POST/PUT/DELETE] and handle the response to [extract/process what].

59. Database Schema

Design a database schema for [application/use case]. Key entities: [list]. Relationships: [describe]. Requirements: [list, e.g., support for multi-tenancy, soft deletes, audit logging]. Database: [PostgreSQL/MySQL/MongoDB/etc.]. Include table definitions, indexes, and constraints.

60. Error Troubleshooting

I am getting this error:

[paste error message]

Context: I am working with [language/framework/tool], trying to [what you were doing]. My environment: [OS, versions]. What I have already tried: [list]. Help me diagnose and fix this.

61. Architecture Decision

Help me evaluate architecture options for [system/feature]. Requirements: [list functional and non-functional requirements]. Scale: [expected load/data volume]. Constraints: [budget/team size/timeline/existing stack]. Compare [option A] vs [option B] vs [option C] with tradeoffs for each.

62. Test Cases

Generate test cases for [function/feature/endpoint]. Cover: happy path, edge cases, error cases, boundary conditions, and [security/performance] scenarios. Format: [table/BDD given-when-then/unit test code in language]. Include expected results for each case.

Communication Templates

63. Difficult Feedback

Help me give [constructive/critical/developmental] feedback to [person/role] about [issue]. Specific examples: [list]. Impact of the behavior: [describe]. What I want to change: [desired outcome]. Use the [SBI/feedback sandwich/direct] framework. Keep it [kind but direct/gentle/firm].

64. Presentation Outline

Create a presentation outline for [topic]. Audience: [description]. Duration: [minutes]. Goal: [inform/persuade/train/inspire]. Include: opening hook, [number] main sections, key points per section, suggested visuals or data, and closing call to action. Format for [PowerPoint/Keynote/Google Slides].

65. Announcement

Write an [internal/external] announcement about [news]. Audience: [employees/customers/public/investors]. Key message: [main point]. Supporting details: [list]. Tone: [excited/professional/reassuring/transparent]. Address potential concerns about: [list]. Length: [brief/moderate].

66. FAQ Document

Create a FAQ document for [product/service/policy/event]. Target audience: [description]. Include [number] questions covering: getting started, common issues, pricing/costs, [topic-specific categories]. Write answers that are clear, concise, and friendly. Flag any questions I should verify the answers to.

67. Stakeholder Update

Write a stakeholder update for [project/initiative]. Audience: [executive sponsors/board/team leads]. Cover: progress since last update, current status (on track/at risk/delayed), key accomplishments, challenges and mitigations, upcoming milestones, and decisions needed. Use [dashboard format/narrative/bullet points].

Personal and Lifestyle Templates

68. Travel Itinerary

Create a [number]-day travel itinerary for [destination]. Travel dates: [dates]. Travelers: [description -- solo, couple, family with ages]. Interests: [list]. Budget: [budget level]. Must-see items: [list]. Include: daily schedule, restaurant suggestions, transportation tips, and practical advice. Note: verify all current prices and hours independently.

69. Recipe Adaptation

Adapt this recipe for [dietary requirement: vegan/gluten-free/keto/low-sodium/allergy-friendly]:

[paste recipe or describe dish]

Maintain the [flavor profile/texture/appearance] as closely as possible. Suggest substitutions for each modified ingredient and note any technique changes needed.

70. Gift Ideas

Suggest [number] gift ideas for [person description: relationship, age, interests]. Occasion: [birthday/holiday/thank you/etc.]. Budget: [range]. They already have/would not like: [list]. Preference for [experiences/physical gifts/practical items/sentimental gifts].

71. Home Organization

Create an organization plan for my [room/space: kitchen, garage, home office, closet]. Current problems: [describe mess/issues]. Items to organize: [list categories]. Constraints: [budget/space limitations]. Suggest: sorting strategy, storage solutions, and maintenance system. Budget: [range].

72. Fitness Plan

Create a [number]-week fitness plan for [goal: lose weight/build muscle/improve endurance/general health]. My current fitness level: [beginner/intermediate/advanced]. Equipment available: [list]. Time available: [minutes per session, days per week]. Injuries or limitations: [list]. Note: consult a healthcare provider before starting any exercise program.

73. Budget Setup

```
Help me set up a budget. Monthly income: [amount]. Fixed expenses: [list with am
ounts]. Variable expenses: [list with estimates]. Financial goals: [list, e.g.,
emergency fund, debt payoff, savings]. Suggest a budget framework ([50/30/20, ze
ro-based, envelope]) and help me allocate.
```

74. Letter of Recommendation Request

```
Help me write a polite request to [person/role] asking for a letter of recommend
ation for [purpose: job, grad school, award]. My relationship with them: [contex
t]. Key points I hope they will address: [list]. Deadline: [date]. Include any r
elevant materials I should offer to provide them.
```

75. Conflict Resolution

```
Help me think through a conflict with [person -- describe relationship]. The sit
uation: [describe]. My perspective: [your side]. Their likely perspective: [your
 best understanding of their view]. What I want as an outcome: [ideal resolutio
n]. Help me plan a conversation that is [direct/gentle/collaborative] and focuse
s on resolution rather than blame.
```

76. Learn a New Skill

```
Create a learning plan for [skill]. My current level: [complete beginner/some ex
perience/intermediate]. Time I can dedicate: [hours per week]. Learning style pr
eference: [reading/video/hands-on/mixed]. Goal: [what I want to be able to do].
Timeline: [weeks/months]. Include milestones and recommended resources.
```

77. Event Planning

```
Help me plan a [event type: party, wedding, conference, fundraiser] for [number]
 people. Date: [date]. Budget: [amount]. Venue: [confirmed/need suggestions]. Ke
y requirements: [list]. Tasks to coordinate: [catering/entertainment/decorations
/invitations/etc.]. Create a timeline working backward from the event date.
```

Tips for Using These Templates

Customize aggressively. These templates are starting points. The more specific detail you add in the brackets, the better Claude's response will be.

Combine templates. Need a business proposal with a SWOT analysis? Use both templates in sequence within the same conversation.

Iterate. Use the first response as a draft, then follow up with specific revision requests: "Make section 2 more concise," "Add more examples to the third point," "Adjust the tone to be less formal."

Save your best prompts. When you customize a template and get great results, save the final version in a Project or a personal note for reuse.

Use Projects for recurring templates. If you use certain prompt patterns regularly, add them to a Claude Project as instructions, so you do not have to paste them each time.

Appendix C: Troubleshooting Common Issues

When Claude does not work as expected, this appendix has your fix. The most common issues are organized into categories with clear solutions. Start with the problem you are experiencing and follow the steps.

Error Messages

"Something went wrong" or Generic Error

This is Claude's catch-all error message, and it can mean several things.

Try these steps in order:

1. Refresh the page (Ctrl/Cmd + R) or restart the app
2. Check your internet connection
3. Try again in 30 seconds — the error is often a temporary server hiccup
4. If the error occurred mid-response, start a new message. Claude often recovers on the next attempt
5. Check status.anthropic.com for ongoing service issues

"This conversation has grown too long"

You have hit the context window limit. Claude can only process so much text in a single conversation.

Solutions:

- Start a new conversation and summarize the key context from your previous chat
- For a long project, break it into smaller, focused conversations
- Use Projects to maintain shared context without repeating it in every message
- Remove or shorten earlier messages by editing them (click the pencil icon)

"I can't process this file"

Claude could not read a file you uploaded.

Check these:

- File size: confirm it is within the upload limits (limits vary by plan)
- File format: Claude supports PDFs, common image formats (PNG, JPG, GIF, WebP), text files, code files, and several document formats. It does not support every format
- File corruption: try opening the file on your own device to confirm it is not corrupted
- Try a different format: convert a Word doc to PDF, or an image to PNG

"I'm not able to help with that"

This is Claude's refusal message. It has determined that your request falls outside its acceptable use guidelines.

Options:

- Rephrase your request with more context about your legitimate purpose
- Break a complex request into smaller, less ambiguous parts
- Provide professional context: "As a [role], I need this for [legitimate purpose]"
- If you believe the refusal is incorrect, try a different approach to the same question
- See Chapter 22 for a detailed discussion of handling refusals

Network or Connection Errors

These appear as timeout messages, "failed to fetch," or the response simply stopping.

Steps:

1. Check your internet connection
2. Disable VPN if you are using one (some VPNs interfere with WebSocket connections)
3. Try a different browser or network

4. Clear your browser cache and cookies for claude.ai
5. If using the desktop app, quit and relaunch it

Slow Responses

Claude Is Taking a Long Time to Respond

Some delay is normal, especially for:

- Complex queries that require extended thinking
- Long responses (Claude generates text sequentially)
- Peak usage times

If responses seem abnormally slow:

1. Check if extended thinking is enabled — it intentionally adds processing time for better results on complex queries. If you do not need it for a simple question, turn it off
2. Check status.anthropic.com for performance issues
3. Try a smaller, simpler prompt to see if the issue is with your specific query
4. Switch to a faster model (Haiku 4.5 is the fastest) for time-sensitive queries
5. Clear your browser cache
6. Try a different browser or the desktop app

Responses Stop Mid-Sentence

Claude has a maximum output length per response. If a response is cut off:

- Type "continue" or "please continue from where you left off" and Claude will pick up where it stopped
- For long content, ask Claude to generate it in sections: "Write Part 1 of 3: [specific section]"
- If this happens often, you may be requesting too much in a single prompt. Break it into smaller requests

The Interface Feels Sluggish

If the entire interface is slow (not just response generation):

1. Close unused browser tabs — Claude's interface uses memory, especially with long conversation histories
2. Clear your browser cache and cookies
3. Try a different browser (Chrome and Edge tend to perform well)
4. Restart the desktop app if applicable
5. Check your device's available memory

Rate Limits

"You've reached your usage limit"

Every plan has usage limits. When you hit them, you will need to wait for the limit to reset.

Free plan: Limited messages per day, with lower limits on more capable models. Limits reset on a rolling basis.

Pro plan ($20/month): Substantially higher limits than Free. You get more messages and priority access during high-traffic periods. Pro limits typically reset within a few hours.

Max plan ($100–200/month): The highest individual limits available.

Team plan ($25/seat/month Standard or $150/seat/month Premium, 5-seat minimum): Business-level limits with administrative controls.

What to do when you hit a limit:

1. Wait for the reset (the interface usually tells you roughly when)
2. Switch to a less capable model if available — Haiku 4.5 has higher rate limits than Opus 4.7
3. If you regularly hit limits, consider upgrading your plan
4. Optimize your prompts to get better results in fewer messages

"Claude is at capacity"

During peak usage, Free-tier users may be temporarily unable to access Claude. Paid subscribers get priority access.

Options:

- Wait and try again in a few minutes
- Try during off-peak hours (early morning or late evening in US time zones)
- Upgrade to a paid plan for priority access

Login and Account Issues

Cannot Log In

Try these steps:

1. Verify you are going to claude.ai (not a lookalike site)
2. Confirm you are using the correct email address — the one you signed up with
3. Try the "Forgot password" flow to reset your credentials
4. Clear your browser cookies for claude.ai and try again
5. Try a different browser or incognito/private window
6. Disable browser extensions that might interfere (ad blockers, privacy extensions)
7. If you signed up with Google or another SSO provider, make sure you are clicking the correct login method

Account Locked or Suspended

If you see a message indicating your account has been locked or suspended:

- Check your email for a message from Anthropic explaining the reason
- If you believe this is an error, contact Anthropic support through their website
- Review Anthropic's acceptable use policy to understand what may have triggered the action

Two-Factor Authentication Issues

If you enabled two-factor authentication and are locked out:

- Use your backup codes (you should have saved these when setting up 2FA)
- If you do not have backup codes, contact Anthropic support

- For next time: always save backup codes in a secure location when enabling 2FA

Billing Issues

If your subscription is not working as expected:

1. Check your account settings to confirm your subscription status
2. Verify that your payment method is current and has not expired
3. Check for any failed payment notifications in your email
4. Contact Anthropic support for billing-specific issues

App-Specific Issues

Desktop App (Windows)

App will not launch: - Restart your computer - Check for Windows updates - Uninstall and reinstall the app from the official source - Run the app as administrator (right-click, "Run as administrator")

App crashes frequently: - Update to the latest version - Clear the app's local cache (check app settings for this option) - Check that your system meets the minimum requirements - Disable hardware acceleration in the app settings if available

Desktop App (macOS)

App will not open ("app is damaged" message): - Go to System Settings > Privacy & Security and allow the app - Re-download from the official source - Check that you are running a supported macOS version

App is unresponsive: - Force quit (Cmd + Option + Esc) and relaunch - Check for app updates - Clear the app cache

Mobile App (iOS)

App crashes on launch: - Force close and reopen: swipe up from the app switcher - Update the app from the App Store - Restart your device - Delete and reinstall the app (your conversations are tied to your account, not the device)

Notifications not working: - Check Settings > Notifications > Claude and ensure notifications are enabled - Verify that Do Not Disturb is not active

Mobile App (Android)

App will not install: - Check that you have sufficient storage space - Ensure your Android version is supported - Clear the Google Play Store cache: Settings > Apps > Google Play Store > Clear Cache - Try downloading over Wi-Fi instead of cellular

App is using too much battery: - Check for app updates - Restrict background activity: Settings > Apps > Claude > Battery > Restricted - App updates usually resolve this — report the issue through the app

Conversation and Feature Issues

Claude Forgot What We Were Talking About

Claude does not have memory that persists between conversations by default. Each conversation starts fresh.

Solutions: - Keep the conversation in a single thread rather than starting new ones - Use Projects to provide persistent context - Summarize key points at the beginning of a new conversation - For long conversations, periodically remind Claude of key context

Claude Gave a Different Answer to the Same Question

This is normal. Claude is not deterministic — it can produce different responses to the same prompt. A feature of how language models work, not a bug.

If consistency matters: - Be more specific in your prompt to narrow the range of possible responses - Use system prompts (via the API) or Projects to set consistent guidelines - Save responses you like and reference them in follow-up conversations

Artifacts Not Appearing

Artifacts (the side panel for code, documents, and other structured content) may not appear if:

- You are using a model or plan that does not support Artifacts
- Your request did not trigger Artifact creation (try asking explicitly: "Create this as an Artifact")
- You are on mobile, where Artifact display may differ
- Your browser is blocking the Artifact panel (try disabling extensions)

File Upload Not Working

If file uploads fail:

1. Check the file size against your plan's limits
2. Try a different file format
3. Try uploading a smaller file to test whether the issue is size-related
4. Ensure your browser allows file uploads (check privacy/security settings)
5. Try drag-and-drop instead of the upload button, or vice versa

When Nothing Else Works

If you have tried everything in this appendix and are still seeing issues:

1. **Check status.anthropic.com** for known outages or degraded performance
2. **Search Anthropic's support documentation** for your specific issue
3. **Contact Anthropic support** through the help option in your account settings or through their website
4. **Try a different device and network** to isolate whether the issue is on your end
5. **Be patient during outages.** Claude serves millions of users, and occasional service disruptions are inevitable. They are typically resolved quickly

Most issues are temporary. A quick refresh, a short wait, or a simple restart resolves the vast majority of problems users encounter with Claude.

Appendix D: Glossary of AI Terms

This glossary covers the key terms you will encounter when using Claude and reading about AI. Definitions are written for general readers, not computer scientists. Where a term has a specific meaning in the context of Claude, that is noted.

AI (Artificial Intelligence) The broad field of computer science focused on creating systems that can perform tasks typically requiring human intelligence — understanding language, recognizing patterns, making decisions, and generating content. Claude is an AI system specifically designed for natural language interaction.

Alignment The challenge of ensuring that AI systems behave in ways consistent with human values and intentions. Anthropic's core mission is focused on AI alignment and safety. Constitutional AI is one of their approaches to this problem.

Anthropic The company that created Claude. Founded in 2021 by former members of OpenAI, including Dario Amodei (CEO) and Daniela Amodei (President). Headquartered in San Francisco. Anthropic's stated mission is the responsible development and maintenance of advanced AI for the long-term benefit of humanity.

API (Application Programming Interface) A set of protocols that allows different software applications to communicate with each other. Anthropic provides an API that developers can use to integrate Claude into their own applications, websites, and services. API usage is separate from the consumer web interface at claude.ai.

Artifacts A Claude feature that creates interactive, standalone content in a separate panel alongside the conversation. When Claude generates code, documents, diagrams, or other structured content, it can present this as an Artifact that you can copy, download, edit, or iterate on. Artifacts launched in June 2024.

Attention Mechanism The core technical innovation behind modern language models. Attention allows the model to weigh the relevance of different parts of the input when generating each word of the output. This is what makes Claude good at understanding context and maintaining coherence across long passages.

Benchmark A standardized test used to evaluate and compare AI model performance. Common benchmarks measure capabilities like reasoning, coding, math, and general knowledge. Examples include MMLU, HumanEval, and GSM8K.

Chatbot A software application designed to simulate conversation with human users. Claude is a chatbot, though the term undersells its capabilities — it functions more as a general-purpose AI assistant.

Claude Anthropic's family of AI assistants. Named after Claude Shannon, the father of information theory. Available in multiple model sizes (Opus, Sonnet, Haiku) and through multiple interfaces (web, desktop, mobile, API).

Claude Code A command-line tool from Anthropic that brings Claude's capabilities directly into a developer's terminal and coding workflow. Claude Code can read, write, and edit code files, run commands, and handle complex software engineering tasks. See the companion book *Claude Code: The Power User Guide (2026 Edition)* from Finnoybu Press for comprehensive coverage.

Constitutional AI (CAI) Anthropic's approach to AI safety and alignment. Rather than relying solely on human feedback to teach the model appropriate behavior, Constitutional AI uses a set of principles (a "constitution") to guide the model's training. The model is trained to evaluate its own outputs against these principles and self-correct. This is a key differentiator between Claude and other AI assistants.

Context Window The maximum amount of text (measured in tokens) that a model can process in a single interaction. Claude's context window is large — up to one million tokens on Sonnet 4.6 and Opus 4.7 (500,000 on Enterprise), meaning it can process the equivalent of multiple full-length books in a single conversation. The context window includes both your input and Claude's output.

Deep Learning A subset of machine learning that uses neural networks with many layers. Claude is built on deep learning techniques, specifically the Transformer architecture.

Embedding A numerical representation of text (or other data) in a high-dimensional space. Embeddings capture semantic meaning — words and phrases with similar meanings have similar embeddings. This is fundamental to how language models understand language.

Extended Thinking A Claude feature that allows the model to reason through complex problems step by step before generating its final response. When enabled, Claude shows its reasoning process (or a summary of it) alongside the answer. This improves accuracy on math, logic, analysis, and other reasoning-intensive tasks. Available on Pro, Max, Team, and Enterprise plans.

Few-Shot Prompting A prompting technique where you provide Claude with a few examples of the desired input-output pattern before asking it to handle a new case. For example, showing three examples of how customer complaints should be categorized before giving it a new complaint to categorize.

Fine-Tuning The process of further training a pre-trained model on a specific dataset to specialize its behavior for a particular task or domain. Anthropic offers fine-tuning options for enterprise customers.

Foundation Model A large AI model trained on broad data that can be adapted to many different tasks. Claude is a foundation model — it was not built for one specific purpose but can handle writing, analysis, coding, math, and many other tasks.

GPT (Generative Pre-trained Transformer) A specific architecture and family of models developed by OpenAI. While Claude uses a similar Transformer-based architecture, it is not a GPT model. The term is sometimes incorrectly used as a generic term for all large language models.

Guardrails Constraints built into an AI system to prevent harmful, inappropriate, or undesired outputs. Claude's guardrails include content filters, refusal training, and Constitutional AI principles.

Hallucination When an AI model generates information that sounds plausible but is factually incorrect or entirely fabricated. See Chapter 22 for a detailed discussion of this limitation and how to handle it.

Inference The process of a trained model generating an output based on an input. When you send a message to Claude and it responds, that is inference. Inference requires computational resources, which is why usage limits exist.

Jailbreak An attempt to circumvent an AI model's safety guidelines or guardrails through cleverly crafted prompts. Anthropic continuously works to make Claude resistant to jailbreaking attempts.

Knowledge Cutoff The date beyond which a model has no training data. Claude's knowledge cutoff varies by model: January 2026 for Opus 4.7, August 2025 for Sonnet 4.6, July 2025 for Haiku 4.5. Claude has no information about events after the relevant cutoff. See Chapter 22 for practical implications.

Large Language Model (LLM) An AI model trained on vast amounts of text data that can generate, analyze, and understand human language. Claude is an LLM. "Large" refers to the number of parameters (often billions or trillions) and the scale of training data.

Latency The time delay between sending a request and receiving a response. Lower latency means faster responses. Haiku models are optimized for low latency, while Opus models prioritize capability at the cost of higher latency.

MCP (Model Context Protocol) An open standard developed by Anthropic that allows AI models to securely connect to external data sources and tools. MCP enables Claude to interact with databases, file systems, development tools, and other services through a standardized protocol. Launched in 2025.

Model In AI, a model is the trained system that processes inputs and generates outputs. Claude is available in several models of different sizes and capabilities: Opus (most capable), Sonnet (balanced), and Haiku (fastest). Each model represents a different tradeoff between capability, speed, and cost.

Multimodal The ability to process multiple types of input — not just text but also images, documents, and other media. Claude is multimodal: it can analyze images, read PDFs, and process various file types. Claude cannot generate images — it is multimodal on the input side but text-only on the output side.

Natural Language Processing (NLP) The field of AI focused on enabling computers to understand, interpret, and generate human language. Claude is an NLP system, though its capabilities extend well beyond traditional NLP tasks.

Neural Network A computing system inspired by biological neural networks. It consists of interconnected nodes (neurons) organized in layers that process information. Modern language models like Claude use neural networks with billions of parameters.

OpenAI The company that created ChatGPT and the GPT series of models. OpenAI and Anthropic are the two leading companies in the large language model space. Several Anthropic founders, including CEO Dario Amodei, previously worked at OpenAI.

Parameter A numerical value within a neural network that is adjusted during training. The number of parameters is a rough proxy for a model's capacity — more parameters generally means more capability, but also more computational cost. Modern LLMs have billions to trillions of parameters.

Prompt The text input you provide to Claude. Your prompt can be a question, an instruction, a piece of text to analyze, or any combination. The quality and specificity of your prompt significantly affects the quality of Claude's response. See Appendix B for prompt templates.

Prompt Engineering The practice of crafting effective prompts to get optimal results from an AI model. This involves techniques like providing context, specifying format, using examples, and structuring requests clearly.

Projects A Claude feature that allows you to organize related conversations, upload reference documents, and set persistent instructions that apply across all conversations within the project. Projects help maintain context and consistency for ongoing work.

RAG (Retrieval-Augmented Generation) A technique that combines a language model with an external knowledge retrieval system. Instead of relying solely on training data, the model retrieves relevant information from a database or document collection before generating its response. This can reduce hallucination and provide more current information.

Rate Limit A restriction on how many requests you can make to Claude within a given time period. Rate limits vary by plan (Free, Pro, Max, Team, Enterprise) and by model. See Appendix C for handling rate limit issues.

Reinforcement Learning from Human Feedback (RLHF) A training technique where human evaluators rate model outputs, and those ratings are used to fine-tune the model's behavior. RLHF is one of the methods used to align Claude with human preferences and values, alongside Constitutional AI.

Responsible AI The practice of developing and deploying AI systems in ways that are ethical, transparent, fair, and safe. Anthropic positions itself as a responsible AI company, with safety research as a core part of its mission.

Safety In AI, safety refers to ensuring that AI systems do not cause harm — either through malicious use, unintended behavior, or loss of control. Anthropic prioritizes safety in Claude's development, which sometimes manifests as cautious refusals (see Chapter 22).

Scaling Laws Research findings showing that AI model performance improves predictably as you increase model size, training data, and computational resources. These laws have driven the trend toward ever-larger models.

System Prompt A special set of instructions provided to Claude before the conversation begins, typically used through the API or Projects feature. System prompts set the model's behavior, personality, and constraints for the entire conversation. Regular users interact with system prompts through the Projects feature.

Temperature A parameter that controls the randomness of a model's outputs. Lower temperature produces more predictable, focused responses; higher temperature produces more varied, creative responses. Temperature is adjustable through the API but not directly in the consumer interface.

Token The basic unit of text that a language model processes. A token is roughly three-quarters of a word in English — the word "hamburger" might be split into "ham," "bur," and "ger" (three tokens). Context windows, pricing, and usage limits are all measured in tokens.

Training Data The text corpus used to train a language model. Claude was trained on a large and diverse dataset including books, websites, academic papers, and other text sources. The specific composition of Claude's training data is not fully disclosed by Anthropic.

Transformer The neural network architecture that underlies modern language models, including Claude. Introduced in a 2017 paper called "Attention Is All You Need," the Transformer architecture uses attention mechanisms to process text efficiently and capture long-range dependencies.

Turing Test A test proposed by Alan Turing in 1950 to evaluate whether a machine can exhibit intelligent behavior indistinguishable from a human. While

Claude can often pass the Turing Test in casual conversation, the test itself is considered an incomplete measure of intelligence by most AI researchers.

Vision Claude's ability to process and analyze images. You can upload photos, screenshots, diagrams, charts, and other images, and Claude can describe, interpret, and answer questions about them. Claude can understand images but cannot generate them.

Zero-Shot Prompting Asking Claude to perform a task without providing any examples — just a direct instruction. For example, "Translate this paragraph to French" without showing any translation examples first. Claude performs well on zero-shot tasks due to its extensive training.

Appendix E: What's New in 2025–2026

The pace of development at Anthropic has been extraordinary. In just over two years, Claude evolved from a capable but limited chatbot into a multimodal AI assistant with advanced reasoning, coding, and collaboration features. This appendix chronicles the major milestones — a timeline of how Claude became the product you are using today.

2024: The Year Claude Grew Up

March 2024: The Claude 3 Family Arrives

Anthropic launched the Claude 3 model family — three models at different capability levels, establishing the naming convention that continues today:

- **Claude 3 Haiku:** The fast, lightweight model designed for quick responses and high-volume tasks. Optimized for speed and efficiency.
- **Claude 3 Sonnet:** The balanced middle-tier model, offering strong capabilities at moderate cost and speed. Quickly became the default for most users.
- **Claude 3 Opus:** The most capable model in the family, designed for complex reasoning, nuanced writing, and demanding analytical tasks.

This tiered approach was deliberate. Rather than a single model, Anthropic gave users the ability to choose the right tradeoff between capability, speed, and cost for each task. The Claude 3 family was a significant leap over Claude 2, particularly in reasoning, instruction-following, and multilingual support.

All three models launched with a 200,000-token context window — large enough at the time to process entire books, lengthy codebases, or extensive document collections in a single conversation. (Sonnet 4.6 and Opus 4.7 have since expanded that to 1M tokens.)

June 2024: Claude 3.5 Sonnet and Artifacts

Two major developments arrived in the summer of 2024.

Claude 3.5 Sonnet launched as a major capability jump over its predecessor. It was notably faster than the original Sonnet while being more capable — in many benchmarks, it matched or exceeded Claude 3 Opus at a fraction of the computational cost. A pivotal moment: it demonstrated that model capability improvements did not always require larger, slower models.

Claude 3.5 Sonnet quickly became the most popular model in Claude's lineup, offering an exceptional balance of intelligence, speed, and availability.

Artifacts launched alongside 3.5 Sonnet, introducing a new interaction paradigm. Instead of just generating text in the chat, Claude could now create standalone, interactive content in a separate panel. Code with syntax highlighting, rendered HTML pages, SVG visualizations, documents, and more could be created, viewed, and iterated on as Artifacts.

Artifacts transformed Claude from a conversational assistant into something closer to a creative workspace. Users could ask Claude to build a web page and see it rendered in real time, create a chart and interact with it, or draft a document and edit it collaboratively.

October 2024: Upgraded Models and Computer Use

The fall brought another round of significant updates.

Claude 3.5 Haiku launched, bringing the 3.5 generation's improvements to the fastest tier. It offered better reasoning and instruction-following than the original Haiku while maintaining the speed that made Haiku popular for high-volume applications.

Claude 3.5 Sonnet received a major upgrade (sometimes called the "new" 3.5 Sonnet), further improving its capabilities across coding, analysis, and creative tasks. The upgraded version set new benchmarks in several evaluation categories.

Computer use entered public beta — one of Anthropic's most ambitious features. Computer use allowed Claude to interact with a computer's graphical interface: moving the cursor, clicking buttons, typing text, and navigating applications. Still in beta and limited in scope, but it pointed toward a future where AI assistants could operate software on your behalf, not just generate text about it.

Throughout 2024: Projects and Platform Growth

Projects rolled out during 2024, giving users the ability to organize their Claude usage around specific workstreams. A Project could hold reference documents, custom instructions, and multiple conversations, all sharing a common context. Particularly valuable for ongoing work — a writing project, a research effort, or a business initiative could live in its own Project with relevant materials always at hand.

The year also saw continued expansion of Claude's platform presence: improvements to the web interface, the launch of mobile apps, and the introduction of the Team plan for collaborative business use.

2024–2025: Claude Code and MCP

November 2024: MCP — The Model Context Protocol

Anthropic announced the **Model Context Protocol (MCP)** in November 2024 as an open standard for connecting AI models to external data sources and tools. MCP defined a standardized way for AI assistants to interact with databases, file systems, APIs, development tools, and other services.

MCP's significance extended beyond Claude. By releasing it as an open standard, Anthropic encouraged the broader AI ecosystem to adopt a common protocol for tool integration. MCP grew rapidly through 2025 into 2026, with a thriving ecosystem of community and vendor-built servers.

February 2025: Claude Code Launches

Claude Code was Anthropic's entry into the developer tools space. Rather than building another IDE plugin, Anthropic took a different approach: a command-line tool that brought Claude directly into the developer's terminal.

Claude Code could read and understand entire codebases, write and edit code across multiple files, execute shell commands, run tests, and handle complex software engineering tasks — all through natural language interaction in the terminal. It quickly became popular among developers for handling substantial coding tasks with minimal hand-holding.

For comprehensive coverage of Claude Code, see the companion book *Claude Code: The Power User Guide (2026 Edition)* from Finnoybu Press.

2025: The Claude 4 Era

Mid-2025: Claude 4 Opus and Sonnet

The Claude 4 generation was another generational leap, with Opus and Sonnet 4 arriving in mid-2025. Improvements landed across the board:

- Substantially better reasoning and analytical capabilities
- Improved instruction-following and reduced hallucination
- Better performance on complex, multi-step tasks
- Enhanced coding abilities
- More natural and nuanced writing

Claude 4 Opus established itself as one of the most capable AI models available, particularly excelling at tasks requiring deep analysis, complex reasoning, and sophisticated writing. Claude 4 Sonnet continued the tradition of offering exceptional capability at the balanced tier.

August–September 2025: Consumer Terms Shift

In late August 2025, Anthropic announced revised consumer terms taking effect in late September. Conversations and coding sessions on Free, Pro, and Max plans would, by default, be eligible to improve future Claude models. Existing users were prompted to make a choice in-app; new users were opted in by default and could opt out at any time. Opting in extended data retention to up to five years; opting out kept the standard 30-day window. Team, Enterprise, and API usage remained excluded from training.

September 29, 2025: Claude Sonnet 4.5

Claude Sonnet 4.5 brought another wave of capability gains at the balanced tier. Notable improvements landed in:

- Creative writing quality and voice consistency
- Complex instruction-following
- Multi-step reasoning accuracy

- Code generation and debugging
- Reduced overrefusal on legitimate requests

Sonnet 4.5 became the new default for most users, again demonstrating that the Sonnet tier could deliver flagship-quality capabilities.

Claude Haiku 4.5

Haiku 4.5 rolled out alongside the broader 4.5 generation, bringing meaningful gains in speed, instruction-following, and cost-efficiency for high-volume and latency-sensitive workloads.

2026: The Current Generation

February 10, 2026: Windows Desktop App

The native **Windows desktop app** shipped on February 10, 2026, joining the existing macOS app. Anthropic positioned it as bringing Claude to roughly 70% of desktop users worldwide — a meaningful expansion for organizations standardized on Windows.

February 17, 2026: Claude Sonnet 4.6 with 1M Context

Sonnet 4.6 launched on February 17, 2026, with two headline changes: a **one-million-token context window at standard pricing** (no beta header, no long-context surcharge) and improved agentic-coding performance. Early Claude Code testing showed users preferred 4.6 over 4.5 about 70% of the time.

The 1M context window was a category shift. A 900,000-token request now bills at the same per-token rate as a 9,000-token one, removing the longstanding tradeoff between context length and cost.

April 16, 2026: Claude Opus 4.7

Opus 4.7 shipped on April 16, 2026. Pricing held steady at $5 per million input tokens and $25 per million output tokens. Headline gains included substantial improvements in advanced software engineering — particularly on the hardest tasks — and notably better vision, with the ability to read images at higher resolution. Opus 4.7 also runs at the 1M-token context window.

Current Lineup

The current model lineup — **Opus 4.7**, **Sonnet 4.6**, and **Haiku 4.5** — is the culmination of more than two years of rapid development.

Opus 4.7 is the most capable model available, excelling at: - Complex, multi-step reasoning and analysis - Sophisticated creative writing and nuanced communication - Advanced coding and software architecture - Higher-resolution vision and document understanding - Extended thinking for thorough problem-solving

Sonnet 4.6 offers the best balance of capability and speed: - Strong performance across all task categories - Significantly faster than Opus with overlapping capabilities - 1M-token context window at standard pricing - The recommended default for most users and use cases

Haiku 4.5 is optimized for speed and efficiency: - The fastest response times in the Claude family - Well-suited for quick questions, simple tasks, and high-volume applications - Lower cost for API users - Capable enough for most everyday interactions

Platform Expansion

Throughout 2025 and into 2026, Anthropic expanded Claude's availability across platforms:

- **iOS app** with full conversation support, image upload, and voice input
- **Android app** with feature parity to the iOS experience
- **macOS desktop app** with system integration features
- **Windows desktop app** (February 2026) bringing native Claude to Windows 10 and later

The native apps are faster and more stable than the web interface, with platform-specific features like file system integration, notifications, and offline conversation history.

Extended Thinking Improvements

Extended thinking — Claude's ability to reason through complex problems step by step before responding — saw continuous improvement throughout this period. Key developments included:

- Longer and more thorough reasoning chains
- Better visibility into Claude's reasoning process
- Improved accuracy on mathematical and logical problems
- More effective use of extended thinking for creative and analytical tasks
- Refinements to when Claude automatically engages extended thinking versus when it responds directly

Extended thinking became one of Claude's most distinctive features, particularly for users working on complex analysis, research, and problem-solving tasks.

Timeline of Key Updates

Date	Milestone
March 2024	Claude 3 family launches (Haiku, Sonnet, Opus) with 200K context
June 2024	Claude 3.5 Sonnet launches — major capability jump
June 2024	Artifacts feature launches
October 2024	Claude 3.5 Haiku launches
October 2024	Claude 3.5 Sonnet upgraded
October 2024	Computer use enters public beta
2024	Projects feature rolls out
2024	Team plan launches
November 2024	MCP (Model Context Protocol) released as open standard
February 2025	Claude Code launches
Mid-2025	Claude 4 Opus and Sonnet launch
August–September 2025	Consumer terms shift — training opt-in by default on Free/Pro/Max
September 29, 2025	Claude Sonnet 4.5 launches

Date	Milestone
2025	Claude Haiku 4.5 launches
February 10, 2026	Native Windows desktop app ships
February 17, 2026	Claude Sonnet 4.6 launches with 1M-token context at standard pricing
April 16, 2026	Claude Opus 4.7 launches

What This Pace of Change Means for You

If this timeline feels dizzying, that is because it is. The pace of improvement in AI capabilities has been unprecedented, and there is no sign of it slowing down. Between the time this book goes to print and the time you read it, there may well be new models, features, or capabilities that we could not have anticipated.

This is exactly why this book emphasizes principles, frameworks, and transferable skills rather than button-by-button tutorials. The interface will change. The models will improve. New features will launch. But the fundamental skills of crafting effective prompts, understanding AI limitations, thinking critically about AI output, and using AI tools ethically — those will serve you well regardless of what version number appears on the screen.

Stay current by following Anthropic's official channels (see Appendix F for links), and remember: the most important update is always the one happening between your ears — your growing understanding of how to work with AI effectively.

Appendix F: Resources and Further Reading

This appendix collects the most useful resources for continuing your Claude education and staying current as the platform evolves. Resources are organized by category for easy reference.

Official Anthropic Resources

These are your primary sources for accurate, up-to-date information about Claude.

Claude Web Interface https://claude.ai The main web application for accessing Claude. Sign up, manage your account, and start conversations here.

Anthropic Documentation https://docs.anthropic.com Comprehensive technical documentation covering Claude's capabilities, API reference, usage guides, and best practices. Oriented toward developers, but the user guides section is valuable for all users.

Anthropic News and Blog https://anthropic.com/news Official announcements, research papers, product updates, and company news. This is where new model launches, feature releases, and policy changes are announced first.

Anthropic Research https://anthropic.com/research Published research papers and technical reports from Anthropic's research team. Covers topics including Constitutional AI, model safety, interpretability, and capability evaluations. More technical than the blog, but valuable for users who want to understand the science behind Claude.

Anthropic Status Page https://status.anthropic.com Real-time information about Claude's operational status, including ongoing outages, performance issues, or scheduled maintenance. Bookmark this for when Claude is not responding as expected.

Anthropic Support Available through the help menu in your Claude account. For account issues, billing questions, and technical support.

Developer Resources

If you are building with Claude or exploring its technical capabilities, these resources are essential.

Anthropic API Documentation https://docs.anthropic.com/en/docs Complete API reference, authentication guides, rate limit details, and code examples for integrating Claude into applications. Supports Python, TypeScript/JavaScript, and direct HTTP requests.

Claude Code Documentation Available through Anthropic's documentation site. Covers installation, configuration, and usage of Claude Code — the command-line tool for developers. For comprehensive coverage, see the companion book *Claude Code: The Power User Guide (2026 Edition)* from Finnoybu Press.

Model Context Protocol (MCP) Specification https://modelcontextprotocol.io The official specification for MCP, Anthropic's open standard for connecting AI models to external tools and data sources. Includes the protocol specification, implementation guides, and a directory of available MCP servers.

Anthropic Cookbook Available through Anthropic's GitHub repository. A collection of practical examples, tutorials, and code samples for common patterns when working with Claude's API.

Anthropic GitHub https://github.com/anthropics Open-source tools, SDKs, and reference implementations from Anthropic.

Community and Learning Resources

The Claude and broader AI communities offer many unofficial but valuable resources for learning and staying current.

Online Communities

Reddit r/ClaudeAI An active community of Claude users sharing tips, prompts, use cases, and discussions about Claude's capabilities and limitations. Good for real-world usage advice and community discoveries.

Reddit r/artificial Broader AI discussion that frequently covers Claude alongside other AI developments.

Discord Communities Several Discord servers are dedicated to Claude and AI discussion. Search for active Claude or AI assistant communities on Discord for real-time conversation and tips.

Newsletters

The AI landscape changes quickly, and newsletters are one of the best ways to stay current without drowning.

The Rundown AI A daily newsletter covering the most important AI news, including Claude updates, in a digestible format.

Ben's Bites A popular daily AI newsletter covering product launches, research papers, and industry developments.

Superhuman AI Focuses on practical AI usage tips and productivity, often featuring Claude-specific advice.

Import AI A weekly newsletter by Jack Clark (co-founder of Anthropic) covering AI research and policy. More technical and policy-oriented than the others.

YouTube Channels

Video tutorials and demonstrations can be particularly helpful for visual learners.

Search YouTube for channels covering Claude tutorials, prompt engineering techniques, and AI productivity tips. The landscape of AI-focused YouTube channels changes rapidly, so searching for recent, well-reviewed content is more reliable than recommending specific channels that may go inactive.

Look for channels that: - Demonstrate actual Claude usage rather than just talking about it - Provide practical, actionable advice - Update their content regularly to reflect new features - Have engaged communities in their comment sections

Podcasts

Several podcasts cover AI developments with varying degrees of technical depth:

- **Latent Space** — Technical discussions about AI development, often featuring industry practitioners
- **Practical AI** — Focuses on real-world AI applications and implementation
- **The AI Podcast (NVIDIA)** — Interviews with AI researchers and practitioners
- **Hard Fork (New York Times)** — Covers AI alongside broader tech news, accessible to general audiences

Books

Companion Titles from Finnoybu Press

This book is part of a series of definitive guides to AI tools from Finnoybu Press. Our companion titles provide the same depth and practical focus for other platforms:

ChatGPT: The Definitive Guide (2026 Edition) The comprehensive guide to OpenAI's ChatGPT. Covers everything from getting started to advanced techniques, with the same conversational, authoritative approach as this book. Essential reading if you use both Claude and ChatGPT — understanding both platforms helps you choose the right tool for each task.

ChatGPT: The Power User Guide (2026 Edition) Goes beyond the basics with advanced prompting strategies, workflow automation, API usage, and power-user techniques for getting the most out of ChatGPT. For users who have mastered the fundamentals and want to push further.

Claude Code: The Power User Guide (2026 Edition) A deep dive into Claude Code — Anthropic's command-line AI coding tool. Covers installation, configuration, workflow integration, advanced usage patterns, and real-world development scenarios. Essential for developers who want to use Claude in their coding workflow.

All titles are available through major book retailers and at press.finnoybu.org.

Other Recommended Reading

The AI field moves fast, and books become outdated quickly. That said, these topics are worth exploring through books that were current at the time of publication:

- **Prompt engineering and AI interaction** — Look for recently published guides that cover general principles; they tend to age better than platform-specific tutorials
- **AI ethics and society** — Books exploring the social implications of AI provide important context beyond technical usage
- **The history of AI** — Understanding where the field came from helps you evaluate where it is going

Staying Current

The single most important resource tip we can give you: **no single source is enough.** Anthropic's official channels give you product news. Community forums give you practical tips. Newsletters give you industry context. Books (including this one) give you depth and structure.

Build a small, manageable information diet:

1. **Bookmark status.anthropic.com and anthropic.com/news** for official updates
2. **Subscribe to one or two AI newsletters** for daily or weekly context
3. **Check a community forum** (like Reddit or Discord) when you have specific questions
4. **Revisit this book's companion resources** at press.finnoybu.org for updates, errata, and supplementary materials

Publisher Information

Finnoybu Press Website: press.finnoybu.org Email: press@finnoybu.org

For errata, supplementary materials, bulk ordering, and information about upcoming titles, visit our website or contact us by email. We welcome feedback from readers — your experiences and suggestions help us make each edition better.

Thank you for reading *Claude: The Definitive Guide (2026 Edition)*. We wrote this book to be the most comprehensive, practical, and honest guide to Claude available. Whether you picked it up as a complete beginner or an experienced user looking to deepen your skills, we hope it has served you well.

The best way to learn Claude is to use Claude. Open a conversation, try the techniques from this book, experiment with the prompt templates in Appendix B, and build your own workflows. The more you use Claude, the more intuitive it becomes — and the more value you will get from it.

Happy prompting.

www.ingramcontent.com/pod-product-compliance
Ingram Content Group UK Ltd.
Pitfield, Milton Keynes, MK11 3LW, UK
UKHW051117290926
15471UKWH00010B/1721

9 798950 533020